D1117584

CLOSING
THE
OPEN
DOOR

CLOSING
THE
OPEN
DOOR

American=Japanese Diplomatic Negotiations
1936=1941

JAMES H. HERZOG

Naval Institute Press
Annapolis, Maryland

Library of Congress Catalog   Card Number: 73-82483
ISBN: 0-87021-728-3

Printed in the United States of America

Contents

Preface

The role of the United States Navy in Japanese-American relations just prior to United States entry in World War II serves as an excellent example of a military branch of one country significantly influencing its government's foreign relations with another country. For five years before the Japanese attack on Pearl Harbor, as the tempo of world affairs reached crises which resulted inevitably in war, the leadership of the United States Navy enjoyed a special position in the highest councils of the United States government unparalleled before or since. One could categorically say that it was the heyday of direct American naval influence in foreign relations. Although that influence affected Britain, the Netherlands, and Germany, it was most pronounced vis-à-vis Japan.

That naval strategic thinking was oriented towards Japan and the Pacific area should not be a surprise. In the Atlantic, only Britain of the European powers had a sizable navy and that was considered more of a complement to United States security than a threat. In the Pacific, since the United States had acquired the Philippine Islands in 1898 after a short war with Spain, the one maritime nation which could threaten United States national interests was Japan. The strategic advantage of Japan over the United States improved exponentially as a result of her opportune participation in World War I. During that war she took from Germany possession of the Caroline, Palau, Gilbert, Marianas (less Guam which was American), and Marshall island groups, and subsequently had her seizures blessed by mandate from the League of Nations. In 1922 the same naval treaty which gave Japan 60 percent parity with the fleets of Britain and the United States also stipulated that Japan would not fortify the mandated islands nor would the United States fortify any of her possessions west of Hawaii.

Almost immediately after the Naval Treaty of 1922 Japan enshrouded the mandated islands in secrecy, denying visits by foreigners who might observe whether in fact she was adhering to the provisions of non-fortification. At the opposite end of the spectrum of what could be observed, the Japanese naval units and their actions in Chinese waters were familiar sights to the officers and men of the United States Asiatic Fleet. As Britain, France, and the Netherlands, in addition to the United States and Japan, competed for their share of commerce with China, so each nation had naval ships on the China Station.

The five senior admirals who were directly involved in the United States strategy with Japan from 1936 to 1941 had each served in the Asiatic Fleet prior to becoming admiral, so each had had a previous conditioning for subsequent events. Admiral Harry E. Yarnell, as Commander in Chief, Asiatic Fleet, dealt directly with the Imperial Japanese naval commanders in China during Japan's war with China commencing in 1937. Yarnell's successor, Admiral Thomas C. Hart, continued direct relations with Japanese officials during a time when, because of the war in Europe, the only occidental naval force in China was American. Hart also tasted the gall of defeat by superior Japanese forces which smashed through the thin Allied defenses en route to rich prizes in the Netherlands East Indies in January and February of 1942. Admirals James O. Richardson and Husband E. Kimmel, as successive commanders of the U.S. Fleet, took exception to the concept of using the fleet in Hawaii to deter Japan from aggression in the Southwest Pacific. The former objected vehemently to stationing the fleet in Hawaii where he thought it could not be properly trained or supported, while the latter doggedly deplored the constant deterioration of the effectiveness of the fleet. But it was Admiral Harold R. Stark, as Chief of Naval Operations, who exerted the most powerful influence on President Franklin D. Roosevelt, Secretary of State Cordell Hull, and Army Chief of Staff George C. Marshall. Stark's strategic plan to do everything possible to assist Britain in her fight against Germany and to keep the peace in the Pacific, at almost any price, would be followed until only weeks before Japan broke the peace with the Pearl Harbor attack which brought the United States into World War II.

This book describes the roles these five admirals and their subordinates played in Japanese-American relations in the five years before the Pearl Harbor attack.

In my research one of the most fortunate aspects was the quality and quantity of original documents made available to me. Within the

Naval History Division I was allowed access to the complete files of the War Plans Division; the Chief of Naval Operations and the Secretary of the Navy files; the unpublished work of Captain Tracy Kittredge which purportedly was to have been a history of the U.S. Navy in World War II; the unpublished narrative of Admiral Thomas C. Hart; and naval orders and documents which were promulgated only within the structure of the Office of the Chief of Naval Operations. From a researcher's point of view, I found most enjoyable the meticulously indexed and cross-referenced classified State Department files in the National Archives. These Washington sources were complemented by the Roosevelt Papers at Hyde Park, records and documents in the Naval War College, and the invaluable volumes of the various investigations of the Pearl Harbor attack.

I am very grateful to a large number of persons without whose help I would never have finished this book. I am particularly appreciative for the assistance of: Lieutenant Commander Arnold S. Lott, USN (Retired) as senior book editor of the Naval Institute Press in making suggestions and for his Job-like patience; Captain F. Kent Loomis, USN, former director of naval history, for expediting my clearances to classified navy records; Commander Burton Robert Truxler, USN, for his prompt work in declassifying those selections which I desired; Dr. Dean C. Allard, of the Naval History Division for his always professional cooperation; Mrs. Patricia Dowling for cheerfully and efficiently supplying the voluminous files in the diplomatic records section of the National Archives and for promptly answering numerous subsequent queries; Dr. Whitney Trow Perkins, as my doctoral adviser at Brown University; Dean Ernest R. May, Harvard University, who encouraged me to write the book; and lastly my wife Jacqueline and daughters who made the sacrifices of their time while I wrote.

Any mistakes or shortcomings are solely mine and should not reflect upon any of my cherished acquaintances who have helped me along the way.

CLOSING
THE
OPEN
DOOR

CHAPTER 1

Tension and Frustration in the Pacific

On December 8, 1936, President Franklin Delano Roosevelt was on board the cruiser USS *Indianapolis* as she steamed north off the coast of Brazil. The President, in the comfort and security of the admiral's quarters, had relaxed on his post-election cruise, yet he was deeply concerned about recent international events.

He had just learned of the Anti-Comintern Pact of November 25, tying Japan to Germany and Italy in agreements ostensibly against communism and the Third International. Germany, the previous spring, had violated the Treaty of Versailles and the Locarno Treaties by reoccupying the demilitarized Rhineland, and the Italians had taken Addis Ababa in July to end the Ethiopian war. The actions of the two European militants seemed to be part of the pattern begun by the Japanese in their seizure of Manchuria in 1931. The news that the three leading aggressors of the time were united was certainly reason enough for the President to express concern.

Roosevelt sent for his naval aide, Captain Paul Bastedo, and asked him about the status of America's war plans. It was a pregnant question, symptomatic of the shift in focus in Roosevelt's second term, and it was not answerable by Bastedo. The aide immediately wrote a memorandum to the Chief of Naval Operations suggesting a complete analysis be given the President on the subject war plans.[1]

Exactly five years after the President queried his naval aide concerning war plans, the United States Navy would be crippled in the greatest naval disaster in American history—the highly successful Japanese attack on the United States Pacific Fleet at Pearl Harbor, Hawaii. That December "day of infamy" would presage a war during which Roosevelt would die in office and the *Indianapolis* would be the

1

last major U.S. naval vessel sunk by the Japanese. In those five years Roosevelt would ask hundreds of questions of his naval subordinates—sometimes heeding and sometimes disregarding their counsel. He would use senior naval officers as special envoys to the British and Dutch and as ambassadors to Vichy France and the Soviet Union. Naval officers would become militarily and diplomatically involved with Japanese officials in China and Washington. They would attempt to influence their counterparts in the Departments of State and War to enlist further support in winning presidential approval of naval analyses and plans.

Early in January 1937, Captain Bastedo received from the Chief of Naval Operations the answer to his memorandum requesting the status of war plans—a six-page synopsis of the war plans situation as envisioned by officers in the War Plans Division, who worked for the Chief of Naval Operations. The review of plans given Captain Bastedo covered the major contingency and supporting plans of the Navy, but emphasized the *Orange Plan,* the plan for war in the Pacific. "Practically all detailed planning [was] confined to this plan as the Joint Board had decided that war in the Pacific [was] more probable than war with any other major naval Power."[2]

The attention of senior officers of the United States Navy through 1936 into 1937 continued to be focused in the Pacific and on future relations with Japan, even though U.S. newspapers in 1936 were filled with accounts of actions by Germany and Italy and the outbreak of the Spanish Civil War. Naval strategists viewed their problems in the light of the traditional roles of the Navy in the Pacific, the theories of Captain Alfred Thayer Mahan, the history of Japanese actions in the Pacific, the restraints of the recent naval treaties, and the attitudes of the statesmen of the nation towards problems in the Orient.

The U.S. Navy's assessment of Japan as the most likely enemy of the United States had obvious historical roots. Almost every month some incident involving Americans and Japanese reinforced this apprehension. In the last six months of 1936, various incidents not reported in the newspapers had done much to condition the thinking of naval leaders.

On May 31, 1936, a party of enlisted men and one lieutenant from the USS *Blackhawk* were sightseeing in Chinwangtao, in northern China. One of them took pictures of a train carrying Japanese military equipment and was then forcibly detained by Japanese army officers who demanded his camera. This he refused to give up, although in their presence he did remove and destroy the film. The U.S.

officer subsequently informed the Japanese officers that he considered their actions totally unwarranted; that any difficulties with American sailors should be first referred to him; and that "above all they just keep their hands off American sailors." One of the Japanese officers said, "Sorry, I didn't know you were in town."[3]

Nearly two months later, in Peiping the American Ambassador, Mr. Nelson Trusler Johnson, learned of the incident. At that time he met with Admiral Orin Gould Murfin, Commander in Chief, Asiatic Fleet. They agreed that it was too late to take any action but that future instances should be promptly reported to the embassy or to the nearest consular office. Commanding officers, Navy and Marine, would have many opportunities in the next few years to do just that.

One of the most frustrating problems facing U.S. naval war planners was the almost complete lack of intelligence on the Japanese activities in the mandated islands. The presence of military bases, even small ones capable of supporting submarines or aircraft, posed a threat to any ship steaming toward Guam or the Philippines. In fact, Guam was effectively surrounded by Japanese controlled potential island bases. Japan had been given a mandate in 1919 under the provisions of Article 22 of the Covenant of the League of Nations to administer all former German islands north of the equator, but the same article also forbade the construction of fortifications. Since Japan had left the League of Nations in 1933 rather than accept a censure over her invasion of Manchuria, there was a strong possibility that the mandate against fortifications might not be honored. Early U.S. war plans had called for immediate reinforcement of the Philippines in the event of war; later plans were more realistic, calling for a progressive movement across the Pacific and seizure of islands as necessary. Under either contingency, effective planning depended on knowledge of enemy capabilities in the islands that stretched along the shortest route to Japan.

On occasion the Navy relieved ships in the Asiatic Fleet with others from "stateside," and such ships, en route to the Asiatic stations, passed near the islands. To get close enough to observe bases and defense works necessitated entering Japanese territorial waters, and that required prior permission. An opportunity to see first-hand what was going on presented itself neatly when the USS *Alden* was scheduled to report to the Asiatic Fleet.

In a letter of June 5, 1936, Secretary of the Navy Claude Swanson presented his case to Secretary of State Cordell Hull, through whose department the request for visit clearance would have to go. He pointed out that for some time there had been "a strong undercurrent of conjecture and suspicion regarding the harbor development or fortification of the Pacific possessions of both the United States and Japan." To allay any such suspicion which might be held by the Japanese government, the Navy Department "would welcome the visits this year by two Japanese public vessels to certain of the Aleutian Islands and other ports not normally open to foreign vessels." And then followed the gambit—would the State Department inform the Japanese government regarding the proposed trip of this destroyer and suggest the desirability of an invitation from that government for the *Alden* "to visit informally certain of the larger unopened ports of the Mandated Islands, as well as the open ports of Saipan, Anguar, Palau, Ponape, Jaluit, and Truk?"[4]

The American ambassador to Japan, Joseph Grew, was so advised. His answer a few days later was not optimistic. He had made an informal suggestion that an invitation be extended to the *Alden* to visit the closed ports of the Japanese mandated islands. However, he observed that "it is quite possible that the Minister of Foreign Affairs will avoid communicating to me the unfavorable reply and will tacitly let the matter drop." If the foreign minister chose the face-saving approach of just not extending the invitation, Grew could see that nothing would be gained by pressing for an answer. He informed Hull that if a definite answer was desired—even though it might be negative—he would seek another interview with the foreign minister a few days before July 21,[5] the date the *Alden* was scheduled to depart Hawaii. The Navy desired an answer if possible before that date.

On July 13, Captain Bruce Livingston Canaga and Captain William Dilworth Puleston of the Central Division of the office of the Chief of Naval Operations inquired of Mr. Max Hamilton of the Far Eastern Division of the State Department if anything further had been heard from Tokyo in regard to the visit of the *Alden* to the closed ports. Hamilton informed the captains that the approach, in this instance, reaction was that if the Japanese did not respond favorably to the approach which had been made by Mr. Grew, then the American government should notify the Japanese government in the usual way that the *Alden* desired to visit the *open* ports of the mandated islands. Mr. Hamilton informed the captains that the approach, in this instance, had been based at least partially upon the thought that the Japanese might wish to extend such an invitation as a good will gesture, and that it would be better to await the outcome of the present approach before requesting visits to the open ports. Both Canaga and Puleston indicated they concurred with Hamilton but that they would discuss the matter with the Chief of Naval Operations, Admiral William Harrison Standley, to see if he wanted Grew to press the foreign minister for a definite answer.[6]

The next day Admiral Standley conferred with his staff from the War Plans and Central Divisions on the subject of the *Alden* visit in the light of Grew's telegram. The following morning, July 15, Commander Harry Wilbur Hill of the central division, on orders of Admiral Standley, called Hamilton to say that Admiral Standley *did* want Mr. Grew to press the Japanese foreign minister for a "definitive reply." The reason given for this hard stand by the Navy was that "in the past we had never been able to get a formal reply from the Japanese Government [granting] permission for American naval vessels to visit *closed* ports in the Japanese Mandated Islands." If the Japanese opposed visiting *closed* ports Mr. Grew was to "notify the Japanese Government that the Navy Department desired to have the U.S.S. *Alden* visit certain *open* ports" and, failing to get this concession, the "Government might have on record any disposition on the part of the Japanese Government to raise objection to visits of American naval vessels to *open* ports of the Mandated Islands."[7]

A formal request at this juncture for the *Alden* to visit the *open* ports would have put Ambassador Grew in an undesirable position. Having entered into informal discussion in a spirit of good will and asking for a mutual exchange of visits to show good faith, he was being asked by the Navy Department to change his approach to a more demanding, formal one in which a definite answer would be required instead of the more discrete diplomatic silence. If the foreign minister, for reasons which he could not disclose, could not give an affirmative answer, he still was in a position to keep friendly relations by remaining silent. To force the issue after having tried to get mutual visits by the informal gambit would most probably embarrass the foreign minister and strain the existing good relations. In addition, requesting to visit the open ports without waiting for an answer to the informal request to visit all ports would make it particularly difficult for the Japanese to accept, for it would show the actual motive was to see the mandated islands and not to promote good will by mutual visits.

On July 16, the U.S. Navy gave up its insistence on forcing a Japanese decision. Admiral Standley, "after some consideration... thought the best thing to do would be to let the case of the... *Alden* run its course; to send no further instructions on this case to Mr. Grew;" and should the *Alden* not receive an invitation to visit to pro-

5

ceed to the Asiatic station. Mr. Hamilton was informed that another attempt would be made after the first of the year when a transport was scheduled to go to the Far East. Then the request would be made to visit open ports through the regular diplomatic channels.[8] For the time being, the naval planners would have neither the benefit of a visit nor the satisfaction of being told "no" for the record.

If the naval officers were frustrated over not being able to force the Japanese through diplomatic channels to allow U.S. naval vessels to visit the mandated islands, their frustrations were to increase to the multiple power over not getting State Department cooperation in closing Hawaiian ports to Japanese visits. For years visits by Japanese naval vessels to the Hawaiian ports of Hilo, and Honolulu, were a cause for much alarm among the intelligence and security officers in the Hawaiian commands. The largest foreign ethnic group in the islands was Japanese and such visits were usually festive with deliberate programs to promote goodwill on the part of the Japanese Navy and the local Japanese citizens. Numerous instances of photographing of facilities, measuring piers and buildings, and exchange of packages were observed by American personnel. In Hilo, lack of customs and immigration officials made the problems of control even worse.

In June 1936, a joint planning committee met in Honolulu to study ways to take action against suspected espionage in the Hawaiian chain. Representatives from the Departments of War, Commerce, Treasury, State, and Navy attended. The Chief of Naval Operations forwarded information of Japanese activities as discussed in Honolulu to the President.

On August 10, 1936, in a memorandum to the Chief of Naval Operations the President expressed himself in very positive language:

> One obvious thought occurs to me—that every Japanese citizen or non-citizen on the Island of Oahu who meets these Japanese ships or has any connection with their officers or men should be secretly but definitely identified and his or her name placed on a special list of those who would be the first to be placed in a concentration camp in the event of trouble.
>
> As I told you verbally today, I think a Joint Board should consider and adopt plans relating to the Japanese population of all the Islands. Decision should be made as to whether the Island of Hawaii could or should be defended against landing parties. From my personal observation I should say off-hand that it would be extraordinarily difficult, as the Island is quite far from Oahu. The chief objective should be to prevent its occupation as a base of operations against Oahu and other islands.[9]

This was the Commander in Chief of all U.S. armed forces speaking about concentration camps for citizens as well as aliens. They would be used, not in 1936 but in 1942, and not in Hawaii but in California. The Japanese threat to Oahu would come not from a base of operations on Hawaii, but from fast and efficient aircraft carriers. Ironically, Oahu would be hit first.

If Roosevelt felt concern over Japanese actions in the Hawaiian Islands, he was equally concerned about the other large group of American islands much closer to Japan's expanding sphere of influence. The Philippine Islands had been guaranteed their independence prior to 1946 by the Tydings-McDuffie Act of 1934. Army planners considered the islands indefensible, whereas Navy planners wanted to build up naval facilities both in the Philippines and in Guam. The expiration of the naval limitations agreements made such possibilities "legal" again.

On November 16, 1936, shortly after his re-election, the President discussed the future of the Philippines relative to Japan with Robert Walton Moore, acting secretary of state, and Francis Bowes Sayre, assistant secretary of state, who was later to become United States high commissioner to the Philippines. The diplomats asked Roosevelt whether he had reached a decision with respect to the retention of a naval base in the Philippines after the granting of independence. Specifically they raised the question of the defensibility of such a naval base, pointing out that an indefensible base "would clearly constitute a liability rather than an asset." Roosevelt's answer was prophetic; "that in case of a Japanese attack upon the Philippines we would have to let the Philippines go temporarily and that we would gradually be moving westward, making our position secure on one Pacific island after another as we slowly moved West."[10] He estimated that it would take at least two years after hostilities commenced before the U.S. would be prepared for an open attack upon the Japanese forces.

Sayre, still not satisfied, suggested that the whole question of Philippine neutralization and our future program there turned on "whether a Philippine naval base is defensible." Roosevelt said that he was not convinced either way and that he would have the War and Navy Departments prepare a memorandum on this question. He added that the War Department would undoubtedly feel such a naval base to be indefensible except by acquiring and making secure an extended area around it. "The Navy, on the other hand, might feel it possible to defend an isolated point such as Gibraltar."[11] Disagreement over defense arrangements would persist until Japanese victories traumatically ended that interservice debate.

7

While Roosevelt discussed the future of the Philippines with State Department representatives in Washington, Admiral Harry Ervin Yarnell, who had just assumed duty as Commander in Chief, Asiatic Fleet, made his first report to the Chief of Naval Operations. He wrote that "the subject that the British intelligence officers and others seemed more concerned with than any other in their conversations with our officers related to the future status of the Philippines." The British were incredulous that the United States would leave the "Philippines to its political fate and withdraw all United States protection from the gateway to Singapore and India." Senior British officers thought that the Japanese menace could only be met with British-American cooperation and that the Japanese "southward expansion policy" could be prevented by a strong naval base in the Philippines plus the Singapore base.[12]

Cooperation with the British as well as the French and Dutch became a consistent theme for Yarnell, as did his request for a tougher United States policy in the Far East. The issue of Singapore, how it would be used and by whom, along with the problems inherent in the defense of the Philippines, would be constantly in the conversations between the United States and Britain for the next five years. Long after Yarnell had left the Asiatic Station, cooperative defense plans for Singapore and the Philippines would still be in the discussion phase. A meeting in Manila, December 4–6, 1941, between General Douglas MacArthur, Admiral Thomas Charles Hart, successor to Yarnell as Commander in Chief, Asiatic Fleet, and British Admiral Tom Phillips was an eleventh-hour attempt to reach agreement on matters which concerned Yarnell and his British contemporaries in 1936.

CHAPTER 2

Japan Commences
Aggression in China

The answer to President Roosevelt's question concerning war plans originated in the War Plans Division of the Office of the Chief of Naval Operations. In addition to being an important part of the CNO staff, that division was also part of the Joint Board and Joint Planning Committee.

The Joint Board, which decided probable enemies, was the oldest of the interservice agencies, established in July 1903, by agreement between the service secretaries without statutory authorization. The need had always existed to coordinate planning between the two services, but the Spanish-American War with its overseas operations and logistic problems brought the urgency of joint planning to the forefront. The board was suspended, strangely enough, in 1913 and 1914 by President Woodrow Wilson because "he did not wish it to enter discussions of subjects that he considered to be the President's preogative and that might lead to political repercussions." The board "renewed its meetings in October 1915, and was finally reconsituted by new orders at the end of World War I."[1] The new charter for the Joint Board specified the membership to be the Army Chief of Staff and his deputy chief of staff and assistant chief of staff for war plans, the Chief of Naval Operations, the assistant chief of naval operations, and the director of the war plans division.

The Joint Board was consultative and advisory to the Commander in Chief and took no executive action unless required to do so by higher authority. There were no required meetings of the Joint Board, en masse, unless there were matters to be discussed. The organization which permitted the Chief of Staff, the Chief of Naval Operations, and their immediate assistants not to waste time in unnecessary meetings was the working arm of the Joint Board, the Joint Planning Committee. Made up of the War Plans Division chiefs and their assistants, the committee met often, discussed their particular problems with other services' representatives, reached an understanding, and presented the tentative agreement to the Joint Board. Usually there was no discussion in the Joint Board meetings on tentative agreements, since both service chiefs kept informed on subjects by briefing and being briefed by their war plans officers. Discussions in the Joint Planning Committee conferences in reality reflected the views of the Chief of Staff and the Chief of Naval Operations. Disagreements which could not be resolved during Joint Board meetings were to be decided by the President, if necessary. The biggest area of dispute between the Army and Navy in 1936 and 1937 was over war plans in the Pacific—whether to plan on taking the offensive in case of war with Japan (Navy's position) or hold a defense line through Alaska-Hawaii-Panama (Army's position). Chief of Staff of the Army General Malin Craig, evidently shared the views of his planners, but he was either unable or unwilling to have the dispute brought before the President for decision.[2]

In the immediate aftermath of World War I, the Joint Board, in an idealistic general staff approach, undertook to prepare detailed plans for action in any conceivable emergency. A color was assigned as the code word for each emergency and applied as well to the country visualized as the enemy in that emergency. *Orange* was the code word for Japan and actions against Japan while *Red* applied to the British Empire. *Blue* for the United States was less a war plan than a plan for the national position of the American military forces in certain contingencies with no particular enemy specified. Most of the hypothetical situations were highly improbable in the peacetime era of the 1920s. The major exception was the *Orange Plan,* for war against Japan. That plan, from its inception, called for moving large Army units to the Philippines and extensive naval operations in the western Pacific.

Partially as a result of the naval staff review of the *Orange Plan* for Captain Bastedo's use in answering the President and partially because of the increased affinity of Japan for Nazi Germany, the Joint Board, on March 17, 1937, restudied the existing *Orange Plan.* There was an obvious need for a reappraisal of the ability of the Navy to protect troop movements to the Philippines and to carry a war to the western Pacific and, even more, the ever-diminishing ability of the Army to muster any level of expeditionary forces to go anywhere. "By successive stages the strength of the Army was cut and cut until in 1935 it had declined to 118,750,"[3] and yet from its initial appearance in 1924 to its cancellation in 1938 the *Orange Plan* called for the Army within ten days of the start of hostilities to have 50,000 troops on the West Coast ready to sail to the Philippines. After months of wrestling with unknown capabilities and known deficiencies the Joint Board agreed on November 16, 1937 to rescind the existing *Orange Plan* and to prepare a substitute. The war planners had tasted another bitter dose of revising plans downward to match existing and foreseeable capabilities against an increasingly stronger enemy whose intentions were changing for the worse.

While the War Plans Division officers grappled with the shortcomings of the *Orange Plan*, the officers in the Central Division continued to maneuver through diplomatic channels for permission to visit the mandated islands. After the Japanese declination of Ambassador Grew's informal bid to get the *Alden* into the islands as part of a mutual visit exchange, the Navy Department decided to try the formal route of request with the next westbound ship. That proved to be the transport *Gold Star*.

In February 1937, the Navy Department requested through the State Department permission for the *Gold Star* to make informal visits at Saipan, Yokohama, Kobe, Miike, Palau, and Truk. After months of waiting for a reply, the American ambassador finally received the inevitable decision. Answering a telegram from the State Department, sent at the request of the Navy Department, "inquiring whether the proposed informal visits of the USS *Gold Star* to certain ports in the Japanese Mandated Islands would be agreeable to the Japanese Government," Mr. Grew stated that he was "in receipt of a reply from the Foreign Office . . . dated July 31, 1937, stating that the Japanese Government is unable to give consent to the proposed visit."[4] No reason was given since none was required, but the fact that earlier in the month Japan had renewed the conflict with China indicated an unwillingness to be involved with American visits at that time. No follow-up requests for other visits appear in the archive files; evidently the Navy gave up trying to get Japanese permission to visit even the open ports in the mandated islands.

In the Japanese home islands the story was different. There United States naval ships visited frequently and generally were well received. Usually during a tour in the China Station, the Commander in Chief, Asiatic Fleet, made a formal visit to Japan. As Admiral Yarnell had not visited Japan since taking command of the Asiatic Fleet,

11

he planned to visit that country in the summer of 1937. In May he also requested authorization from the State Department through Navy Department channels to visit Vladivostok in July. Since the visits of an admiral of a fleet had political ramifications in the diplomatic sense, especially if a second country was involved in the visit, the State Department advised the ambassador in Tokyo of Yarnell's tentative plans. The State Department message also stated that it might possibly be advantageous from the point of view of "psychological effects, both positive and negative, upon Soviet and Japanese officialdom, for Yarnell to make the visits to Vladivostok and to Japan on and as part of one trip rather than as separate and therefore more conspicuously special visits."[5] Mr. Grew was directed to discuss the matter with his naval attache and then to pass the suggestion for a combined visit to Admiral Yarnell for his consideration.

The ambassador replied the following week that the naval attache concurred in his opinion that a naval visit to Japan during the summer months should be avoided, and that he had recommended to Admiral Yarnell that he consider a visit between October 1 and October 20 or after November 15 due to Japanese naval and military maneuvers between those dates. If those dates were not convenient a spring visit was suggested. The naval attache further advised Admiral Yarnell, with Mr. Grew's concurrence, that the same political ends would be gained if the announcements of the proposed visits to Vladivostok and to Japan be concurrent but that the visits themselves need not be concurrent.[6]

The recommendation that the summer months should be avoided was very prophetic. On July 7, 1937, the Japanese invaded China following an incident near Marco Polo Bridge, which spanned the Yunting River just south of Peiping and on the strategic Peiping-Hankow railway. Admiral Yarnell had to forego his formal visits for more active relations with the Japanese in China.

Fleet exercises had kept Admiral Yarnell from visiting Japanese ports in the late spring of 1937. By coincidence the same situation in reverse gave the U.S. Navy an excuse to deny visits by Japanese ships to San Francisco. Visits by four naval transports to West Coast ports had been proposed by the Japanese for May and June. Since the United States Fleet was scheduled to arrive in San Francisco May 28 and depart June 4, the Navy Department had the pleasure of telling the State Department to inform the Japanese "that they neither arrive at nor depart from San Francisco on the two dates mentioned."[7]

The year before the Marco Polo Bridge incident ushered in the last phase of the Sino-Japanese War a third and final revision had been made in Japanese national defense policy. The Japanese counterpart to the American *Orange Plan* was in actuality two plans, one by the Navy portraying the United States as the enemy and one by the Army which focused on the Soviet Union. After years of competition with the Army, the Navy had won its case with an imperial ruling approving its rationale for building up strength for a southward expansion. The Army would build up its strength to counter the Soviet Union and to secure the empire's position on the continent and, concomitantly, the Navy would advance Japanese military and economic interests to the south. The threat of British, American, and Dutch opposition and even the possibility of a clash of arms were recognized. To meet such opposition the naval budget in 1936 was sharply increased to provide for an additional two battleships, two aircraft carriers, fifteen destroyers and thirteen submarines. Having formally denounced the naval treaties with Britain and the United States, the Japanese Navy obviously was entering into a buildup of capital ship forces for supremacy in the western Pacific. Control of the western Pacific against the United States Fleet was considered possible only with a force of twelve battleships and twelve aircraft carriers. The ships funded with the increase in 1936 provided the final increment for the force goals.

The inauguration of the war in 1937 in northern China was planned and executed by the Japanese Army. The objective was to annex more territory for expansion—hopefully at as cheap a price as the Army had paid for Manchuria—and to gain a strategic advantage over the Soviet Union and China, while Premier Joseph Stalin ruthlessly purged his general officers and before Generalissimo Chiang Kai-shek became any stronger. It was not the intent of the Army at the time to engage in a general offensive against China. However, agreement had been reached in 1936 between the general staffs of the Army and Navy that the Army would protect Japanese nationals and interests in Shanghai if needed and would deploy three divisions to central China if relations with China were further strained. After action started in northern China the Navy lost no time in invoking the Army promise for help in Shanghai and central China. The southern expansion plan was under way.

The Navy plan urged upon the general staffs by Vice Admiral Kiyoshi Hasegawa, commander of the Japanese Third Fleet in Shanghai, involved immediate occupation of Shanghai and Nanking and the destruction of the Chinese air force. This, reasoned the Navy, would force China to surrender. More was at stake than a quick victory over China. Shanghai, with its International Settlement, was the economic nerve center of the Far East. France, Italy, Japan, the United States and, especially, Britain had sizable investments in Shanghai and the Yangtze valley which they managed from their respective sectors in the International Settlement. A Japanese-controlled Shanghai and a subservient China would give Japan definite economic advantages over its western rivals.

The 40,000 foreign residents of the International Settlement were self-governed by an elected council, although each of the foreign powers considered its own sector to be part of its national territory. *In toto* there existed a system of extraterritorial rights uniquely and inextricably woven, with each power protecting its sector with a small military force. Just as the American sector was patrolled by American Marines, the Japanese sector was protected by a naval landing party of 2,000. In July this force was reinforced by 300 sailors from Japanese ships in Shanghai and by an additional 1,000 from a squadron of fifteen ships which arrived on August 11. An incident over the shooting of a Japanese lieutenant and seaman, supposedly by the Chinese, provided the *cause célèbre* for pouring troops into Shanghai. The mayor of Shanghai, O. K. Yui, protested the increase in Japanese forces while the Japanese consul general, Suemasa Okamoto, objected to Chinese troop movements near the Japanese sector. Civilian control on both sides rapidly gave way to military control and operations. Unexpected Chinese resistance accelerated the influx of troops into the Shanghai area. On August 15, the Japanese government decided to send troops to Shanghai, in what appeared to be more than just a rerun of a similar plot in 1932.

At this time Admiral Yarnell, aboard the flagship *Augusta* in Shanghai, asked for "about 1000 Marines from the United States, as soon as practicable."[8] The United States then had in China 528 U.S. Marines at Peiping, 786 Army troops at Tientsin in accordance with the Boxer Protocol of 1901, and the Fourth Marine Regiment of 1,073 men in Shanghai. The Marines had been in Shanghai since 1927; they had been augmented by an army regiment during the 1932 disorders. The Asiatic Fleet under Yarnell's control was more a collection of ships to show the flag in the Far East than a balanced or even operational fleet. It consisted of one cruiser, approximately twelve destroyers, six submarines and six specially-built shallow draft river gunboats and auxiliaries. Only the gunboats remained exclusively in Chinese waters. The only modern ship in the entire fleet was the heavy cruiser *Augusta*. The fleet usually spent winter months in the Philippines and the summer months in Chefoo and Tsingtao in northern China.

The President agreed to a proposal to send the Sixth Marine Regiment from San Diego to Shanghai in answer to Admiral Yarnell's request. The decision was due in no small measure to the reasoned memoranda of Dr. Stanley K. Hornbeck, adviser on political relations in the State Department, and the fact that the British and French were reinforcing their garrisons also.[9]

While Admiral Yarnell had a box seat for the sparring around Shanghai, he became directly involved in the Japanese attempts to muscle into the area. An order from Vice Admiral Hasegawa closing part of the Yangtze to all shipping during hours of darkness without prior notification was sent through the Japanese and American consuls general. Admiral Yarnell shot back an indignant reply via the reverse of the route through which he had learned of Hasegawa's oral order. He took Hasegawa to task for not having conferred with him on the matter and then informed him that he was unable to comply because he must have freedom of action to move on short notice to visit men-of-war, merchantmen and U.S. Marines and bluejackets in the American sector. However, in order to facilitate identification in darkness he would arrange for each American ship to burn "navigation lights and fly her ensign or national flag as the case may be and to pass as close as practicable to the first Japanese man-of-war encountered up or down stream, reducing speed while passing her."[10] Yarnell's reply, which was paralleled by similar replies from the British and French naval commanders in chief, had several effects. For one, Admiral Hasegawa began to correspond directly with the other senior naval officers. One week later, on August 26, when Hasegawa proclaimed via the press that the lower Yangtze and coast of central China would be closed to Chinese shipping, he made a point to specify that his action "does not affect foreign . . . shipping."[11]

The third and most positive reaction to Yarnell's reply to Hasegawa was from Mr. Hull. On August 10, Mr. Hull had sent to Ambassador Johnson the State ". . . Department's concept of the mission and function of the United States armed forces in China." The key words in a rather long telegram were:

> . . . The primary function of these forces is to provide special protection for American nationals. Incidental to protection of life comes protection of property, but protection of property as such is not a primary objective. These forces are in no sense expeditionary forces. . . . nor are

15

they defending territory of the United States. They are expected to protect lives but they are not expected to hold positions regardless of hazards.[12]

At the end of Hull's message he directed Ambassador Johnson to

...repeat this telegram to Peiping, Tientsin, Shanghai, and Tsingtao, and instruct the officers in charge at those places to bring the contents of this telegram informally and in confidence to the attention of the commanding officers of American armed forces at those places.[13]

In view of the telegram of August 10, Mr. Hull was quite perturbed to receive directly from Admiral Yarnell nine days later the gist of Admiral Hasegawa's oral order and Yarnell's reply thereto. Within hours of the receipt of Yarnell's telegram Mr. Hull had sent to Mr. Clarence Edward Gauss, the consul general Shanghai, the first in a series of what were to become increasingly acrimonious messages meant for Admiral Yarnell. Hull referred to the August 10 telegram and said that he assumed "that the contents of that telegram were brought to the attention of the commanding officers of American armed forces." It was the desire of the government to protect its nationals, but also to avoid becoming in any way involved in the conflict between the Chinese and Japanese or to interfere with their military operations. More specifically, Mr. Hull assumed that "our armed forces will to as great an extent as possible avoid coming into or remaining in line of fire between Japanese and Chinese armed forces and, if in such line of fire, will not make assumption that fire is being deliberately directed against them unless such is with reasonable clearness the case." Then followed: "This is not an instruction or an order; it represents an effort to be of assistance ... Please bring the above to the attention of the Commander-in-Chief at once."[14]

On September 1, Admiral Yarnell reported to the Chief of Naval Operations, Admiral William Daniel Leahy, progress on preparations to deny entrance of armed Chinese and Japanese troops into the American sector of the International Settlement. The Marines had barbed wire and multiple machine guns along the front facing the Japanese sector. The anticipated "enemy" can be surmised by the last sentence in the message: "Unarmed Chinese soldiers will be permitted to enter and will be segregated under guard."[15]

On September 2, the Japanese announced a tightening of the blockade of the Yangtze and requested notification of the intended entry and exit of American commercial vessels. Mr. Hull's instruction to the consul general at Shanghai, meant directly for Admiral Yarnell,

16

was that there need be no objection "to the giving of such notifications, but that if and as notifications are given they should be given on the basis of courtesy and practical expediency rather than on the basis of a waiving of the right to immunity from interference which the giving of an express promise on our part would imply."[16] Admiral Yarnell was told that he should neither refuse nor agree to comply but should state that notification would be given to both Chinese and Japanese when and so far as practicable. Yarnell chafed under these instructions for the next three weeks. The vagueness of orders, a subsequent prohibition against giving general directions to American shipping in China, and disagreement over actions relative to the Japanese prompted Yarnell to issue his own policy statement. On September 22, he sent a copy to the Chief of Naval Operations, after having issued it to officers in the Asiatic Fleet and releasing it to the press in China. Admiral Leahy conferred with Dr. Hornbeck in the State Department and decided to release Yarnell's policy statement to the press in Washington since it had already been given to the press in Shanghai. Immediately afterward President Roosevelt sent a memorandum to Secretary of State Hull saying that he was "disturbed by the newspaper story a few days ago . . ." He could not "understand why this statement by Admiral Yarnell, relating to American policy in China, should have been handled by the Navy press room, nor [did he] know whether its release had [Hull's] approval beforehand or not."[17] The feelings of the President and Mr. Hull were made known to Admiral Leahy, who promptly told Admiral Yarnell that it was "desired that hereafter any statement regarding 'policy' contemplated by the Commander-in-Chief Asiatic Fleet be referred to the Secretary of the Navy for approval."[18]

Admiral Yarnell's policy statement which caused so much furor read in part:

> The policy of Cincaf during the present emergency is to employ United States naval forces under his command so as to offer all possible protection and assistance to our nationals in cases where needed . . . Most American citizens now in China are engaged in businesses or professions . . . these persons are unwilling to leave until their businesses have been destroyed or they are forced to leave due to actual physical danger. Until such time comes our naval forces can not be withdrawn without failure in our duty and without bringing discredit on the United States Navy. In giving assistance and protection our naval forces may at times be exposed to dangers which will in cases be slight but in any case these risks must be accepted.[19]

Though the statement might have been bothersome to President Roosevelt and Mr. Hull, it was in actuality quite an accurate blueprint for policy followed by Yarnell and his successor, Admiral Hart.

While the Japanese forces advanced up the Yangtze River in the fall of 1937, the Secretary of State received two letters which presaged a crisis involving the United States and Japan. On September 14, the Chief of Naval Operations reported that, except for occasional purchases in Netherlands Borneo and Oha in North Sakhalin, the Japanese imported all their oil from the United States.[20] Two weeks later the Secretary of the Navy passed to the State Department information on an order for 3,500,000 barrels of crude oil for the Japanese Navy to be shipped from the United States between November 1, 1937 and March 1, 1938. The contract called for an export rate of 875,000 barrels per month which was $2\frac{1}{2}$ times the rate of the preceding eighteen months. In addition to building up her capital ship inventory Japan had started in earnest to build up her oil reserves. For four years she would be allowed to draw upon American resources, much to the consternation of those in and out of government who wanted to restrict her imports from the United States.

By September the Japanese were in position to hit Nanking with the full strength of their naval air force. Admiral Hasegawa gave notice that bombing would begin after twelve o'clock noon on September 21. Upon receipt of this information Admiral Yarnell sent his Japanese counterpart a letter telling him that the United States Navy had at Nanking two gun boats, the *Luzon* and *Guam* and that "as long as the United States Embassy and U.S. nationals remain in Nanking, it [was] necessary for these two vessels to remain there also." These two vessels had a large United States flag spread horizontally on "the upper works." Yarnell requested that the Japanese naval air force be given instructions "to avoid dropping bombs in the vicinity of these vessels."[21] Through September, October, and November the gun boats enjoyed immunity from bomb damage.

The month of October 1937 emphasized the tenor of the time. A frustrated President Roosevelt made a speech on October 5, in which he stated that international lawlessness and war, declared or undeclared, should be treated as contagious and quarantined. His implication was that the United States was considering action to assist other nations in the quarantine. Pressure from Mr. Hull, reaction from the many isolationist congressmen, and disapproval by most of the press forced a recantation of the initiation of international restraints just one week later. Hard on the heels of Roosevelt's about-face, Admiral

Yarnell sent the Secretary of State a message that caused more than just a ripple in the sea that Mr. Hull had lately helped calm down. Admiral Yarnell's message was a copy of instructions given to the Commanding General, U.S. Marines, at Shanghai:

> In case of attack on the defense forces or noncombatants in the United States sector by planes of any nationality fire may be opened on such planes in self defense.[22]

Admiral Yarnell pointed out to the Secretary of State that his order was just an extension of one already given to vessels of the Asiatic Fleet authorizing them to take such action in case of attack. In a concurrent message to Admiral Leahy, Yarnell stated that he believed such attacks were improbable but "issuance and publicity of this order will undoubtedly result in more care being observed in avoiding such action by planes of opposing forces."[23]

The day after receiving the Yarnell order, Max Hamilton of the Far Eastern Division on orders from Mr. Hull called on Admiral Richardson, the assistant chief of naval operations, not "to raise the question as to the merits of the order issued by Admiral Yarnell" but to point out "that the Secretary of State felt that the giving of publicity to such an order [created] serious embarrassment to the Secretary of State in the moderate course which he was endeavoring to follow in foreign relations." Hamilton pointed out that "public sentiment and sensational newspaper reports in regards to such orders played into the hands of the critics of the Administration," and that in the past when Admiral Yarnell had issued certain orders with sensational publicity in the American press the President had spoken to the Secretary of State about the matter. Admiral Richardson was told "if Admiral Yarnell could not be directed to refrain from giving publicity to such matters, Mr. Hull would lay the whole matter before the President for decision."[24] Admiral Richardson discussed the question of muzzling Admiral Yarnell with Admiral Leahy who in turn informed the Secretary of the Navy. The decision was relayed back to the State Department that Admiral Yarnell had a great many troubles of his own and that the Navy did not wish to send him the instruction requested by Mr. Hull. The next morning, October 30, Mr. Sumner Welles, the under secretary of state, called the President and received concurrence that the Navy Department should send a telegram to Admiral Yarnell asking him to endeavor to avoid publicity in such matters. The President, as Commander in Chief had made his decision and the Commander in Chief, Asiatic Fleet, was so ordered.[25]

As the Japanese closed in on Nanking in the fall of 1937 Chiang Kai-shek's Foreign Office advised the American ambassador, Mr. Johnson, to evacuate. On November 22, the ambassador and most of the embassy staff departed on the *Luzon* up the Yangtze to Hankow, while the *Panay*, which had replaced the *Guam,* remained in Nanking to evacuate the remainder of the staff. Mr. Grew notified the Japanese government of the *Panay*'s planned movements on December 1, 1937. On December 12, the *Panay,* carrying embassy personnel and escorting three American-owned self-propelled oil barges, was bombed and strafed by Japanese aircraft despite the weather being clear and sunny and the large American flags at the masts and painted on the awnings. The attack sank the *Panay* and two oil barges, wounded eleven officers and men, and killed two sailors and a civilian.

On orders of Admiral Yarnell the United States held a court of inquiry in Shanghai into the facts of the sinking while the State Department, on orders from the President, demanded "an apology, indemnities, punishment of officers involved and assurances that similar incidents would not happen again." The findings of the court of inquiry were sent by the State Department to the Japanese government on December 23, on which date the Japanese accepted the four demands originally ordered by Roosevelt. Indemnities of $2,214,000 were paid by the Japanese on request of the State Department after agreement with the Navy Department on valuation of the various items in the claims.

In the latter part of November Admiral Yarnell had suggested withdrawing the Sixth Marines. Fighting had progressed up the Yangtze and the British had indicated that they were reducing the size of their force. The State Department agreed but requested that a formal announcement not be made until the transport was actually in China in the event that something might occur and that the Navy Department get in touch before giving the press release "to safeguard against any statement which would imply that the Marines had been sent to Shanghai for 'fighting purposes.' "[26] On December 10, a press release from Shanghai carried the story that the Sixth Marines from San Diego would return on the *Chaumont* in January. Since Yarnell had asked for the Marines in the first place, the State Department acquiesced in his decision to send them home.

On December 21, the Commander in Chief of the Japanese fleet in China issued a letter to the European and American naval commanders that "it is the desire of the Japanese Navy that foreign vessels including warships will refrain from navigating the Yangtze except when clear understanding is reached with us."[27] The joint letter from the American, French, British, and Italian commanders said in reply that with regards to the movements of warships, they would of course notify the Japanese authorities on the river of intended movement whenever practicable, but that they could not accept the restriction suggested by the Japanese letter that foreign men-of-war could not move freely without prior arrangement with the Japanese and that they reserved the right to move their ships whenever necessary without notification.[28]

Four days after Admiral Yarnell had reported the exchange with the Commander in Chief, Japanese Fleet in China, the Secretary of the Navy informed him that his "continued presence . . . in Shanghai [was] thought to be desirable from the political and diplomatic point of view." Admiral Yarnell was to remain in Shanghai until March 1938 when, by order of the President, he was released from the geographical restrictions on his movements.

As 1937 drew to a close, Secretary of State Hull could take some satisfaction in having avoided a direct confrontation with the Japanese despite Admiral Yarnell's propensity for taking positive stands against each of the Japanese restrictions. Hull assiduously parried each suggestion by the British that—jointly with the United States—economic sanctions be taken against the Japanese and, even more horrifying to Hull, that jointly a naval show of strength be made in the Far East. In the United States the tide of isolationism was running strong and Hull correctly read the signs of the time. A case in point was the sinking of the *Panay*. Unlike the sinking of the *Maine* in Havana, Cuba, in 1898, which triggered a war cry, the attack on the *Panay* precipitated a hue and cry to get the United States military out of China. In fact, a Gallup poll one month after the sinking showed 70 percent of the American people in favor of *all* Americans, including missionaries, leaving China.

There was no satisfaction or comfort in the ranks of the military planners in December. As the joint planners struggled with the *Orange Plan* in the light of Japanese successes and impudence, it was readily apparent how weak the United States was. The only military strength available was the Navy—a one-ocean navy. Parsimonious congresses had appropriated such meager funds for the Army that after pay, which was fixed by statute, and repair and maintenance costs for the surplus World War I equipment, little was left to improve the weapons inventory. The Navy had fared slightly better since President Roosevelt had taken the initiative to build it up to treaty strength, but the Congress did not authorize any increase in personnel strengths.

Admiral Leahy and his staff, aware of British interests and responsibilities in parts of the western Pacific and the possibility of future cooperation against a militant Japan, decided to conduct private conversations with the Admiralty. Actually, the conversations were to have a twofold purpose: to find out what could be done if the United States and Britain found themselves at war with Japan and to take up with the British the question of limitations on battleship displacement which had been stipulated in the London Treaty of 1935 and 1936. President Roosevelt agreed with the approach and the purpose of the visit. Leahy, with this approval, decided in late December, 1937, to send Captain Royal Eason Ingersoll, then chief of the War Plans Division, to converse with war planners in the Admiralty. His preparation was indicative of the significance of his trip, for in addition to being briefed by Admiral Leahy, he was also called to the White House for a briefing. His visit would set a precedent for similar meetings between representatives of the two navies which would in future years draw them together, not against Japan or in the Pacific, but against an enemy elsewhere. Interestingly, four years later, Ingersoll in the rank of admiral assumed duty as Commander in Chief, Atlantic Fleet, when British-American cooperation was the closest.

CHAPTER 3

American War Plans
Against Japan

Upon his arrival in London, Captain Ingersoll met with the British Secretary of State for Foreign Affairs, Sir Anthony Eden, who had cancelled a post-Christmas holiday for the occasion. Ingersoll told Eden that the United States Navy's plans for action in the Pacific were based on certain assumptions about the fleet dispositions the British might be able to make and that the same was probably true about British plans. President Roosevelt and Admiral Leahy thought the time had come "to carry matters a stage further by exchanging information in order to co-ordinate our plans more closely." Ingersoll was free to disclose the American dispositions under certain eventualities and desired to learn what the British dispositions would be under similar circumstances. In answer to Secretary Eden's question on possible courses of action then or in the future, Ingersoll replied that the discussions which were to be held between himself and the Admiralty "would be limited to future incidents against which joint action might later be taken, [but that] no move could be made at all in the Pacific, unless full preparation had been made for every eventuality, including war." Ingersoll thought the technical examination between the two countries should come first, after which any considerations on political decisions should be easier.[1] He left with the impression that Eden was more interested at the time in immediate gestures to impress the Japanese than he was in long-range planning. corresponding opposite in the War Plans Division of the Admiralty,

The technical talks were held between Captain Ingersoll and his Captain Tom Phillips. Ingersoll recorded his impressions during these talks in a daily report to the Chief of Naval Operations. As Ingersoll saw it, the British were not counting on any assistance from Russia,

France, or the Netherlands. They were interested in Manila as a base, because they feared Hong Kong was too vulnerable to land attack, and they were sure the Japanese would not attempt to take the Philippines while they were involved in China. They believed their positions in the Pacific would be safe with units of their fleet based at Singapore and the United States Fleet based at Hawaii or, better yet, to the westward of Hawaii. For an effective show of strength against the Japanese, the British proposed that their fleet start for Singapore and the United States Fleet for Hawaii to arrive approximately at the same time. Should the two governments decide to blockade Japan from further southward expansion, the two navies would hold a line roughly from Singapore through the Netherlands East Indies past New Guinea and the New Hebrides eastward of Australia and New Zealand. (This was the genesis of a plan of defense which would be debated, revised, and disputed until two days before the Pearl Harbor attack.) British officers believed that such a show of strength by the two navies might be necessary—even if there were no hostilities with Japan—in order to bring about peace terms between China and Japan which would have continued the principle of the "open door."[2]

Captains Ingersoll and Phillips signed the official "Record of Conversations" on January 12, 1938, and agreed therein to recommend British-U.S. cooperation in case of war with Japan, the British basing a fleet at Singapore and the United States concentrating a fleet at Pearl Harbor.[3]

While Captain Ingersoll was still in London, Admiral Yarnell in Shanghai was taking exception to the actions of Admiral Hasegawa. The first of the year Yarnell had learned through the British Navy of a new Japanese policy allowing only Japanese merchant ships to proceed up the Yangtze. He pointed out in a letter to Admiral Hasegawa on January 5 that, as recently as December 28, Ambassador Grew had informed the Japanese government "that the United States claimed absolute freedom for their ships to move and trade on the river and that the United States government looks to the Japanese authorities to give prior warning in regard to any area on the Yangtze becoming, through steps taken by them, a dangerous area." Then followed the strong language for which Admiral Yarnell would be criticized by Hull later: "I can not accept a policy which prevents the free navigation of the Yangtze River by United States naval or merchant vessels."[4] Yarnell's letter was ignored by the Japanese. They controlled the river above Nanking and in the name of military operations they also controlled ship movements on the river in that area for the rest of the year.

One week after Captain Ingersoll returned to Washington from London, his war planners—with their U.S. Army counterparts—rejected the latest version of the *Orange Plan* which had been prepared by the Joint Planning Committee. On January 19, the two service authorities on Pacific problems, Major General Stanley D. Embick and Rear Admiral James O. Richardson, were directed to make a further Pacific study. Embick, as a brigadier general, had designed the defenses of Corregidor and formerly commanded the harbor defenses of Manila and Subic Bays. In 1933 he wrote while in the Philippines, and later reiterated in 1935 while serving in the Army War Plans Division, that "to carry out the present *Orange Plan*—with the provisions for the early dispatch of our fleet to Philippine waters—would be literally an act of madness."[5] Richardson, who was then assistant chief of naval operations, was thoroughly familiar with the Navy's position and *Orange Plan* evolution. He also had first-hand experience in the Far East, having served two tours of duty with the Asiatic Fleet. The efforts of the pair were accepted as a new *Orange Plan* by the Joint Board on February 21 and by the service secretaries a week later.[6] On the basis of this latest plan, the Navy asked for and received from the President and Congress authorization for a 20 percent increase in size.

Concurrently, while the *Orange Plan* was being rewritten in Washington, Admiral Leahy wrote his two key fleet commanders to revise their supporting war plans. He told Admiral C. C. Bloch, Commander in Chief, United States Fleet, and Rear Admiral H. E. Yarnell, Commander in Chief, Asiatic Fleet, that in the event the United States and British governments should "at some indefinite time in the future" decide that parallel action be taken concerning policy in the Far East, certain assumptions would have to be made "in order to adopt existing *Orange* plans to changed situation"—in other words, "*Blue* and *Red* against *Orange*."[7]

Among the assumptions made by Admiral Leahy were three significant ones affecting future planning: (a) Should the British government decide to send a naval force to the Far East, it would send a force as a single tactical unit of sufficient strength "to engage the Japanese Fleet under normal tactical and strategical conditions" but in the event of a general war in Europe there would be a considerable reduction of British naval strength in the Far East. Under such conditions there would probably be required direct tactical cooperation between the United States and British fleets in the Pacific; (b) should the British government send its fleet to Singapore, the United States would send its fleet "to Truk or some other position in the same general area" after the decision is made "to dispatch the United States Fleet beyond the Hawaiian Islands;" and (c) should parallel action be decided upon by the two governments, "it can be assumed that the British will withdraw their garrisons in North China and the major units of the British China Fleet to Hong Kong or Singapore and that such withdrawals would probably be timed with the movement of the British Main Fleet to the Far East."[8] As events were to prove shortly, the assumptions that the British could station and maintain strong naval forces in Singapore or that the United States Fleet would or could move westward from Hawaii were short-lived dreams.

Through February and March 1938, a discussion brewed in the State Department over the advisability of the annual summer seasonal visit of Asiatic Fleet units to the northern China ports of Tsingtao and Chefoo. Both ports had been occupied rather peacefully by the Japanese since the visits of the year before. Max Hamilton, chief of the Far Eastern Division, in a memorandum to Secretary of State Hull on March 10, reasoned that although both cities were relatively free of disturbances—Chinese versus Japanese—there were possibilities of friction between Japanese troops and American sailors. The long campaign in China had tended "to affect adversely the morale and conduct of various units of the Japanese Army." The Japanese bombing of the *Panay* and other incidents involving the Japanese and American military units may also have tended "to ruffle the tempers of the rank and file of the American fleet."[9] The decision was made, however, for regular summer visits to Chefoo with occasional short visits from Chefoo to Tsingtao. The summer visit was to be shorter than in the past with fewer units participating. With the vantage point of hindsight one could have forecast the inevitable incidents.

While the degree of tension and likelihood of incidents increased in China between the Japanese and American military, the diplomats in Japan were writing the final chapter to the *Panay* tragedy. On April 22, Ambassador Grew received a check for $2,214,007.36 "as indemnification for losses to American property and for death and injuries of American citizens" incident to the *Panay* sinking. In presenting the check, the Japanese minister for foreign affairs raised some interesting points which truly rankled the officers in the Navy Department. Having paid indemnification, the Japanese government assumed it could, with propriety, salvage the sunken gunboat and two barges for conversion into scrap metal. After asking Ambassador Grew for American consent to these intentions, the Japanese minister had the effrontery to suggest that if "the American Government should at some later time decide to replace the *Panay*, the Japanese Government would appreciate receiving [the] contract for construction in Japan."[10] The answer was a diplomatically polite ignoring of the latter and a denial of the former relative to the *Panay*. The United States did acquiesce in the Japanese salvage of the barges on the understanding that Standard-Vacuum Oil Company representatives would be present and the books, documents, logs, and papers recovered would be turned over to the American consular authorities in China.

Not long after he had been given "liberty to leave Shanghai with his flagship at his discretion" Admiral Yarnell was in the middle of another controversy with the Japanese and the State Department. In June he announced to the American ambassador to China, Mr. Johnson, who promptly relayed the information to the Secretary of State, that he intended to visit Nanking and Wuhu about June 24 to 25 in the *Isabel*. How long he would be there depended on whether American nationals in the area needed assistance. After having asserted that he would give due notice of his movements to the Chinese and Japanese authorities and that he would take due care "to avoid unnecessary exposure in dangerous areas," he told the ambassador that the paramount mission of the U.S. Navy was to assist American nationals in the evacuation of such areas as Wuhu. The warning by the Japanese minister at large, Masayuki Tani, for foreign men-of-war to keep clear of combat areas did not, according to Admiral Yarnell, relieve "that nation in [the] slightest degree of responsibility for damage or injury to United States naval vessels or personnel." He would not even consider another suggestion by Minister Tani that United States naval vessels be painted scarlet or other colors to make them more distinguishable from the air. United States naval vessels on the Yangtze were the only ones of their type; they were painted white with large American flags painted on their awnings and that was identification enough.[11]

Whether Hull's reaction was due to the ambassador's message citing Admiral Yarnell's views or to the newspaper headlines over the United Press story dated Shanghai, June 12, is not known, but it was immediate. In a message back to Ambassador Johnson he quoted from the "sensational headlines" of June 13, such as: "Yarnell defies Japan"; "Says Navy will go where it is needed"; and "Won't bar U.S. ships in war zone." Hull pointed out again the public opinion against involvement in China and a growing insistence "upon the removal of all armed forces." Any suggestion of a bellicose attitude by Americans, official or unofficial, in China played into the hands of those opposed to an American presence. After having conferred with officers in the Navy Department, who had no indication of what motivated the proposed Yarnell visit, Hull questioned the advisability of the visit "at a time when active hostilities [were] imminent."[12]

He might well have been surprised by Ambassador Johnson's reply. Neither he nor Admiral Yarnell had given the press information on the visit. The ambassador suspected "that United Press was able to intercept the message which Yarnell [had sent] through naval wireless circuit and used it in its story." He personally saw "no reason why Admiral Yarnell should not make the visit contemplated." He felt there was no more risk of danger or embarrassment than visits to Tsingtao or Chefoo.[13] Admiral Yarnell elected not to go to the Wuhu area, but remained at Shanghai. History undoubtedly would have been more colorful had the Japanese river operations trapped Yarnell's flagship, the heavy cruiser *Augusta,* instead of the little gunboat *Monocacy.*

Second only to the *Panay* case in volume of messages, and perhaps exceeding it in the amount of resulting negotiations, was the incident involving the *Monacacy.* As the Japanese advanced up the Yangtze in the summer of 1938, the area of active fighting approached the city of Kiukiang where the *Monocacy* was located. Each of the key officials concerned with the *Monocacy* had evaluated her future safety relative to the Japanese advance. The Commander, Yangtze Patrol, Rear Admiral David McDougal Le Breton, after conferring with Ambassador Johnson and getting concurrence from Admiral Yarnell, had decided to leave the *Monocacy* in the vicinity of Kiukiang, though fighting was inevitable there.

Hull, on July 5, challenged the wisdom of the decision. He wanted to know how many Americans were in the vicinity and what were the future plans concerning the gunboat.[14] The immediate response from Johnson was that sixty American missionaries and businessmen in the area were "not casuals but persons with interests and property." They did not intend to leave their all to the Japanese.[15] Hull persisted. Back went another telegram to Ambassador Johnson via Frank P. Lockhart, the consul general, who was instructed to pass its contents to Admiral Yarnell also. Among other things, Hull said:

Would not giving by the *Monocacy* of notice of intended departure, with offer of transportation, lead to embarkation by such nationals as are willing to leave? Would any further standing by of the *Monocacy* serve any useful purpose in regard to those not willing to leave?[16]

The answers were sent to the State Department on July 12. The *Monocacy* was and would remain anchored in an open stretch of the Yangtze, "probably the safest place on the river between Kiukiang and Yochow at the present moment." The gunboat could not move upstream because the Chinese had heavily mined the river to stop the Japanese. Movement downstream was blocked by Japanese operations. Mr. Johnson pointed out that for months he, his staff, and the Navy had prepared for such a situation. The gunboats were "not interlopers in this area," and sooner or later they must pass through these hostilities or have the hostilities pass by them. The only course to follow then was to keep the Japanese completely and currently informed of the whereabouts of the vessels, insist upon the rights of noncombatants, and trust the Japanese "desire to do us no harm."[17]

Mr. Hull was not the only one who wanted the *Monocacy* moved upstream. On July 17, Ambassador Grew telegraphed from Tokyo that Japanese naval officials were quite worried over her presence near Kiukiang, and while they were taking every precaution to prevent the recurrence of another *Panay* incident, they could not cover all eventualities. Through Ambassador Grew it was requested that the gunboat be moved to Hankow. Acknowledging that such movement might be impossible due to mines or a boom, it was further requested that the ship be "especially marked or otherwise be made distinctly recognizable from afar and from high aloft."[18] There apparently was bona fide concern to prevent another *Panay* incident.

During the exchange of information and advice concerning the *Monocacy,* Mr. Hull received two other messages from different parts of China pertaining to relations between the United States and Japanese navies. On July 9, Consul General Lockhart at Shanghai forwarded to the Secretary of State a long statement which he had received from his Japanese counterpart. It was at once roses and thorns. The profuse gratitude was for "the hearty cooperation" the United States had shown by giving detailed reports concerning ship movements and avoiding areas of fighting in order to prevent incidents or casualties to life or property. This Admiral Yarnell had certainly done, whether or not it was completely of his own choosing. The stings of criticism, however, were definitely aimed at him, for they were over the issue of whether to make the gunboats more recognizable. He had continued emphatically to reject exotic paint schemes or other proposals to distinguish gunboats from other vessels on the river. The Japanese regretted that some powers considered "the flags printed on the awnings to be sufficient." Their pilots had found it impossible to distinguish flags without coming in "so low as to be greatly exposed to enemy anti-aircraft artillery fire." In addition, recognition depended on the relative position of the ship to the sun and how faded or soiled the flag had become.[19]

On the same day that Mr. Lockhart reported the Japanese consul's double-edged message, Mr. Samuel Sokobin, consul at Tsingtao, gave the final summary of an incident commencing on June 20. On that date Mrs. T. H. Massie, wife of Lieutenant Massie of the *Tulsa,* was slapped by a Japanese sentry on a pier in Tsingtao—even though she was being escorted at the time by two United States Navy enlisted men, one of whom was on shore patrol duty. Although the incident was reported to the American consul and notes were exchanged between Mr. Sokobin and his Japanese colleague, the two navies mutually smoothed over the repercussions of the event.

By coincidence, Captain R. F. McConnell, chief of staff, Asiatic Fleet, arrived in the *Augusta* on July 3 and immediately the Japanese chief of staff made an official call on him. He expressed the regrets of the Japanese Navy, admitted the actions of the sentry were unjustified, and sought ways to cooperate to prevent recurrence of such incidents and to settle them locally without reference to home governments. Captain McConnell accepted the apology, assured his visitor that the U.S. Navy would cooperate to prevent incidents of this kind, but pointed out that the present case was "being handled by the United States State Department" and that the United States Navy "had neither made nor received any communications with Japanese authorities in regard to the incident."[20]

Admiral Yarnell, in transmitting a summary of the discussions between the chiefs of staff to Mr. Sokobin, commented that it was "not exactly accurate to say that understanding had been reached between the American and Japanese authorities with regard to the final settlement of the case." However, since the Japanese naval authorities had shown a conciliatory attitude and appeared willing to cooperate to prevent recurrence, Yarnell could see nothing was to be "gained by continuing the controversy and that the incident should be considered closed."[21] Hull, probably pleasantly surprised to read such a report for a change, acquiesced in Yarnell's suggestion to consider the incident closed.

The presence of the *Monocacy* in the war zone, and the repeated suggestions by the Japanese to improve recognition techniques, prompted another communiqué to Ambassador Johnson, but it was meant as much for Admiral Yarnell as for anyone. Expressing his hope again that no unfortunate incidents would occur, Hull desired that intensive thought be given to the problems of operating naval vessels in the areas of fighting. His own words best describe his feeling of responsibility.

> I suggest that there be avoided express refusals to comply with Japanese and Chinese requests, suggestions or notifications; that if and when replies are made, their tone be made conciliatory; and that movements and operations of vessels be at all times such as to avoid fact or implication of being obstructive. I have neither authority nor desire to give commands regarding naval operations, especially at long range; but I am responsible in regard to the conducting of the foreign relations of the United States as a whole, and I am extremely solicitous that important efforts in other connections be not jeopardized by possible occurrence of unfortunate incidents in the local situation.[22]

Hull's telegram had just been sent when an incoming message, originated in Chefoo by Consul Quincy F. Roberts, reported the latest incident between the Navy and Japanese authorities. Intoxicated American sailors had assaulted four policemen and the Japanese chief of police. Preliminary investigation fixed the blame on the sailors and an acceptable basis for settling the matter had been worked out with the Japanese consul. On behalf of the Commander in Chief, Asiatic Fleet, Consul Roberts expressed regrets, promised that the naval personnel would be punished and that reimbursement for medical costs and torn uniforms, amounting to $55, would be made. During the investigation, however, a new incident occurred. The Japanese chief of police insulted Americans in general, the consul and senior naval officers in particular, and threatened them by flourishing an automatic pistol. This phase too was resolved by Mr. Roberts and the Japanese consul with the acceptance of a full apology from the bellicose chief of police in the presence of the ranking naval officers, the American consul, and puppet Chinese police officials.[23]

Roberts, who had acted promptly to settle the dispute locally, was criticized by his superior, the first secretary of the embassy in Peiping, Mr. Salisbury—first, for waiting five days after the incident before making the report; second, for acting on his own without prior approval of his seniors in the diplomatic system, and finally, for expressing the regrets of Admiral Yarnell which "would have more appropriately have been made by an American naval officer."[24] Fortunately for Mr. Roberts and future Japanese-American relations at Chefoo, Secretary Hull, Ambassador Johnson, and Admiral Yarnell all supported the actions of the consul. Yarnell came to his defense by asserting that Roberts had, in fact, cleared his actions with the Navy before agreeing with the Japanese to settle the matter locally. Johnson and Hull agreed with Yarnell that it was highly desirable to resolve minor differences locally. Again the Japanese diplomats appeared genuinely to want to maintain amicable relations with the United States.

On July 27, the *Monocacy* was present at the Japanese capture of Kiukiang in the course of which a Japanese gunboat approached the *Monocacy,* rendered honors, and departed back downstream. It was the last friendly gesture by the Japanese toward the *Monocacy* for weeks. The harbinger of future treatment came with a letter from the Japanese senior naval officer at Kiukiang denying the *Monocacy* permission to contact the American nationals in the Kiukiang area or to move the vessel to the Standard Oil installation nearby.[25] The next day the Japanese Navy representative at Kiukiang informed the commanding officer of the *Monocacy* that he would like to cooperate, but his orders came from the Army command at Nanking and future movements of the *Monocacy* were in the hands of higher authority at Nanking.[26] By this time Admiral Yarnell was very perturbed over the treatment of the *Monocacy;* little did he realize that much worse treatment was yet to come.

Since Admiral Yarnell was located in Shanghai and he wanted to communicate directly with the senior military commands in Nanking, he sent his messages through the *Oahu* at Nanking. Preferring to deal with the Japanese naval command rather than their army, Admiral Yarnell pointed out the obvious: the fighting was over and duty demanded that *Monocacy* officers promptly gain touch with American nationals and assist them in every way. The ship also required fuel. He requested that Admiral Koshira Oikawa, Commander, Third Fleet, issue the necessary instructions for the *Monocacy* to proceed to the Standard Oil installation by the end of the week.[27] The Japanese Army's authority over naval ships' movements was reemphasized in the answer to Yarnell's request. Rear Admiral Kusaga, the chief of staff of the Third Fleet, strongly objected to any shift of berth by the *Monocacy*, although he expressed sympathetic understanding of the desire to contact nationals and promised active cooperation to that end. He was unable, however, to forecast a date when such would be possible. Rear Admiral Nobutake Kondo reported on July 31 from Kiukiang that *Monocacy*'s movement from her berth to the city would interfere with Japanese operations and that consent of the army would have to be secured.[28]

On August 5, Commander Tanaga in Nanking informed the commanding officer, *Oahu*, that the Japanese Navy had no objection to the *Monocacy* berthing at the Standard Oil installation, but would not agree to her "doing so until permission had been obtained from General Shunroka Hata in Shanghai because of the previous 'unfortunate experience in Nanking,' "—the *Panay* sinking. The Japanese Army's answer was forthcoming. The *Monocacy* was refused permission to shift berth on the grounds that the new location would "permit close observation of their transports anchored in that vicinity and other military operations."[29] The United States Navy representative in Nanking made a strong protest against this attitude on the grounds that "we had no real interests in their military operations, were deeply conscious of our neutral status, and that their illogical objections to our reasonable request were incompatible with their repeated official protestations of respect for American rights and interests in China." Since they had allowed the *Monocacy* officers to contact the American nationals by letter, the Japanese Navy representatives in Kiukiang considered the matter settled except "to try to obtain permission from military headquarters for the *Monocacy* to . . . get fuel and then return to present anchorage."[30]

At this stage, Admiral Yarnell had almost exhausted the peaceful courses of action he could follow in the China area to get the Japanese to cooperate on the *Monocacy* question. On August 15, he called upon the Navy Department to seek the help of the State Department. It was necessary for the *Monocacy* to proceed to Shanghai on account of shortage of fuel and provisions and for relief of personnel. Yarnell stated that he was reluctant to bring about an incident by directing the *Monocacy* to proceed without Japanese consent, and he requested that the State Department take the matter up with Tokyo to secure permission for the passage to Shanghai.[31] The Secretary of the Navy immediately relayed Yarnell's message to the State Department for appropriate action. In instructions to the ambassador in Tokyo the American position on Japanese control of the Yangtze was spelled out by virtue of their possessing a captured boom across the river at

Matung. The Japanese claimed that because the boom was a prize of war, their control of traffic through the river naturally and legally followed. Hull told Ambassador Grew that the government of course could not "admit any such right or the validity of the basis invoked in support of that asserted right." Grew was directed to approach the Foreign Office to get the Japanese government to put an end to the "opposition of the Japanese military authorities" to the *Monocacy*'s passage to Shanghai.[32]

Both Hull and Grew still operated under the long-established basis of international relations that responsible governments either controlled or were held accountable for the actions of their military forces. They soon found out that, under existing arrangements in the government of Japan, the military commanders in China had the authority for ultimate decisions in the China area. A report of this development reached Washington on the same date via two routes. Ambassador Grew reported to the Secretary of State on August 19 that his efforts to obtain authority for the *Monocacy* to proceed to Shanghai had "proved abortive." He had been advised that it was the intention of the Japanese government not to intervene in the exercise by Admiral Oikawa of the discretionary powers vested in him. Having been thus rebuffed, Ambassador Grew took his case to the minister for foreign affairs and made strong oral arguments, basing his approach upon practical considerations and legitimate rights. He told the foreign minister that it was difficult to believe that the Japanese government "would leave entirely to the discretion of one of its subordinate officers the decision in a matter involving one of the primary rights of the United States." The foreign minister immediately consulted Admiral Oikawa, whose reply, relayed to Ambassador Grew, was that military operations precluded moving the *Monocacy* at the time, but that the Japanese Navy would provide logistic support to the gunboat until such time as it could be moved. Grew considered this "as a categorical refusal" and, while fully appreciating the seriousness of the issue involved, thought that there was no doubt but that he had "exhausted diplomatic resources."[33]

On August 19, Admiral Yarnell learned from Japanese naval sources in Nanking that decisions concerning the *Monocacy* would be made in China. Admiral Oikawa offered the same logistic support which the foreign minister had mentioned to Grew, but reiterated the previous objections to the gunboat's moving downstream. Admiral Oikawa emphasized to Admiral Yarnell that moving the *Monocacy* would interfere with Japanese strategy and tactics, that there was a danger of a chance mine, and that—because of possible mistaken identity—there was a danger of being fired upon by "excited Japanese gun crews." Finally, the Matung barrier was a prize of war and third powers had no more right to expect passage through it than they would have had if it remained an intact barrier under Chinese control.[34]

The attempts to put the negotiations concerning the *Monocacy* into the diplomatic system had failed and Admiral Yarnell's bargaining position was back to that of four days earlier with two new developments bearing on the situation. In the first, Admiral Oikawa's hand was strengthened considerably by the Japanese foreign office deferring ultimate authority to the Japanese military forces in China. Admiral Yarnell had no immediate countermove, since he had just exhausted the possibilities of diplomatic assistance in obtaining a clearance for the *Monocacy* to move. The second development was the assertion of cooperation and understanding by the Japanese admiral to Admiral Yarnell. Japanese restrictions on the freedom of movement had not changed; they controlled the passage through the boom at Matung in the river and in this case possession equaled ten-tenths of the law. The offer of Japanese logistic support had possibilities, and Admiral Yarnell recognized that the future of the *Monocacy* necessitated his cooperation with the Japanese naval commanders on the Yangtze.

The day after receiving the offer of help from Admiral Oikawa, Admiral Yarnell informed Admiral Leahy that, unless he was directed otherwise, he would reply to Admiral Oikawa and accept his offer. Without relinquishing any rights of freedom to navigate the Yangtze and recognizing the "special situation now existing below Kiukiang," he would delay sailing the *Monocacy* until a later date.[35] Admiral Leahy answered immediately that Yarnell's proposal was approved except for the acceptance of transportation of fuel and provisions from the Japanese. Also, the State Department recommended the words "in view of navigational difficulties" in lieu of "recognize special situation" which had been proposed originally.[36]

As the *Monocacy*'s fuel supply dwindled to its very end, Admiral Yarnell advised the Chief of Naval Operations, before informing Admiral Oikawa, "*Monocacy* must proceed Shanghai prior 10 September due shortage fuel and provisions request your view."[37] Yarnell had his answer the next day. He was to discuss with the Japanese command on the Yangtze "the necessity for the USS *Monocacy* to either proceed to Shanghai or to obtain coal from mill belonging to Anderson Myers, and that you very much prefer having the *Monocacy* proceed to Shanghai." At the same time it was suggested that an escort through the boom at Matung be requested. Admiral Leahy's suggestions were promptly passed via the *Oahu* to Admiral Oikawa.[38]

Admiral Yarnell's message setting September 10 as a deadline for the *Monocacy* to move down river motivated Admiral Oikawa, in a most unusual show of trust in Admiral Yarnell's integrity, to confide in the Americans the difficulties experienced by the Japanese in their river operations and to show the inconvenience of moving the *Monocacy* at the time. The Japanese had swept only a narrow channel between Wuhu and a point 15 miles above Kiukiang, in the process of which more than 700 mines had been destroyed and numerous casualties sustained by their ships. Below Kiukiang and at six locations pointed out on charts, Chinese detached units were very active. Above Wuhu it was necessary for all ships to proceed in convoys with a destroyer escort and all convoys were subject to sniping and indirect fire from Chinese field and heavy artillery located inland from the river. Congestion on the river was caused by the operation of hundreds of large ships and thousands of small craft. Their numbers presented a serious problem which would be complicated by the passage of even one small gunboat. In addition, passage down of the *Monocacy* would undoubtedly be followed by similar British demands for HMS *Cockchafer* and passage up of reliefs and ships of third powers. Admiral Oikawa believed the Japanese had never questioned the fundamental right of third powers to free navigation of the Yangtze but that the Japanese Navy did claim control of the passage through barriers by virtue of their capture and military nature.[39]

Admiral Yarnell, the following day, thanked Admiral Oikawa for the courtesies and frankness of his confidence and assured him that the trust would be respected. In view of Oikawa's consideration and friendly attitude, Yarnell was "willing to accede to his wishes and hold the USS *Monocacy* at Kiukiang for the time being."[40]

Meanwhile, in Washington, liaison between the working levels of the State and Navy Departments showed agreement that the Navy Department "would send no reply to Admiral Yarnell: In other words, the Navy Department would leave Admiral Yarnell free to accept the Japanese offer to transport mail, supplies, and possible personnel."[41] Yarnell did accept the Japanese offer to support the *Monocacy,* and on September 8 the flow of provisions upstream began from Shanghai. The first shipment of 16,000 pounds of naval stores, motion picture films, and mail was forwarded via HIJM *Steshio Maru*.[42] A few days later, HIJM *Azuchi Maru* departed Shanghai with sixty-eight packages of refrigerated provisions, ship's service and medical stores and one bag of mail.[43]

Coal continued to be a critical item. The *Oahu* was ordered to inform Japanese naval authorities that while periodic access to the Anderson Myers coal pile was "now permitted," *Monocacy* had no adequate equipment for the transportation of this fuel." The senior naval officer, at Kiukiang, agreed to deliver fuel but then stated that the navy had no facilities and was unable to arrange with the army to do so. "Request arrangements be made to supply the gunboat with coal of about 25 tons per week."[44] So coal was added to the shopping list of supplies being delivered by the Japanese.

In mid-September, one of the most interesting airlifts of the Sino-Japanese War took place. On September 14, a dozen sailors relieved from duty on the *Monocacy* were returned to Shanghai by a Japanese airplane provided by Admiral Oikawa. On September 24, two officers and thirteen enlisted replacements were flown in to Kiukiang, and on September 25, two officers and thirteen men relieved from duty on the *Monocacy* were returned to Shanghai by the Japanese plane.[45]

Further cooperation in Kiukiang was evidenced by a report from the *Monocacy* on September 26 that arrangements had been made with the Japanese Army for *Monocacy* to visit various missionaries to ascertain their needs and to explain the method of obtaining the same from Shanghai. All contact since August 6 had been by letter through the Japanese. The following day, two months after the Japanese had taken Kiukiang, a *Monocacy* officer, accompanied by a Japanese army officer and vice consul, visited Americans in the city. They were comfortable and, except for a scarcity of staples, there was no food shortage. The isolation of the *Monocacy* and the missionaries was over.[46]

The *Monocacy* episode pointed up a number of factors which would bear on future Japanese-American relationships over the Asiatic Fleet forces. First, the Japanese military forces in China were the ultimate authority on relations with third powers where military operations were involved. Second, the Japanese Army held higher authority than the Navy and was prone to be less cooperative with the Asiatic Fleet. Third, the Japanese were meeting unexpectedly stubborn Chinese resistance, which necessitated heavier Japanese effort than had been planned. Convenience to third powers would have a low priority. Finally, the Asiatic Fleet forces had to rely upon diplomatic representations to a government whose authority over its army in China was limited at best. The safety of American naval vessels and citizens and the security of property were in the hands of the Japanese military forces in China. In 1938 the Japanese still needed American oil, machinery, and iron for her war machine, so limited cooperation with the Asiatic Fleet was to their national interest. The understanding between Admiral Oikawa and Admiral Yarnell in the fall of 1938 was the high point of that cooperation.

While there might have been a flurry of cooperation in China with the Japanese Navy, there were also concurrent maneuverings within the United States Navy for possible better positions vis-à-vis the Japanese. Through the depression years the Japanese had been allowed to operate a very old transport, the *Mariana Maru,* in the copra trade in and out of Guam's only harbor. Since the administration of the island was a naval responsibility, the governor in July sought authority from the Navy Department to terminate the privileges of entry on September 30, 1938, the expiration date of the then current permit. The governor had information that, upon renewal of permission of entry authorization, the Japanese planned to replace the *Mariana Maru* with a bigger, more modern transport and to ask that the entry privilege be transferred to the newer vessel.

The Secretary of the Navy reviewed the Guam situation in the light of Japanese ship visits and United States defense requirements in a letter to the Secretary of State on July 28. The harbor at Guam had, by an Executive Order of September 23, 1912, been made a closed port to "any commercial or privately owned vessel of foreign registry [or] to any foreign national vessel, except by special authority of the United States Navy Department in each case." The Navy Department had approved the recommendation of the governor to revoke the privilege of entry of the *Mariana Maru* when the term of her permission expired. Admiral Leahy suggested that the Secretary of State inform the Japanese ambassador "that no action on his request to replace the *Mariana Maru* appeared necessary since the Navy Department [had] recently decided to close Guam to the entry of all vessels of foreign registry."[47]

The Hepburn Board studies contributed heavily to the actions by the Navy relative to the *Mariana Maru.* Congress, in May 1938, had directed the appointment of a board to survey the requirements for additional submarine, destroyer, minecraft, and naval air bases in the United States and its possessions. Rear Admiral A. J. Hepburn and his board were in Guam at the time of the initiation of the governor's letter. The Navy did not care to give the Japanese a ringside seat to view possible improvements in Apra Harbor. The board published its report on December 1, 1938. Pointing out concomitantly the defenseless position of Guam and its great potential, the board recommended that a strong air and submarine base be built there. With such a base, it reasoned, operations against the Philippines by Japan would be "a precarious undertaking"; extensive hostile naval operations to the southward would be impeded, if not denied, to Japan and "in time of sudden emergency Guam would provide for security of our Asiatic Fleet." The board's recommendations relative to bases in Alaska, Wake, Midway, and Oahu were eventually fulfilled, but, ironically, the first step in improving Guam as a base—a bill to authorize the dredging of Apra Harbor for submarines—failed to pass Congress.

In the fall of 1938 on the opposite side of the world, the threat of war in Europe grew heavier day by day. The German demands on Czechoslovakia in September, the ensuing Munich conference, and the hopeful "peace in our time" bought by Britain's Prime Minister Neville Chamberlain and France's Foreign Minister Edouard Daladier focused attention on Europe. The meteoric rise of Adolph Hitler in Germany had caught the war planners unprepared. The only current plan was the latest *Orange Plan* which, of course, related only to Japan. It was obvious to the planners that the European situation would increasingly bear upon the American strategic position. On November 12, 1938, the Joint Board instructed the Joint Planning Committee to make exploratory studies of practicable courses of action open to the military and naval forces of the United States "in the event of (a) violation of the Monroe Doctrine by one or more of the Fascist powers, and (b) a simultaneous attempt to expand Japanese influence in the Philippines."[48] Although the war planners would not finish their study until well into 1939, the product of their efforts would be the start of a new family of war plans to meet the vastly more complicated problem of multiple potential enemies hemispheres apart.

CHAPTER 4

British-American Strategic Planning

The opening days of 1939 found the Japanese very much stalemated in their Chinese conquest drive. The seizures of Canton on the south coast of China and Hankow on the Yangtze in October 1938 were the last significant achievements. Chiang Kai-shek's withdrawal of the Nationalist capitol further upriver to Chungking irretrievably eliminated the possibilities of an early end to the war. The drain on resources and the loss of prestige by the Japanese Army gave the Japanese Navy the additional leverage it needed to gain concurrence in executing the next phase of the southward expansion policy.

On February 10, 1939, the Japanese occupied the island of Hainan off the coast of Indochina and nearly midway between Hong Kong and Singapore. As pointed out by Ambassador Grew at the time, possession of this strategic real estate enabled the Japanese to "check all traffic into and out of Hanoi," to control the South China Sea between China and Luzon in the Philippines, and to limit the "sphere dominated by Singapore."[1] The token objection by the French government, which had had an understanding with the Japanese that the status quo of the island would be maintained, was largely ignored.

While the Japanese were leap-frogging well to the south of their home islands, the United States House of Representatives debated and defeated an appropriation bill of $5 million to dredge Apra Harbor in Guam. Fear of appearing to be taking a stand against the Japanese prompted a number of votes against the bill. The isolationist tide in the United States then was very strong indeed.

Meantime, in Shanghai, the Japanese stepped up pressure on the municipal council to obtain control over the police matters in the International Settlement. A number of assassinations in the area gave the Japanese the excuse for demanding joint authority, ostensibly to control the terrorists. Admiral Yarnell, whose Asiatic Fleet command included the Fourth Marines at Shanghai, specifically ordered Colonel Joseph Charles Fegan, United States Marine Corps, not to enter into any agreement with the Japanese over sharing authority: "Either the commander of the Fourth Marines must have full authority or this force must be withdrawn entirely."[2] For the time being Japanese demands were ignored by the council. The International Settlement, because of the legal nature of the extraterritoriality of its component parts, was still considered American, British, Italian, and Japanese land. The French concession adjacent to the settlement was likewise considered part of France. The Japanese were not yet ready to take control of the national territory of such powers and certainly not all at the same time.

No such restraints deterred their annexing the Spratley Islands on March 30. These scattered bits of coral, located approximately 700 miles southwest of Manila, had been claimed by both France and Japan since the 1920s. Their strategic importance was that they afforded excellent anchorages for light naval forces and possible sites for airfields, but even more, they were midway between Hainan and Singapore—less than 700 miles from the most powerful British base east of Suez.

While the Japanese were moving southward, they were also pressing hard in Shanghai to test foreign reactions. On March 8, the Shanghai municipal police and the Japanese gendarmerie raided the American sector and arrested some Chinese without either American or council permission. Admiral Yarnell protested vigorously to the chairman of the municipal council, Mr. Cornell S. Franklin, who likewise protested to the Japanse consul general.[3] The American consul general, Mr. Clarence Edward Gauss, very adroitly kept the disputes within diplomatic channels. As the legal maneuverings continued it was apparent that, without any successes against the Chinese in the war, the Japanese were anxious to control commercial and financial interests in Shanghai and especially to deny to the Chinese the International Settlement as a haven from which to conduct their lucrative businesses.

In the spring of 1939, the United States Navy was involved in an unusual display of goodwill which came close to producing some undesirable results. Ambassador Hiroshi Saito had died in Washington at the end of February. As a friendly gesture President Roosevelt offered to make the heavy cruiser *Astoria,* commanded by Captain

Richmond Kelly Turner, available to transport Saito's ashes to Japan. The Japanese not only accepted the offer, but, trying to get maximum mileage out of the event, portrayed the visit as the start of a new era of understanding and friendship and as an approval of their policies vis-à-vis China. Lavish gifts and entertainment were planned for Captain Turner and his officers. It taxed the diplomatic ability of Ambassador Grew, with Secretary of State Hull giving advice from Washington, to decline, without offending, all but a tactful level of entertainment and participation by Captain Turner and his crew.

While Captain Turner was having an audience with the Japanese emperor, an interesting operation—especially in the light of latter-day relationships—was taking place on the Yangtze. On April 23, 1939, the Asiatic Fleet ships *Isabel* and *Oahu* departed Hankow, which had been in Japanese hands since the previous October, for Shanghai, taking twenty-four Americans, eleven Russians, four Swedes, and a Norwegian. The Russian contingent consisted of the counselor of the Soviet embassy, his wife, eight staff members, and a Tass journalist. The Japanese at the time were literally in control of all passenger traffic on the river since their commercial ships were the only ones moving freely up and down the river. In addition, foreign nationals had to get Japanese military "permission" to leave and to return to river ports even on naval vessels of their parent country. In previous weeks Grew and Hull had protested to the Japanese their controlling the movement of Americans, especially between Shanghai and Hankow where there was no fighting. In this particular move Admiral Yarnell had informed the Japanese admiral at Hankow of the identity of the Russian passengers, while the American, Swedish, and Norwegian consuls had identified their respective nationals to the Japanese consul general only so that their applications for passage on Japanese vessels might be withdrawn. Japanese authorities were not asked for permission to leave nor did they intimate that it was necessary. Evidently moves to Shanghai were acceptable since they were departures. On returns of Americans to Hankow and Kiukiang the consuls had to argue for each on a case-by-case basis with the Japanese consul general at Shanghai.[4]

In less than a month the Japanese were putting new pressures simultaneously on the International Settlements at Shanghai and Amoy. On May 12, at the insistence of the French consul general at Shanghai as head of the French concession, a joint proclamation was issued in conjunction with the chairman of the Shanghai municipal council. Its purpose was concomitantly to answer the Japanese complaints about Chinese "terrorist" activities in the foreign settlements and, at least in words, to serve notice on Japan that its own activities in the same areas would be controlled. The proclamation cautioned the "public that the neutrality of the foreign areas must be strictly respected and that unless political activity ceases immediately it will be necessary, without warning, to introduce strict curfew measures, and to expel all persons engaging in political activities." Finally notice was given by the French concession and the International Settlement administrators that they would take "the most drastic steps within their power to punish any person who at this time commits any act prejudicial to the preservation of peace, order and good government."[5]

Admiral Yarnell was quite concerned over possible Japanese reaction to the proclamation. He recommended to Admiral Leahy that the State Department notify the Japanese foreign office that "any unilateral action against the present Government of the International Settlement will be viewed with grave concern." Yarnell believed that the State Department should make public its notification to the Foreign Office "in order that the Nipponese Army will know, without being informed by their Foreign Office, of the views and attitude of the United States Government." This recommendation was made out of fear that the Japanese army "may take action without knowledge or approval of the Tokyo Foreign Office."[6] Hull did not publicize the decision to act on Yarnell's suggestion, but he did send instructions immediately to Grew to confer with the foreign minister on the subject. The foreign minister assured him categorically that "Japan had no intention whatever to occupy the International Settlement in Shanghai."[7]

On the same day that Admiral Yarnell requested the State Department to caution the Japanese against precipitously taking control of the International Settlement at Shanghai, the American consul at Amoy, Mr. Karl deGiers MacVitty, reported that the Japanese had landed 150 marines in the International Settlement at Kulangsu opposite Amoy. The next day, by coincidence, the Asiatic Fleet destroyer *Bulmer* arrived and two days later Captain John Taylor Gause Stapler, Commander, South China Patrol, Asiatic Fleet, arrived in the cruiser *Marblehead*. Admiral Sir Percy Lockhart Harnam Noble, in HMS *Birmingham*, with three destroyers, arrived the following day. For a show of joint strength, the American and British naval officers and consuls decided to land naval parties equal in number to the Japanese troops in the settlement. The French joined the show the following day with the arrival of a gunboat and subsequently landed a naval force equal in number to each of the others. Hull was perturbed over the landings and requested that the consul give him "by priority radio a statement setting forth how the landing of American naval units may contribute toward protecting American lives against excited and lawless elements," and to provide him with "more detailed daily radio reports than those thus far received."[8]

For the next five months a contingent of United States sailors and Marines, along with an equal number of Japanese forces, remained in Kulangsu, the British and French having withdrawn their forces to Europe after the commencement of hostilities with Germany in September. The persevering Japanese tried to coerce the municipal council into agreeing to turn over to them control of the police and administration of the council by cutting off food and fuel supplies from the mainland. It was truly a dress rehearsal in miniature for action in Shanghai. Diplomatic pressures by the British and Americans and a continued naval presence on the part of the United States, which allowed enough food to enter the International Settlement to negate the effect of the blockade, contributed immeasurably to the resulting impasse. Final resolution of the standoff occurred in October when the council reached agreement with the Japanese consul general to appoint one Japanese inspector of police, to suppress terrorists, and to hire ten additional Formosans as police at a later date. The day following the signing of the agreement, the Japanese and American forces were withdrawn simultaneously. In Kulangsu, as in Shanghai, the administrative rights of the council were protected, at least for the time being. The failure of the Japanese to carry their objective of complete control was due in no small measure to the collective action by the interested powers.

Cordell Hull, who was uncomfortable enough over the participation of American naval forces in the international confrontation at Kulangsu, was even more so when he read an Associated Press report on June 23 that eight American sailors from the destroyer *Pillsbury* were patrolling the entrances to the American Baptist Mission in Swatow. After giving his consul a lesson on the "Department's concept that naval units are landed for the purposes of protection of American citizens from individual acts of lawlessness and dangers incident to serious disorder," Hull asked for details of the landings. In identical language used on Mr. MacVitty at Amoy a month earlier, he also said he "would appreciate receiving if possible somewhat more detailed daily radio reports than those thus received."[9] A prompt reply to the Secretary of State told of several hundred panicky Chinese in the mission compound, a total absence of Chinese police protection, and insufficient Japanese protection to safeguard American property and citizens. The Japanese did not object at any time to the American landing force which was withdrawn in a few days, much to Hull's relief. No force had been necessary since the presence of American military strength alone was enough to restore order.

In June, while the international naval forces glared at each other in Kulangsu, the British were having second thoughts on long-range British-American naval force cooperation in the Far East. The assumptions which Admiral Leahy had passed to his fleet commanders for planning purposes in February 1938 were invalidated by events in Europe. The situation there had again drawn the major units of the British fleet to European waters. What would have been suspected by even an amateur strategist studying the deepening crisis in 1939 was confirmed by informal talks in Washington. The British naval attache, Captain L. C. A. St. J. Curzon-Howe, and Commander T. C. Hampton of the Admiralty met with Admiral Leahy and Rear Admiral Robert Lee Ghormley, chief of the War Plans Division in June. Commander Hampton, who was en route to duty in the Asiatic Station, had been sent to tell the Chief of Naval Operations that the situation in Europe and the Far East had changed so much during the past year-and-a-half that the Admiralty now had to give priority to the threat of Germany and Italy. If "Japan threatened, the British would not be able to send the force to the Far East that had been contemplated in the conversations with Rear Admiral Ingersoll."[10] This information was reaffirmed days later when Ambassador J. P. Kennedy reported from London on an all-day session of the cabinet on June 27 over the possibility of sending capital ships to Singapore as a threat to Japan for the humiliation of British subjects in Tientsin. The decision had been made in that case to weather the storm in Tientsin because the British fleet could not take on the Japanese and protect England against the German threat simultaneously.[11]

The British strategy, according to Commander Hampton, was "to maintain a portion of their Fleet in home waters and the remainder, except part of the China Detachment and the Dominion Forces, in the Eastern Mediterranean." In case of war in which Japan became involved, they would concentrate on Italy, the supposed weak link, and as soon as Italy was reduced, send naval reinforcements to the Far East. At the time, officers in the Admiralty were inclined to believe that Japan was less likely to join Germany and Italy than she was eighteen months earlier. Admiral Leahy informed his British visitors

45

that he could not commit the United States Navy to any definite agreement, that he did not know what action Congress would take in case of trouble, nor could he discuss any action other than "parallel action." Leahy did say that the United States would undoubtedly send most of its naval forces to Hawaii in case of a European war in which Japan was involved and the United States was neutral.[12] Following the meeting, Admiral Leahy directed his fleet commanders to change their war plans to reflect the inability of Britain to send a large force to Singapore due to the world situation.[13]

A far-reaching move by President Roosevelt was made the following month. By issueing a Military Order on July 5, Roosevelt transferred the Joint Board into the newly established Executive Office of the President. The effect was that the Chief of Staff, Army and the Chief of Naval Operations were raised above their immediate civilian superiors and given a position of influencing national as well as service strategies. Roosevelt had earlier designated the two service chiefs to work directly with the under secretary of state in a standing liaison committee, which had been proposed by Hull to deal operationally with Latin American problems. The timing of these organizational changes was significant. The military service chiefs were in an unparalleled position to influence presidential decisions just before the start of war in Europe, just as new war plans were evolving and just as Admirals Leahy and Yarnell were being relieved as Chief of Naval Operations and Commander in Chief, Asiatic Fleet, respectively.

Meanwhile, the Japanese appeared to have taken a new tack in China during June and July. Having failed to crush Chiang Kai-shek's elusive armies, they launched a relentless campaign of bombing open, definitely non-military cities and hamlets, apparently to terrorize the Chinese people into submission. The effects were opposite to those desired—a stiffening of the will to resist and adverse world public opinion. As for the United States, there was more than public opinion involved. Concurrently, there was a marked increase in incidents of bombing of property, schools, and churches flying the American flag. On June 12 and again on July 6–7 bombs were dropped close aboard the USS *Tutuila,* and near the embassy office and embassy residential quarters in Chungking. After nonresponsive replies and inaction, even the pacific Cordell Hull had had enough. The President, Hull, and a unanimous Senate agreed upon the termination of the Treaty of Commerce and Navigation between Japan and the United States which dated from 1911. On July 26, Hull notified Japanese Ambassador Kemsuke Horinouchi that, according to the terms of the treaty, it would be ended six months later, in January 1940. The United States had finally taken a positive step—one which would allow economic sanctions to be used against Japan. The Japanese paused to weigh the significance but, in the absence of anything further, were not deterred from their course.

Through the early months of 1939, while the Japanese advanced southward to Hainan and the Spratley Islands and increased the tempo of activity against the International Settlements in China, in Washington the war planners of the Joint Planning Committee labored at reviewing plans in the light of the increasing German menace to the world. They presented their study in April, five and a half months after receiving the directive. The decision of the British to concentrate naval forces in Europe to check the Germans and Italians was a difficult one to make, for it meant weakening their position against the Japanese at a time when strengthening that position was the order of the day. The American war planners, in a more limited sense, found themselves in the same position. If the Western Hemisphere were to be defended against a rising German and Italian threat, naval forces would have to be used because they were the only existing military force. Force to be used in the Western Hemisphere could not be used against Japan also and a one-ocean navy could not be spread around the world and be effective.

The war planners concluded that Germany and Italy could violate the Monroe Doctrine by supporting Fascist revolutions in Latin America. The relegation of such countries to the status of colonies would give to their European exploiters the advantages of trade, access to raw materials, and military and naval bases. From such bases the Panama Canal possibly could be attacked. Finally, the planners discounted the possibilities of German or Italian action in Latin America unless: (a) Germany believed that Britain and France would not intervene and (b) Japan moved to attack the Philippines and Guam and even then only in case the United States had responded to the Japanese attack by counterattack in the western Pacific.[14]

However, to overcome glaring deficiencies in existing war plans concerning concerted action by Germany, Italy, and Japan, the Joint Planning Committee recommended that future plans reflect new possibilities. That recommendation received immediate approval and action. In less than three weeks, four of a new family of tentative plans were offered to the Joint Board for approval. The most limited plan, *Rainbow 1,* provided for the defense of the Western Hemisphere south to the bulge of Brazil, 10° S. Two other plans provided alterna-

47

tively for the extension of operations from this area: *Rainbow 2*, to the western Pacific, and *Rainbow 3*, to the rest of South America. *Rainbow 4* envisaged Great Britain and France at war with Germany and Italy and possibly Japan, with the assumption that the United States would be involved as a major participant.

Reexamination of the possibilities under *Rainbow 4* led the planners to the conclusion that if all the major powers were at war using their current forces, operations in Latin America would probably be very limited in scope whereas operations by Japan in the Pacific would probably be extensive in scope. The recommendation was made that there be two plans covering United States participation with Britain and France against Germany, Italy, and Japan. One plan provided for the United States to furnish armies for a maximum effort in Europe against Germany and Italy, while the other plan called for not providing maximum effort in Europe, maintaining the Monroe Doctrine, and carrying out "allied Democratic Power tasks in the Pacific." The Navy by that time, June 1939, had completed talks with the British over cooperation in the Pacific against the Japanese and unofficial agreements had been reached. The joint planning committee recommended that the plan for the United States to concentrate war effort in the Pacific be moved up in priority to the *Rainbow 2* position where it might "conceivably press more for answers" than plans other than *Rainbow 1* would. Part of the justification for the change in priority read:

> Whether or not we have any possible intention of undertaking a war in this situation, nevertheless we may take measures short of war, and in doing so should clarify the possible or probable war task that would be involved.[15]

A week later, on June 30, the Joint Board approved the recommended change in priority. The revised description of the new five *Rainbow* plans read:

1. To prevent violation of the Monroe Doctrine, and to protect the United States, its possessions, and its sea trade.

2. To carry out No. 1, and also to sustain the authority of democratic powers in the Pacific zones.

3. To secure control of the Western Pacific.

4. To afford hemisphere defense, through sending U.S. task forces if needed to South America, and to the eastern Atlantic.

5. To achieve the purposes of 1 and 4, also to provide ultimately for

sending forces to Africa or Europe in order to effect the decisive defeat of Germany or Italy or both. This plan assumed U.S. cooperation with Great Britain and France.[16]

With the definitions of strategic objectives having been clarified, the Joint Planning Committee had the basis for all future planning until the United States entered the war in December 1941. Shifting emphases in the priority of developing the five *Rainbow* plans resulted from changes in the international situation. All the plans in one way or another had a bearing on the two plans against Japan, *Rainbows 2* and *3*.

As should be expected, the security of the Western Hemisphere received first priority. *Rainbow 1* was submitted to the Joint Board on July 27, 1939, where it was studied, slightly changed, and submitted directly to President Roosevelt in accordance with his Military Order of July 5; he approved the plan orally on October 14, 1939.

On August 14, while the plan was before the President, Admiral Harold Raynsford Stark, who had become Chief of Naval Operations on August 1, sent to Sumner Welles, under secretary of state, a secret memorandum relative to the political aspects of *Rainbow 1*. He believed it was necessary that Welles should read it for background information, but felt that since it quoted joint basic war plans it should be destroyed or otherwise protected after it had been read. This was an opening move for future close personal relations between Admiral Stark and Mr. Welles. Part of the secret memorandum read:

> ...The *General Situation* under which these plans are being prepared is as follows: Germany, Italy and Japan, acting in concert, violate the letter and spirit of the Monroe Doctrine. Japan, supported by Germany and Italy, violates by armed aggression vital interests of the United States in the Western Pacific. It is to be assumed that aggression initiated by one or two of these powers will be eventually supported by the concerted action of all three.[17]

The next priority after *Rainbow 1* applied to *Rainbows 2* and *3*, the two Pacific area plans. "The Joint Board had directed the Joint Planning Committee in June to give priority to the development of plans for United States naval offensive in western Pacific (*Rainbow 2* and *3*) in the event of war with Japan."[18] Even after war began in Europe a few months later, the strategic thinking continued to emphasize the plans against Japan. Since Britain and France controlled the Atlantic, and to a lesser degree the North and Mediterranean Seas, the most likely action to involve the United States in war would be an attack by Japan in the Pacific. Planning for such an eventuality was much more complex than planning for *Orange* plans in the past. Not only were other "democratic powers" involved in the Pacific, but additional potential enemies who might act in concert existed in the Atlantic.

Another problem facing the planners was how far the Japanese would advance and in which direction before the United States and the "democratic powers" could take action. The navy planners of the joint planning committee set up three alternative hypotheses:

- Japan had not begun to move southward from Formosa. The United States Fleet might move to Manila Bay with detached units to Singapore, Cam Ranh Bay, and Hong Kong with ground troops either accompanying or following later to the western Pacific. These acts hopefully would prevent a war in the Pacific.

- Japan had already taken Hong Kong and Cam Ranh Bay and had begun operations in the Netherlands Indies. In this case the United States would react by moving forces to the Far Pacific, whereupon the Japanese would move against Guam and the Philippines.

- Japan had already taken the Netherlands Indies and isolated Singapore and was in a position to take the Philippines. The Army planners on the committee pointed out the obvious: in this case "the principal advantage of Allied participation will have been lost and the problem becomes essentially that of an *Orange* War."[19]

The last hypothesis was most prophetic, considering it was two and one-half years in advance of the actual performance. Only the inability of the planners to fathom the lurking vulnerability of Singapore to land attack marred a classic prophecy.

A bit of the color left the China scene when Admiral Yarnell was relieved by Admiral Thomas Charles Hart on July 25, 1939. A few days before being relieved, Admiral Yarnell sent the Secretary of the Navy his evaluations of the effectiveness of American foreign relations in the Far East and his military recommendation for strengthening the hand of the diplomat. He observed that, during his tour in China, the rights of Americans in the Far East had been "upheld vigorously by the State Department," and the position and policies of the United States could not have been stated more clearly or more positively. On the other hand, Yarnell thought the Tokyo government was generally impotent to deal with or give decisions regarding affairs and incidents in China, because in many cases it was entirely ignorant of what was going on there. Then the admiral offered the advice which he would consistently repeat until war came, namely:

> ... that for every note written, there should be some increase in the United States armed forces in the Far East. When dealing with a nation whose policies are determined by a ruthless military clique which worships the sword and understands nothing but force, such a procedure may have merit.[20]

Just days before war commenced in Europe, Admiral Stark received advice from two different directions relative to his policy toward Japan. His own staff in the War Plans Division observed that in the event Britain and France entered war against Germany, "the invitation to aggression by Japan in the South China Sea Area would prove so promising that [it] ... would be hard for that country to resist even if they so wanted." Without suggesting how to do it, the war plans staff thought "that the United States [should] take immediate steps as may be practicable to provide a deterrent effect against such aggressive measures by Japan."[21]

The next day Admiral Yarnell gave Admiral Stark, the new Chief of Naval Operations, the benefit of his experience in the Far East. In language reminiscent of similar advice given to Admiral Leahy a year before, Admiral Yarnell volunteered that:

1. We should never engage in a war single-handed against Japan if at all possible. Great Britain, France, and the Netherlands are vitally interested and should take part.

2. In case of a single-handed war, we cannot move our fleet to Eastern waters due to lack of a base.

3. I do not believe our government will ever build a first class Naval base in the Philippines.

4. We can never compete with Japan in transporting U.S. troops to the Far East.

5. The war should be a Naval war,—cruisers, submarines, and aircraft operating against lines of communications.[22]

Admirals Stark and Hart and the War Plans Division would attempt right up to the start of war to develop and put into operation plans encompassing Yarnell's perceptions.

Meanwhile, in China, the Japanese lost no time in exploiting the European war to their advantage vis-à-vis the British and French. On September 5, the Japanese government informed the European belligerents that the continued presence of their warships and troops in China "might result in unfortunate incidents and in a condition of affairs ill adapted to Japan's 'non-involvement policy'."[23] Consequently, Japan gave them "friendly advice" to withdraw these forces voluntarily and offered to undertake the protection of the lives and property of their citizens.

Secretary Hull learned of the Japanese action from two sources. Consul General Gauss in Shanghai reported that the British and French military there had told Admiral Hart of the squeeze, while in Washington the British and French diplomats had sought advice and support from Hull. On September 7, Hull did see the Japanese ambassador and told him that although his government was trying to force the Western powers out of China, American troops would remain there. He also implied that the congressional proponents of economic reprisals might have their way. That was all he could or would do. On September 11, he advised the British to make no reply but "to keep them guessing."[24]

In Shanghai, Admiral Hart took the position that *any* change in the nature of the International Defense Plan definitely affected his forces and a full revision of the plan with United States representatives participating would have to be made before any change was consummated. The International Defense Plan, made originally in 1931 and amended in 1934, was an agreement among the commanding officers of the British military forces, the U.S. Fourth Marines, the Japanese naval landing party, the chairman of the Shanghai Municipal Council, the commandant of the Shanghai Volunteer Corps, and the commissioner of the Shanghai Municipal Police, with the commanding officer of the French military forces accepting the plan—as long as it made provision for cooperation and mutual aid between the French forces and the forces of the International Settlement. As far as the Western powers were concerned it was a military rather than a diplomatic agreement.

At a September 14 meeting of defense commanders, the Japanese commandant in Shanghai urged a revision of the defense plan "pointing out that it was originally intended to protect foreign nationals from the Chinese and that this necessity no longer existed."[25] The participants agreed to submit the matter to a committee to draft proposals. Neither at this meeting, at another on September 23, nor at a showdown on November 14 did the Japanese bring up the issue of British or French withdrawal. In the November meeting, the Western military leaders took the attitude that if there could be no agreement among them it would be best to await the results of diplomatic efforts before proceeding further. One reason the Japanese were not pushing for British withdrawal from Shanghai was that Britain had withdrawn five gunboats from the Yangtze and cut her garrisons in Peiping and Tientsin to token levels sufficient only to preserve her rights under the Boxer Protocol. Through the rest of 1939, France and Italy also drew down their respective forces in Peiping and Tientsin to a mere handful at each legation and, like Britain, France withdrew its gunboats from the Yangtze River. As 1940 approached, only the United States had maintained former force levels in North China and on the Yangtze.

CHAPTER 5

The Rainbow War Plans

Shortly after Admiral James Otto Richardson broke his flag as Commander in Chief, United States Fleet, in the battleship *Pennsylvania* on January 6, 1940, he received a letter from Admiral Stark, Chief of Naval Operations, pointing out that events in the Far East might "be far more important to us than the troubles in Europe, especially if something should break and break quickly and without warning."[1] It was, Stark told Richardson, "something ... for which you should be mentally prepared." Stark also indicated that Admiral Hart, Commander in Chief, Asiatic Fleet, thought that the situation in the Far East was serious and that the year 1940 "may prove to be a crucial and critical one." It was apparent that the senior naval commanders in Washington and China were more concerned at the start of 1940 over the explosive potentials in the Far East than in the lingering standoff in the European war.

Richardson did not completely share the concern of Stark and Hart. First, he was not pleased with the fact that a large detachment of the fleet, consisting primarily of cruisers and destroyers, had already been sent to Hawaii. Now he found Stark's comments on something breaking without warning and being mentally prepared "somewhat disquieting." In a letter dated January 26 Richardson outlined his views on the naval role in national strategy and especially relative to Japan. He told Stark that as assistant chief of naval operations he had constantly pushed Admiral Leahy, then CNO, to impress upon the President that "we do not want to be drawn into this [the China incident] unless we have allies so bound to us that they cannot leave us in the lurch." He estimated that war with Japan would last five to ten years and cost 35 to 70 billion dollars. He evaluated the *Orange Plan* as good only as a training device for war planners and as a basis for asking for appropriations. The Navy needed time and money to develop bases for the fleet "to put on any real pressure" and "should not go into a thing like this unless we expected to see it through."[2] Richardson would reiterate many times the value of a trained and supplied fleet based on the West Coast rather than one without proper logistic support, based in Hawaii. Doggedly, he urged his position on Stark, and later on President Roosevelt, until he was finally relieved by Admiral Husband Edward Kimmel in February 1941.

In answer to a letter of March 8 from Richardson asking why there was a Hawaiian detachment of cruisers and destroyers, Stark reviewed the requests of the previous fall from Admiral Hart that the Asiatic Fleet be reinforced with a division of heavy cruisers, or if they were not available, light cruisers. The situation in the Shanghai area at the time of the request was very tense; war had commenced in Europe and the Japanese were becoming increasingly more belligerent toward the British on the Yangtze and in Shanghai and Tientsin. The State Department and the President agreed with Stark to send the cruisers only as far as Hawaii, and to reinforce the Asiatic Fleet with one tender, a squadron of patrol aircraft, and six new submarines. Stark favored leaving the detachment in Hawaii indefinitely, because "no one can measure how much effect its presence there may have on *Orange* foreign policy." The State Department, according to Stark, strongly supported his deterrent concept.[3]

On March 31, 1940, American newspapers carried the news that the annual fleet exercises would be held in Hawaiian waters. In 1935, the last time the exercises had been held in that general area, American pacifists had led the claim that such an act was hostile to Japan. This time the exercises were kept to an area well eastward of the 1935 exercise area, yet the Japanese newspapers were filled with accusations that the exercises were threatening. Despite the Japanese attitudes the fleet left West Coast ports on April 2 and conducted Fleet Problem XXI in the Hawaiian area.[4] While the United States Navy exercised in fleet war games, the German war machine suddenly came to life. After an immediate occupation of Denmark on April 9, the Germans invaded Norway and defeated a spirited though weak British attempt to hold northern Norway.

Meanwhile, in Washington, the war planners continued their

work on the *Rainbow* family of plans. One of the hypotheses the Navy planners used as a basis for *Rainbow 2* was that the Japanese had seized Hong Kong and begun operations against the Netherlands East Indies. On the possibility that the start of the German spring offensive might be paralleled by Japanese actions, the Joint Board on April 10 "directed the Joint Planning Committee to proceed immediately with the completion of plans for an immediate projection of U.S. forces into the Western Pacific."[5] The initial movement of forces was planned for Singapore and the Netherlands East Indies, to be supported, if the hypothesis held true, across the Atlantic, by way of the Cape of Good Hope and Indian Ocean. To insure that Singapore would be available to the U.S. Fleet, the Navy recommended that the British be asked to send a division of capital ships to reinforce their naval forces in the Far East. It was further recommended that the British, Dutch, and French authorities be contacted diplomatically to ascertain their proposed actions in the Pacific vis-à-vis Japanese aggression. Another explosive political question was whether United States forces would be used to defend the European colonial possessions.[6] Before these questions could be answered, events in Europe turned attention away from the Pacific for the time being.

While the war planners worked on *Rainbow 2*, Admirals Stark and Joseph Knefler Taussig, a previous assistant chief of naval operations, testified before the Senate Naval Affairs Committee for more appropriations for the Navy. Taussig created quite a furor in Japan by asserting that war with Japan was inevitable. Despite a special press conference by Secretary of State Hull and denials by Navy Department spokesmen to the press that Taussig's statements were his own opinions and not the government's, the impact in Tokyo was considerable. Naval attaches reported from Tokyo that evidently strict orders had "been issued to Japanese officers not to discuss either naval matters or relations with the United States. Friends of many years duration refused to speak of Admiral Stark's and Admiral Taussig's testimony in front of the Senate Committee and declined to comment on same even in informal conversations."[7]

On May 7, Stark wrote a hurried letter to Richardson, who was at Pearl Harbor with the fleet after the exercises. He had "just hung up the telephone after talking with the President" and wanted to explain in more detail by letter the order sent by dispatch "to remain in Hawaiian Waters for a couple of weeks." Richardson was told that when the fleet returned to the West Coast ports, he was to keep enough fuel and stores aboard all ships so that on short notice it could return to Hawaii *en masse*. The primary concern on May 7 was whether or not Italy would enter the war against Britain and France and trigger a move by Japan against the Netherlands East Indies. Stark called the "Italian situation ... extremely delicate, the two weeks ahead regarded as critical."[8]

The next move in Germany's blitzkrieg came suddenly and soon. The Chamberlain government fell on May 10 over dissatisfaction with the British performance in the Norwegian campaign. On the same day, Winston Churchill became Prime Minister and Germany turned its juggernaut against the Netherlands and Belgium.

In Hawaii, Richardson chafed at tying the fleet to the inadequate base at Pearl Harbor. He considered the assumptions upon which past plans had been based to be completely different in the light of the deteriorating European situation. On May 13 he wrote to Stark:

> It seems that, under present world conditions, the paramount thing for us is the security of the Western Hemisphere. This, in my opinion, transcends everything—anything certainly in the Far East, our own or other interests.
>
> South America is the greatest prize yet remaining to be grabbed ...

He added that any move to the west meant hostilities and would be a grave mistake since U.S. interests there were not vital. The ability of the fleet to protect the Western Hemisphere should not be reduced; however, if higher authority decides that "we should go west, all of us are ready to give all we have." In an interesting postscript to the letter, Richardson told Stark that he had sent a detachment to simulate a raiding force against Pearl Harbor to test the efficiency of Navy patrol planes and Army bombers. The Navy planes had seen the group, but the Army bombers had not.[9] In the spring of 1940 at least one admiral was thinking about the possibility of an attack on Pearl Harbor.

The Netherlands government, on May 14—after four days of fighting which included the devastating bombing of Rotterdam—surrendered to Germany. The next day Churchill, referring to himself as a "Former Naval Person," wrote to President Roosevelt of the seriousness of the situation. His list of immediate needs to fight the war against Germany was almost all-inclusive, except manpower. He wanted

> First of all, the loan of forty or fifty of your older destroyers to bridge the gap between what we have now and the large new construction we put in hand at the beginning of the war. This time next year we shall have plenty. But if in the interval Italy comes in against us with an-

other one hundred submarines, we may be strained to the breaking point. Secondly, we want several hundred of the latest types of aircraft, of which you are now getting delivery. These can be repaid by those now being constructed in the United States for us. Thirdly, anti-aircraft equipment and ammunition, of which again there will be plenty next year, if we are alive to see it. Fourthly, the fact that our ore supply is being compromised from Sweden, from North Africa, and perhaps from Northern Spain, makes it necessary to purchase steel in the United States. This also applies to other materials. We shall go on paying dollars for as long as we can, but I should like to feel reasonably sure that when we can pay no more, you will give us the stuff all the same. Fifthly, we have many reports of possible German parachute or airborne descents in Ireland. The visit of a United States Squadron to Irish ports, which might well be prolonged, would be invaluable. Sixthly, I am looking to you to keep the Japanese quiet in the Pacific, using Singapore in any way convenient.[10]

Eventually everything on the order was filled, with the glaring exception of the use of Singapore and visits to Irish ports.

After the fall of the Netherlands, concern within the Navy Department over expected Japanese moves into the East Indies reached a fevered pitch. In retrospect, it appears that the officers in the War Plans Division, in particular, were grasping at straws in desperation to counter the expected southward advance. On the day Churchill wrote to Roosevelt about his needs, Captain Russell Sydnor Crenshaw, chief of that division, convinced Admiral Stark that certain of the proposals from the planners should at least be taken up with the State Department and the President. One proposal was that, if the Japanese Navy moved into the area of the Netherlands East Indies, that the United States Navy make similar moves—or, an interesting variation on that proposal, that the U.S. Navy participate in "courtesy calls" *with* the Japanese, by sending a division of *Omaha*-class cruisers to the East Indies to be under the operational control of Commander, Asiatic Fleet, for as long as needed.[11]

With Admiral Stark's approval, the chief of the Central Division, OpNav, Captain Roscoe Ernest Schuirmann, visited the Far Eastern Division of the State Department on the same day, May 15. There he discussed with Dr. Hornbeck and Mr. Hamilton the proposals "that if Japan sends a small occupation force for the protection of the Dutch East Indies" that the United States send a similar force, or, that the United States should "suggest or notify Japan that if they occupy the islands that the United States share in the occupation." Hornbeck and

Hamilton were in positive agreement that unless the United States "were prepared to go to war, if necessary, in the event such a joint occupation were opposed by Japan that [the United States] should not make such a move." The proposal of suggesting to Japan some joint occupancy would not be feasible according to the diplomats, since Japan had already stated that it wished the status quo preserved in the East Indies. Schuirmann explained that these were merely suggestions that the Navy was exploring and the reactions of the State Department to them was desired "in order to clarify our own ideas."[12] Now, having gotten the reactions from Hornbeck and Hamilton, the navy proponents abandoned the ideas.

Nevertheless, the Joint Army and Navy Board recognized that the United States was the only power in a position to restrain the Japanese from taking action in the Netherlands East Indies. In connection with the studies of possible cooperation with the Allies, the naval attache in London, Captain Alan Goodrich Kirk, was instructed by the board just before the Netherlands fell to obtain full information as to facilities that might be available at Singapore for a naval detachment, should the United States decide to support British and Dutch resistance to any further Japanese move to the south.[13] The Admiralty expressed a strong desire "that the United States Government guarantee the Netherlands East Indies."[14] On May 17, Kirk reported an Admiralty proposal that the United States send naval forces to Singapore. Admiralty staff officers pointed out that, if the Japanese moved southward for any reason, they could easily cut British lines of communications between Australia and India.[15]

Meanwhile, from the Far East came a report that Japan too was in the dark over Italy's future moves. On the day the Netherlands capitulated, First Secretary Robert L. Smyth in Peiping reported to Secretary Hull that the Japanese in Peiping were "displaying keen interest in regard to the question of Italian entry into the European war." The analysis of the United States attaches and Smyth was that the Japanese would again request the "belligerent powers to withdraw their armed forces from China as in September last."[16] Unknown to the diplomats were concurrent actions being taken by Admiral Hart to get an "agreement between the European forces in Shanghai to maintain the peaceful status quo." The informal oral agreement reached among the senior military commanders of the European powers was accomplished "without consultation with . . . civil authorities." Admiral Hart thought that the Italians in Shanghai were "fully disposed to keep their word, even though there [were] signs that their local civil authorities [were] rather put out over the Italian commander's having entered into the agreement." By design, the agreement was reached without knowledge of the Japanese, although they were informed after the fact. Hart thought the effect on them was "even amusing." He wrote Stark:

> ... our move caught the local Japanese authorities quite flat-footed and they have been trying to recover from the surprise and to answer criticism from their own higher-ups ever since. Our initiative in the matter was, I am sure, a very good and profitable move. An incident between white troops which the Japs could call disorder would give them just the pretext which they may be looking for.[17]

Secretary Hull, having learned about the agreement made in Shanghai, furnished the details to Ambassador Grew in Tokyo. In addition, he advised, "the commanders of the detachments of European forces at Peiping have manifested a completely cooperative attitude in keeping with the agreement reached at Shanghai, and that the United States Government assumed that the agreement included the detachment at Tientsin also." Grew was told to inform the Japanese Foreign Office that the United States expressed satisfaction with the development.[18]

On May 22, Admirals Richardson and Stark each originated a letter to the other. In Stark's previous letter of May 7, he had mentioned to Richardson that the "Italian situation is extremely delicate, the two weeks ahead regarded as critical." Now on May 22 Stark admitted to Richardson that two weeks earlier "it looked as if Italy were coming in almost immediately and that a serious situation might develop in the East Indies and that there was a possibility of our being involved." However, the recent blitzkrieg events in Europe had certainly altered the picture for the time being. Stark thought events had made "more remote [for the moment, at least] the question of a westward movement of the fleet." Although the possibility was remote, planning for such an eventuality was going full speed ahead. Stark told Richardson that *Rainbow 2* was nearing completion and would be sent to him by officer messenger as soon as possible. Richardson was instructed "to go ahead with the preparation of a tentative Fleet Operating Plan for *Rainbow 2*," but to keep "constantly in mind the possibility of a complete collapse of the Allies, including the loss of their fleets." Such a catastrophe was considered in *Rainbow 1*. Should the Allied fleets pass into the hands of the Germans, however, an entirely different, and far more serious situation would exist. Richardson was asked to give his views regarding the best disposition of U.S. fleet forces in such an event. In a postscript Stark indicated the pressures of his job. He wrote:

> Have literally lived on the Hill—State Dept.—& White House for last several days. Thanks God yesterday I finally swung support for 170,000 men and 34,000 marines.[19]

Admiral Richardson's letter of May 22 was his most perceptive in the series exchanged with Stark. The fleet was still in Hawaii—past the "couple of weeks" it was to have stayed after the fleet exercises. He pointed out to Stark that since he had to plan the fleet schedule and employment for the next few months he had to know more about why the fleet was there and how long it would remain. Even curtailed gunnery training would require wholesale movement of targets, tugs, drones, and utility aircraft. Richardson then asked two most poignant questions:

(a) Are we here primarily to influence the actions of other nations by our presence, and if so, what effect would the carrying out of normal training . . . have on this purpose? . . .

(b) Are we here as a stepping off place for belligerent activity? If so, we should devote all of our time and energies to preparing for war. . . .

As it is now, to try and do both (a) and (b) from here at the same time is a diversification of effort and purpose that can only result in the accomplishment of neither.

At the end of his letter Richardson pleaded with Stark to push for more enlisted men, to operate the training stations at full capacity, and to train men as quickly as possible in order to fill the complements of new ships being built and others being recommissioned.[20] While Richardson's letter was enroute to Stark, the highest council in Washington again reviewed the war plan situation in the wake of the German victory over the Netherlands and in the face of the impending fall of Belgium and possibly France. The President, Under Secretary of State Welles, Army Chief of Staff General George Catlett Marshall, and Admiral Stark on May 23 agreed that "we must not become involved with Japan, that we must not concern ourselves beyond the 180th Meridian, and that we must concentrate on the South American situation."[21] Work was suspended on the two plans involving Japan, *Rainbow 2* and *3,* but evidently only by the Army. After years of having worked on the *Orange Plan,* the navy planners were not ready to write off the Philippines and Guam. They continued to work on *Rainbow 3* throughout the fall of 1940, and not until August 6, 1941 were *Rainbow 2* and *3* cancelled.

In line with the May 23 agreement the Joint Planning Committee gave top priority to *Rainbow 4*—the defense of the Western Hemisphere. The purpose of the plan was:

> To provide for the most effective use of United States' naval and military forces to defeat enemy aggression occurring anywhere in the territory and waters of the American continents, or in the United States, and in United States' possessions in the Pacific westward to include Unalaska and Midway.[22]

Rainbow 4 was finished the end of May and forwarded by Secretary of War Harry H. Woodring and Acting Secretary of the Navy Lewis Compton to the President on June 13.

The evolution of the strategic thinking in Washington in the spring of 1940 made Stark's answers to Richardson's what-are-we-doing-here letter all the more interesting. The agreed-upon emphasis, as of May 23, was upon the defense of the Western Hemisphere, and not to become involved with Japan or actions west of 180° longitude. Yet on May 27 Stark answered the question as to why the U.S. Fleet was in Hawaii:

> You are there because of the deterrent effect which it is thought your presence may have on the Japs going into the East Indies. . . . Along the same line as the first question you would naturally ask—suppose the Japs do go into the East Indies? What are we going to do about it? My answer is that . . . , I don't know and I think there is nobody on God's green earth who can tell you. I do know my own arguments with regard to this, both in the White House and in the State Department, are in line with the thoughts contained in your recent letter.
>
> I would point out one thing and that is that even if the decision here were for the U.S. to take no decisive action if the Japs should decide to go into the Dutch East Indies, we must not breathe it to a soul, as by so doing we would completely nullify the reason for your presence in the Hawaiian area. . . .
>
> You ask whether you are there as a stepping off place for belligerent activity? Answer: obviously it might become so under certain conditions but a definite answer cannot be given as you have already gathered from the foregoing.
>
> I realize what you say about the advantages of returning to the West Coast for the preparation at this time is out of the question. If you did return it might nullify the principle reasons for your being in Hawaii. This very question has been brought up here. As a compromise,

however, you have authority for returning ships to the Coast for dock-ing, taking ammunition, stores, etc., and this should help in any case. . . .[23]

Richardson was also given permission to curtail or to change the scheduled gunnery exercises in any manner he saw fit. He was re-minded again that, should the situation change in the Atlantic, some ships from the U.S. Fleet at Pearl Harbor would be ordered to the Atlantic. Stark's reading of the situation on May 27 was that the force so ordered would not be extensive—"a division of cruisers, a carrier, a squadron of destroyers, possibly a light mine layer division, possibly Patrol Wing One, and possibly, but more unlikely, a division of sub-marines with a tender." He closed with another estimate of Italy's entering the war in Europe—June 5.[24]

A side issue arose at the same time Stark issued his guidance to Richardson over possible movements to the Atlantic. It was minor, in retrospect, but indicative of the pressures on the President, the inter-relationships of the requirements for naval forces in the Pacific and Atlantic Oceans, and the influence Stark had with the President. The United States minister to Uruguay, Mr. Edwin C. Wilson, was deeply concerned about open and very active Nazi propaganda efforts in Latin America, especially in Uruguay. Fear of a coup along the lines of successful tactics just used in Norway generated one message of panic after the other. To counter the German moves as he foresaw them, Wilson proposed that the United States send—as a one-time show of force—forty or fifty ships to the South Atlantic and then leave a powerful squadron along the eastern coast of South America in-definitely. Roosevelt's immediate response was to order the heavy cruiser *Quincy,* then at Guantanamo, Cuba, to Montevideo, the capi-tal of Uruguay, and to refer the matter to Stark for advice. Mean-while, Under Secretary Welles argued for much heavier forces than just the *Quincy*—at least three or four cruisers and a reasonable num-ber of destroyers.[25]

Stark, in a memorandum of June 2, reviewed the defense prob-lems and in the Western Hemisphere ended with the immediate solu-tion to Wilson's and Welles' request for more forces. He wrote:

I offer the following solutions:—
(a) Dispatch one additional 8″ cruiser to South America.
(b) Continue destroyer shakedown cruises to South America.—
(c) If desirable at a later date;—Reinforce the above by another heavy cruiser and/or a squadron (9DD) of destroyers.

63

(d)   For the present utilize ships now in the Atlantic, thus not weakening the fleet in the Pacific....[26]

Roosevelt passed the Stark memorandum to Welles the following day with a covering memorandum which read:

Please read enclosed from Admiral Stark sent me last night, Sunday. Stark is absolutely right and gives in paragraph #13 the only solutions possible.[27]

Stark did send another heavy cruiser, the *Wichita,* to join the *Quincy* and the crisis came to a head and passed with the actions of the Uruguayan congress on June 13 dissolving all "illegal organizations." Stark had not had to touch his Pacific forces.

From the Asiatic Station Admiral Hart, on June 7, reviewed his first ten months of duty there. He observed that delays in moving the gunboats still continued, caused in almost every case by requests from the Japanese Navy made at the insistence of the Japanese Army. Two months before, he had reported on the problems that Rear Admiral William Alexander Glassford, Commander, Yangtze Patrol, was having with the Japanese over getting clearance to move U.S. gunboats from place to place. At that time Hart admitted that giving in to the Japanese so often "irked him considerably" but that he "would risk [his] personal reputation as long as the respective cases ... in themselves [were] unimportant." He did not want to have "an *incident* over something which did not amount to much, per se." Now in June Glassford wanted to relieve the gunboat at Hankow. After two months of postponements by the Japanese Navy, Hart decided to put his foot down. A threat to report the delays to Washington induced cooperation on the proposed gunboat trip to Hankow. Hart told Stark that it was obvious to him that the Japanese "Army and Navy in Central China did not want any discussions of [delays] by the respective capitols ..." Hart's self-evaluation of his record for the first ten months was that in every instance he had had his way "though quite frequently having to delay a bit to get it."[28]

On the same day Hart wrote Stark about the comparatively peaceful relations with the Japanese, the American consul in Canton received from his Japanese counterpart a letter charging the United States Navy with a violation of international law on the high seas. Four destroyers were reported to have ordered a Japanese military transport, HIJM *Shinko Maru,* to heave to off the South China coast near Amoy at longitude 118°13′ East and latitude 23°54′ North on May 7 at 8:05 A.M. (The destroyers were Destroyer Division 59—the

Pope, Peary, Pillsbury, and *John D. Ford.*) After four months of exchanging notes through diplomatic channels at Canton the incident was termed a misunderstanding. Through examination of the deck and signal logs of the destroyers involved and conferences with United States naval officers, it was determined that a small International "K" flag was being flown as a tactical signal just high enough above the bridge of each ship for the adjacent ships to see it. It was not flying at the yardarm and it was not displayed with the "International Code" pennant necessary to make it the international signal to heave to as read by the Japanese commanding officer. The destroyers had passed the transport on an opposite course at least one mile to starboard. They had not made a run in on the transport and then veered away after signalling, as alleged. The investigative report by the Commander in Chief, Asiatic Fleet, was either acceptable to Japan or it effectively checkmated the initial allegations, since no further action was taken by the Japanese consul general at Canton. The incident differed from previous cases involving the two navies in two significant ways: (a) This time it was Japan who initiated the complaint; and (b) the complaint, until resolved, was handled in proper diplomatic channels rather than between military commanders directly, as in the Yarnell era. It was just one year after the *Monocacy* incident.[29]

Admiral Hart had written on June 7 that he had gotten his way with the Japanese military in China in every instance though having to delay at times a bit in doing so. The prognosis for relations between other occidental powers and Japan appeared much less favorable in the event Italy entered the war. Rear Admiral Walter Stratton Anderson, the director of naval intelligence, reported to Admiral Stark on June 8 that he had "thoroughly reliable information" that if Italy entered the war Japan would take the following actions in China:

(a) Use force to remove or disarm the European belligerents' forces in China if any fighting occurs between them.

(b) Reissue the warning of 5 September 1939 to France and Britain regarding maintenance of peace and withdrawal of armed forces.

(c) Issue the same warning to Italy, after first confidentially informing her and negotiating and arranging for withdrawal of Italian troops on condition that France and Britain evacuate.[30]

As events developed in China in the summer of 1940 the assessment proved to be quite accurate.

Despite Japanese anticipation of trouble among the European belligerents, the relationships worked out by Admiral Hart to continue the status quo peacefully were successful in every quarter. In Tientsin British, French, and Italian commanders agreed on June 11, the day after Italy entered the war, to avoid friction. The Italian concession was "out of bounds" to British and French liberty parties. All other concessions were to be open to all nationals except that military personnel were to be in civilian clothes and military vehicles were to fly no flags. Any incidents between European troops were to be resolved by the senior United States Marine Corps officer present.[31] Very much the same arrangement was made in Peiping the following day. Liberty would be on alternate days for Italian and Anglo-French enlisted men with certain places of amusement "out of bounds" and the senior commandant present to be the arbitrator of any disputes.[32] Since the senior commandant was Marine Colonel Allen Hal Turnage, the "keeper of the peace" at Peiping, as in Tientsin, was an officer who reported to Admiral Hart. By August, after the French-Italian armistice, the commandants of the French and Italian embassy guards had reached a supplemental agreement to lift the restrictions on alternate-day liberty in Peiping. By the end of August when the supplemental agreement was signed, there were in Peiping on duty with the embassies only two French officers and 15 men, one Italian officer and 36 men, and nine British men.[33] There were fewer European troops yet in Tientsin, while U.S. Marines numbered sixteen officers, a warrant officer, and 315 men in Peiping and thirteen officers, a warrant officer, and 225 men in Tientsin.[34] In Shanghai, cooperation among the European powers paralleled that in Peiping and Tientsin; however, Japanese pressures to force out the British and French were more persistent and successful in the latter part of June.

In Washington the collapse of France caused more concern than any other foreign event at the time. President Roosevelt gave his hypothesis of the war situation in the fall of 1940—six months in the future—to Rear Admiral Anderson, director of naval intelligence, and to Brigadier General Sherman Miles, director of military intelligence, for their evaluation. Roosevelt foresaw that Britain and the British Empire would still be intact; that the French government and surviving French forces would still be resisting in North Africa; that British and French navies, in conjunction with the U.S. Navy, would control the Persian Gulf, Red Sea, western Mediterranean, and the Atlantic from Morocco to Greenland, having probably been driven out of the eastern Mediterranean; that Japan and Russia would not be active in the war but that the United States would be active, though with naval and air forces only.[35]

The intelligence chiefs, who received the President's hypothesis on June 13, turned for recommendations as to how to answer to the War Plans Divisions of their respective services. Colonel Frank S. Clark and Captain Charles Johnnes Moore, the senior Army and Navy members, respectively, of the Joint Planning Committee wrote a report to the Chief of Staff and Chief of Naval Operations entitled *Views on Questions Propounded by President on War Situation.* They took exception, in part, or completely, to each of Roosevelt's forecasts. They thought that Britain, as distinguished from the British Empire, would probably not "be an active combatant" in six months. Likewise, they reasoned that France could not continue to resist in North Africa since she would be cut off from supplies, weapons, and ammunition there. The war planners had information that Japan and the Soviet Union on June 9 had settled a longstanding dispute over the border between Manchuria and Outer Mongolia and they read this as an omen that not only would the two enter the war, but that they might take concerted offensive action in the Far East. Roosevelt's forecast of naval strength appeared reasonable to the planners with the exception that the situation in the Mediterranean would be the reverse of that foreseen by him. The last item, that the United States would be active in the war, really disturbed the planners. The limited arms production in 1940, a one-ocean navy, presidential insistence that munitions be furnished Britain at a time when American requirements were increasing—in contrast to a desire to deter Japan from further aggression in the Far East—all made the assumption that the United States would be an active participant within six months seem dangerous to the planners. They urged their superiors to discourage the President from getting the country involved as a belligerent before it was adequately prepared. They spelled out what would probably happen if the United States entered the war prematurely:

> Belligerent entry by the United States in the next few months would not only disperse and waste our inadequate means, but would result in leaving the United States as the one belligerent to oppose the almost inevitable political, economic, and military aggression of totalitarian powers.
>
> Early entry of the United States into the war would undoubtedly precipitate German subversive activities in the Western Hemisphere, which we are obligated to oppose. Our ability to do so, or to prepare Latin American countries to do so would thus be ham-strung.
>
> Our entry into the war might encourage Japan to become a belligerent on the side of Germany and Italy, and might further restrict our efforts on behalf of the Allies.[36]

The report was never sent to Roosevelt. It was overtaken by events of

June 17 and a subsequent study originated by the Navy on June 22, which incorporated most of the expressed ideas and ultimately became, on June 27, a document entitled *Basis for Immediate Decisions Concerning the National Defense.*

The day of June 17 certainly was one of the busier days in 1940 for decisions, actions, and the commencement of significant events. Early in the morning (2:00 A.M.) Ambassador Anthony J. Drexel Biddle reported from Bordeaux, the temporary capital of France, that a new French government—formed just the day before under Marshall Philippe Petain—had asked Germany for armistice terms. Fear that the French fleet might surrender to Germany was so strong that Roosevelt, the day before, had urged the French government through its ambassador, Count St. Quentin, to continue the war from North Africa or at least to send the fleet to British ports. News of the request for armistice terms increased fears of Germany getting the fleet and triggered further American actions later in the day.

Later in the morning of June 17, by coincidence, naval intelligence reported that, should Germany and Italy gain control of the French fleet, their combined naval strength would be about one-third greater than the British fleet and greater also than the U.S. Fleet, most of which by design was in Hawaii. The same report pointed out that with the French fleet at his disposal Hitler had a much better chance of a successful invasion of Britain.[37]

The potential disparity in naval strength also bothered Mr. Churchill. On June 15 and again on June 17, he repeated his request for thirty-five destroyers. On May 15 he had requested forty to fifty destroyers. All the requests went unanswered for the time being because there did not seem to be a legal way to make the transfer and the Navy Department insisted that they could not be spared.[38]

On the same day, again by coincidence, Roosevelt sent a request to Congress for new construction for a two-ocean navy. The Navy General Board had already proposed that the United States Navy be expanded drastically so that it would be dominant in both the Atlantic and Pacific Oceans. The Roosevelt request on June 17 was for 1,300,000 tons of new shipping. The belated start of the race for naval supremacy was on, just eighteen months before many of the existing capital ships would be sunk or damaged at Pearl Harbor. In budget terms, the amount made available by Congress for contract authority in fiscal year 1941, which began two weeks later, jumped to $946,098,-112 from $22,450,000 the previous year—a level almost forty-three times higher. Increased personnel, training, and base support expenditures necessary to man the new construction likewise increased. Total appropriations approved by Congress for fiscal year 1941 for the navy rose to 3.5 billion dollars. The previous year the appropriations were only 0.9 billion dollars.[39]

Three other actions taken by Roosevelt on June 17 followed relative to the French situation. First, he ordered a freeze on all funds of the French government. Since France had already transferred most of her gold stocks to the United States for safekeeping and had also deposited funds to pay for heavy defense contracts for aircraft and ammunition, the funds frozen were considerable. Second, Roosevelt— in anticipation of favorable congressional action—served notice that European possessions in the New World could not be transferred as a result of the war. By joint resolution on June 17 and 18 the Senate, unanimously, and the House, 380–8, so voted. Roosevelt sent notes to Germany and Italy, with information copies to Britain, France, and the Netherlands of the United States' stand on hemispheric integrity.[40]

The last action again concerned the French fleet. Late in the afternoon (5:00 P.M.) a note, which Secretary Hull himself described as "almost a brutal message,"[41] was telephoned to Ambassador Biddle at Bordeaux to be passed to the French government. Churchill, who had requested Roosevelt to intercede with Petain not to surrender the French fleet, had sent a parallel message in much more diplomatic language and had received Petain's answer that he could not send the fleet to Britain, but that Germany would not get it and, if necessary, it might be scuttled. Ambassador Kennedy's telephone call from London at 7:00 P.M. concerning this information arrived too late to stop the instructions given Biddle. Biddle was told, among other things:

> The President desires you to say that in the opinion of this Government, should the French Government, before concluding any armistice with the Germans fail to see that the Fleet is kept out of the hands of her opponents, the French Government will be pursuing a policy that will fatally impair the preservation of the French Empire and the eventual restoration of French independence and autonomy. Furthermore, should the French Government fail to take these steps and permit the French Fleet to be surrendered to Germany, the French Government will permanently lose the friendship and goodwill of the Government of the United States.[42]

In reply, French Foreign Minister Paul Baudouin told Biddle that the last sentence of the Roosevelt message "deeply pained" the French government, but assured him that the fleet would never be surrendered, but that it might be sent overseas or sunk.[43]

69

Two separate items of intelligence originated from Tokyo on June 17 to intensify even more the confusion and coloring of the kaleidoscopic situation of that day. One was to presage further Japanese activities in the Pacific, while the other was to meld with additional bits of intelligence and cause an immediate reaction in Washington affecting United States forces in the Pacific. On June 17 (possibly on June 18), the Japanese director of military intelligence told the British military attache in Tokyo that "the Japanese people would be cowardly if they failed to take advantage of the opportunities presented by the disasters suffered by the French and British. Nothing could stop Japan from seizing French Indo-China, the Netherlands Indies, or Hong Kong—any or all of them." Britain could avoid war only by closing the Burma Road and the Hong Kong frontier and by prompt withdrawal of British troops from Shanghai. These blunt forecasts became realities when formal demands along these lines were made of Britain on June 24 and June 27.[44]

The other intelligence item was from Ambassador Grew. To understand its significance better, other intelligence reports which preceded it should be examined. On May 27, Japanese newspapers published an official note from Germany to Japan giving Japan carte blanche to take control of the Dutch East Indies. On June 3, Ambassador Grew sent a long five-section message analyzing the future actions of the Japanese government and the increasing rivalry between the three major factions: the pro-German, pro-Russian, and the pro-democratic groups. The country was in a "state of political turmoil of unusual intensity." The pro-Russian militants, made up of reactionary societies and younger army officers, planned to overthrow the existing government by autumn. They advocated a partition of China along Polish lines and then an immediate "seizure of the Netherlands East Indies before a German victory in Europe would give Germany a similar opportunity." They discounted the possibility of war with the United States and believed that in any case "the Japanese fleet had nothing to fear from the use of force." Germany, meanwhile, was exploiting its European successes to gain support among its followers in Japan. Their plan was to intensify anti-American demonstrations so that "the United States will be less prone to enter the European War against Germany." The pro-democratic group was the least vocal and politically most vulnerable of the three groups. The crux of the June 3 message was found in Grew's words: ". . . a complacent view of the future would no longer be warranted."[45] On June 10, Japan and the Soviet Union had reached a rapprochement in settling the Manchukuo border dispute. On June 14, the Japanese-sponsored Wang Ching-wei government in Nanking demanded the recall of British, French, and Italian troops and warships from China.

In addition to the preceding chronology, the Office of Naval Intelligence acquired two additional bits of unsupported information that influenced the evaluation of the June 17 message from Grew. On May 1, there was a lead that German sabotage of the Panama Canal was planned and on June 13 there was a report from a Brazilian crew that Japanese ships would be scuttled in the canal if the United States mobilized. The preceding items were all bits of a mosaic taking on particular characteristics before June 17. With the Grew message the mosaic was complete—at least to the War Department officers. In the context as they read it, the United States was in imminent danger.

Grew's message to the Secretary of State originated from Tokyo on June 17, was received in Washington during the evening of June 16–17, due to the time difference, and was passed almost immediately to the naval and military intelligence offices. In the War Department General Marshall and his top advisers held a conference at 8:30 A.M. June 17 to discuss the international situation in light of the Grew message, which read:

> Confidential reports have been coming to us from various sources of considerable concentration of Japanese military forces in Hainan, Formosa and Kyushu, but these reports are not subject to confirmation. Soviet and British attachés here are speculating with regard to a possible Japanese invasion of French Indo-China in the event of the capitulation of France in Europe.[46]

In reviewing the "various possibilities" General Marshall remarked that the United States "may suddenly find Japan and Russia appear as a team operating to hold our ships in the Pacific." Then he speculated on the effect of the French navy going to Germany and Italy: "...we will have a very serious situation in the South Atlantic. Germany may rush the South American situation to a head in a few weeks." During the conference Marshall favored "a purely defensive action in the Pacific, with a main effort on the Atlantic side." To this end they unanimously recommended bringing the fleet to the Atlantic. If this were not possible, then they asserted the need for additional long-range bombers to patrol the approaches to the Hawaiian chain, because "opponents in the Pacific would be four-fifths of the way to Hawaii before we knew that they had moved."[47]

Later in the morning General Charles D. Herron, Commanding

General, Hawaiian Department, received the following message from the War Department:

> Immediately alert complete defensive organization to deal with possible trans-Pacific raid, to greatest extent possible without creating public hysteria or provoking undue curiosity of newspapers or alien agents. Suggest maneuver basis. Maintain alert until further orders. Instructions for secret communications direct with Chief of Staff will be furnished you shortly. Acknowledge.[48]

A similar message was sent to the Commanding General, Canal Zone.

Admiral Stark sent no such message to Richardson, who at the time was aboard the fleet flagship *Pennsylvania,* in Lahaina Roads, Maui. In fact, Stark apparently sent no message to any naval commander paralleling the Army alert or even telling them that the Army had called an alert. Years later Stark testified that he "was not impressed so far as the Navy was concerned, with any particular gravity at that time." He "looked on it largely as an Army affair."[49] It is possible that Stark had a fixation on getting the fleet to the Atlantic and saw no reason to alert the commander about an enemy to the west when the fleet was going to be moved to counter another enemy in another ocean. Already he had ordered some ships from Hawaii to the Atlantic in anticipation of Germany gaining the French fleet. On June 18 by note he urged Roosevelt to return the fleet to the Atlantic. In this he had the complete support of Welles and Marshall with whom he had discussed the matter on June 17. Roosevelt delayed his answer. Stark sent Richardson a message to take the fleet out of Hawaii on or about June 24, after having leaked that the destination was the Canal Zone. The objective was to test the report that "any movement in force by major Fleet units toward Atlantic will occasion extensive sabotage in Canal." Richardson was told the Army in the Canal Zone was on alert, but no mention was made of the alert in Hawaii. After proceeding toward the canal for two days, maintaining radio silence, he was to return the fleet to Hawaii and to anticipate coming to Washington for a conference.[50]

What to do with the United States Fleet was the question of the day on June 18. Marshall and Welles agreed with Stark that it should be brought to the Atlantic to deter German action and to protect South America. Churchill, through his ambassador, Lord Philip Ken Lothian, had found support in Dr. Stanley K. Hornbeck, who was Secretary Hull's chief adviser on affairs in the Far East. The British reasoned that as long as the British fleet could control the eastern

Atlantic, it was an advantage to deter Japan by naval force in the Pacific—and the corollary to that, if the fleet withdrew from Hawaii, Japan would feel free to do whatsoever she wanted in the Pacific, thereby aggravating the international situation all the more. Should the British Isles become untenable, the British had indicated that their fleet would proceed to Singapore and *then* the United States Fleet could move to the western Atlantic and the Caribbean Sea. Roosevelt on June 18, when urged by Stark to move the fleet, did not know what to do and is reported to have said to Stark: "When I don't know how to move, I stay put."[51] On June 24, he told the navy that the "decision as to return of the Fleet from Hawaii is to be taken later."[52]

In the immediate wake of the June 17 decisions Roosevelt made two major changes in his cabinet. At some point in time during the preceding two or three months Roosevelt had decided to run for an unprecedented third term as president. With an eye to the future workings of the government as it geared for war, and certainly with an eye to the elections in the fall and to gaining bipartisan support should the United States enter the war, he brought into his cabinet on June 19 two prestigious Republicans. Colonel Frank Knox, editor of the *Chicago Daily News* and unsuccessful vice presidential candidate in 1936, was named Secretary of the Navy, while Mr. Henry L. Stimson, was named Secretary of War.

Both Knox and Stimson were much more vocal on foreign policy recommendations than the President could afford to be at the time. In fact, both had made major speeches on June 18, the day before they were appointed to the cabinet. Knox in Detroit had advocated compulsory military training, an army of one million men (In June 1940 the army strength was 230,000 men and 13,500 officers.), either the building of an enormous fleet or close cooperation with the British to control the Atlantic, and the construction of the most powerful air force in the world, providing as many planes as possible to Britain. Stimson's speech in New Haven paralleled that by Knox. He too was for compulsory military training, for opening U.S. ports to the British fleet for repairs and servicing, and for the United States Navy to convoy supplies and munitions to Britain.[53] These two activists were Roosevelt's kind of men and complemented his cabinet ideally for his wartime needs.

On June 22, Richardson and Stark each originated letters to the other. Stark's short letter to Richardson said that his trip to Washington "was held in abeyance because of uncertainty as to movements of the fleet in the immediate future." Richardson had planned to return to the West Coast on May 9 after the fleet exercises. After he had been ordered to remain in Hawaiian waters "a couple weeks," Stark had written his why-are-you-in-the-Hawaiian-area letter on May 27. In the order to execute a feint toward the Canal Zone Richardson had been told to anticipate coming to Washington upon his return with the fleet to Hawaii. Now in the latter part of June he was again being told "to stay put." Tentatively, the decision had been made for the fleet to remain where it was, but the decision was conditional, based on what happened to the French fleet.[54]

Richardson's letter to Stark on June 22 was a much longer one than he had received. In it Richardson reviewed how he, as Commander in Chief, United States Fleet, with his fleet in Hawaii, had received the information about the June 17 army alert. General Herron, upon receipt of the War Department message alerting the army forces in Hawaii had asked Rear Admiral Claude Charles Bloch, Commandant, Fourteenth Naval District, who was also Commander, Base Force, for help in long-range patrols against "possible carrier and plane attacks." Bloch informed Vice Admiral Adolphus Andrews, Commander Scouting Force and the senior officer present afloat (SOPA) at Pearl Harbor, about the request for patrol assistance. Richardson, Commander in Chief, U.S. Fleet, was at the time in the *Pennsylvania* in Lahaina Roads, Maui. When he was told about the alert and patrols, he asked Bloch by dispatch whether the request for "additional air patrol" was "part of an army exercise" or was "it based on information from the War Department." Bloch's answer was that the request by Herron "was based on a directive from the War Department." Herron had no information as to whether or not it was an exercise. Since Herron did not know and none of the admirals had the slightest hint as to what was going on, Richardson flew back to Pearl Harbor and, after conferring with his subordinates and General Herron, he sent a dispatch to Stark on June 22.[55]

> Commanding General Hawaiian Department received orders War Department placing forces on alert against hostile trans-Pacific raid and since no information received Navy Department have assumed this exercise. Navy patrol planes are participating.[56]

Stark replied by priority dispatch:

> War Department directive concerning alert issued as precautionary measure after consultation with Navy and State Department. Request you continue cooperation.[57]

Richardson closed out his letter of June 22 by observing that "the Army 'alert' and action caused" him some concern though he was "positive that any Army intelligence bearing on the above would be available to and evaluated by the Navy" and that he would be provided with this information. Since "anything of this character tends to aggravate the tenseness of the situation and to interrupt training" and a "serious situation may again arise," Richardson offered the Chief of Naval Operations the following advice:

> ... a remedy would be to insure that where possible, when joint action is involved, even in drills, that the Commanders of the Army and Navy be jointly informed, with definite information to me as to whether the alarm is real or simulated for the purposes of training.[58]

In Washington, on the same day as the Richardson-Stark exchange, the draft of *Basis for Immediate Decisions Concerning the National Defense* was discussed by Stark, Marshall, and Roosevelt. After the oral review Roosevelt ruled on the question of returning the fleet from Hawaii. That decision "would be taken later." The rest of the draft needed revision—a task given to the Joint Planning Committee. On June 27, Stark and Marshall presented Roosevelt with the revised edition which incorporated the Roosevelt comments of June 22. The recommendations for the immediate future were:

> (1) a defensive position by the United States; (2) nonbelligerent support of the British Commonwealth and China; (3) hemisphere defense, including possible occupation of strategic bases on the soil of Allied Nations' western colonies in case of those nations' defeat; (4) close cooperation with South America; (5) speeding of production and training of manpower, including a draft act and "progressive" mobilization; and (6) preparation of plans for the "almost inevitable conflict" with the totalitarian powers, to assure concerted action with other nations opposing Germany, Italy, and Japan.[59]

Each week which passed without German invasion of the British Isles made the strategy of June 27 look more attainable, and through the summer and into November when Admiral Stark wrote his *Plan Dog*, it was the strategy followed.

As the military leaders of the United States were presenting their commander in chief with strategy guidance, Japan was presenting the final in a series of demands forecast earlier by its military intelligence director. On June 24, Britain was asked to close the Burma Road to war materials and other goods and to take similar action relative to the Hong Kong frontier. To make their point that they meant business,

Japanese forces in China massed 5,000 troops on the Kowloon border —the strip of British territory on the China mainland immediately opposite Hong Kong. The move on June 27 was an additional demand that British troops leave Shanghai.

The demands of June 27 prompted the British ambassador, Lord Lothian, and the Australian minister, Mr. Richard G. Casey in Washington, to ask Secretary of State Hull for help in standing up to the Japanese forces in China. Lothian pointed out that since the collapse of France, Britain alone was having to fend off Japanese demands. Would the United States either join in an embargo or send ships to Singapore to show a cooperative front against Japan, or, if not, would the United States join Britain in mediating a peace settlement between China and Japan. Hull's answer to all items was negative. "Sending the fleet to Singapore would leave the entire Atlantic seaboard, north and south, exposed to possible European threats. Our fleet is already well out in the Pacific, near Hawaii." "As to the embargo proposal, we have been progressively bringing economic pressure on Japan since last summer..." Concerning making peace with Japan, the United States had nothing to offer Japan in the way of concessions or assistance and "no properties or interest of China should be offered to Japan by Britain or the United States. In other words, we do not make peace with Japan at the expense of China..."[60] At this stage there was no help in the offing from the United States for the British in the Far East. The British maneuvered for time, but by July 14 had worked out an agreement to vacate Shanghai, to close the Burma Road for three months during which time they would work towards a Sino-Japanese peace agreement.

The same bitter medicine experienced by the British was forced on the Vichy French. Japan also asked France to close the border of Indochina next to China and to withdraw its forces from Shanghai. Ambassador St. Quentin asked Under Secretary of State Sumner Welles for help in Indochina since additional demands included the admission of Japanese agents to inspect imports and exports to insure compliance by the French. He received no satisfaction. When Welles was asked then if the United States was interested in taking over the French concession in Shanghai, his answer was that the United States "would make no commitment of any character to the French Government at this time with regard to this question."[61] The recent failure to get France to move its fleet well out of the reach of Germany was still fresh. There was no thought of helping the French in Indochina now.

Admiral Hart on June 25 had recommended, in the event that the British and French troops were forced out of Shanghai, that the United States at least take over the Defense Sector B, controlled by British forces, which contained the American Consulate General and numerous other important American interests. Hart was willing to concede to Japan the British Defense Sector D, the second of two being vacated by the British, if U.S. Marines could control Sector B. At that time in Shanghai the Marines numbered 47 officers, 7 warrants, and 1,011 men.[62]

On August 9, Britain announced that her forces would be withdrawn from Shanghai, Tientsin, and Peiping. Immediately thereafter, Colonel DeWitt Peck, commanding the Fourth Marines, requested a meeting of the Shanghai Defense Committee on August 12. Representatives from British, French, American, and Italian forces, Shanghai Volunteer Corps, and the municipal police attended. The Japanese command, apparently waiting for instructions from Tokyo, did not send a representative, but by letter requested another meeting on August 15. At the August 15 meeting the proposal made by Colonel Peck that Japan take over Defense Sector D and the United States take over Sector B was approved by a majority vote. Only the Japanese voted "no" while the Italians abstained. The Japanese contended that any changes had to be agreed upon unanimously, that they had a right to submit an alternate plan, and that the British forces had to leave by August 19.[63]

Peck tried to reach an understanding with his counterpart, Rear Admiral Moriji Takeda, commander of the Japanese naval landing party in Shanghai, but to no avail. Both sides asked for help through the diplomatic channels. From Hull, through Welles, Grew, and the consul in Shanghai, Richard P. Butrick, the State Department officials gave complete support to the military negotiators in Shanghai. Mr. Grew was informed in Tokyo on August 18 that if American troops tried to enter Sector B after the British departure they would be "opposed by Japanese forces."[64] Each side stiffened its resolve not to back down, yet not to challenge the other directly. The discussions in Shanghai developed into meetings between Rear Admiral Glassford, Commander, Yangtze Patrol, representing Admiral Hart, the Commander in Chief, Asiatic Fleet, and Vice Admiral Iwamura, representing Admiral Shigetaro Shimada, the Commander in Chief, China Sea Fleet. An interim arrangement, namely, to assign Sector B to the Shanghai Volunteer Corps until further agreement could be reached, became in actuality the existing arrangement until U.S. Marines were finally withdrawn from Shanghai to the Philippines during the first week in December 1941.

Just as the fall of France in June, with Italy's eleventh-hour entry to contribute to the coup de grace, upset the balance of power in Europe, threw American planners into a near-panic and compounded the turmoil in international relations in China, so did it affect the Japanese government. The pro-German elements, primarily in the army, were elated at the turn of events in Europe and, as might have been expected, the previously suppressed smouldering insistence on closer military ties with Germany flared into open flame. Moderates in the Yonai government and generally the Japanese admirals countered that Hitler could not easily overcome British sea power and that the end was not yet in sight. Despite the cautiousness on the part of the moderates and the admirals, the Army was determined not to let pass the golden opportunity to join with an obviously winning team. The war minister, General Shunroka Hata, was forced by the pro-Axis element of the army to resign on July 16 and, quite deliberately, there was no recommendation for a replacement. A new Cabinet was formed under Prince Fumimaro Konoye, who had been prime minister from 1937 to 1939. The new war minister was General Hideki Tojo. who was destined to become prime minister in October 1941 and take his country into war with the United States. Yosuka Matsuoka became the foreign minister ostensibly to counterbalance the influence of the army, but he was instrumental in Japan's joining the Axis in the Tripartite Pact within a few months. The fourth Cabinet member was Admiral Zengo Yoshida, the navy minister.

Meanwhile, Admiral Richardson finally had his trip to Washington, from July 7 to 11. After conferences with the CNO and the President, he conferred with Hornbeck, adviser on political relations in the State Department. He reaffirmed to each one what he had written and said many times before: that "neither the Navy nor the country was prepared for war with Japan" and if such an eventuality did happen it would be costly, drawn out, and with doubtful prospects of ultimate success. He returned to the fleet "with three distinct impressions":

> *First* That the Fleet was retained in the Hawaiian area solely to support diplomatic representations and as a deterrent to Japanese aggressive actions;
>
> *Second* That there was no intention of embarking on actual hostilities against Japan;
>
> *Third* That the immediate mission of the fleet was accelerated training and absorption of new personnel and the attainment of a

maximum condition of material and personnel readiness consistent with its retention in the Hawaiian area.[65]

Being out of the Washington mainstream, Richardson retained these impressions through September when the newly appointed Secretary of the Navy, Colonel Frank Knox, visited him and the fleet. On the request of Knox, Richardson prepared a long memorandum of points which they had discussed. The main points Richardson drove home during the Secretary's visit concerned the deficiencies of enlisted men, both in numbers and training; the location of the fleet inhibiting its ability to train and to prepare for war; his low appreciation of "Navy Publicity;" and even worse opinion of cooperation between the Executive, State, and War Departments with the Navy Department. To emphasize his personal evaluation of the State Department's role in the fleet's location, Richardson asked the rhetorical question:

> .... what is the State Department's conception of our next move? Does it believe that the Fleet is now mobilized and that it could embark on a campaign directly from Hawaii or safely conduct necessary training from the insecure anchorage of Lahaina which is 2000 miles nearer enemy submarine bases than our normal Pacific bases?[66]

Richardson's comments on navy publicity were a direct slap at Stark's handling of the service party line in Washington. Richardson had been assistant chief of naval operations under Admiral Leahy and knew the Washington routine quite well. He was particularly concerned about those actions which were creating a "false sense of security" in the United States: "... practically all Navy Publicity, hearings before committees, speeches in Congress and handouts from the Navy Department...."[67] It was Stark and his immediate subordinates in the Office of the Chief of Naval Operations, who were responsible for navy publicity, who were doing the testifying before committees in Congress and giving handouts from the department. Richardson took a dim view of what he saw from the sidelines—that too much emphasis was placed on the defensive nature of the Navy; on the Navy as a "mobile Maginot Line behind which people can reside in peace;" on the fleet being "fully manned, fully trained and ready to fight at the drop of a hat;" on solely "material things" being used as the basis for measuring comparative strengths of navies; and on "aviation as a cheap means of defense." This type of publicity statement he thought weakened "the moral fibre" of the country and created an "unhealthy national morale in a country which may be drawn into war on very short notice." The sincerity and alarm of the

79

Commander in Chief, United States Fleet, is best illustrated in his closing statement of that part of the memorandum:

> For a people, who may actually be involved in war in a comparatively short time, to be told that they can risk war without danger or wage war without risk, may be fatally detrimental to the determined prosecution of the very war towards which such conceptions inevitably lead.[68]

Nor did Richardson confine his critical comments to navy publicity. He did not consider that coordination and mutual understanding between the "Executive, State and War Departments with the Navy Department" was as close as was "necessary for effective action." He was responsible for the efficiency of the Navy "upon which the government relies to enforce National policy, when its aims cannot be secured by diplomatic means." To Richardson the existing policy appeared "to be headed towards forcing our will upon another Pacific Nation by diplomatic representations supported by economic measures, a large material Navy in process of construction, and the disposition of an inadequately manned *Fleet in being.*" Then he asked if the country were prepared to face war or the inevitable loss of prestige if it were not. Had objectives of such a war been formulated and its costs considered and compared with the value of victory? He ended his long memorandum with observations on the Atlantic scene.

> Are objectives being formulated and plans made for our active participation in the European war? We cannot long remain half in and half out of such a war. We should decide now on definite objectives and plans and should not assume that we will fight this one like we did the last, i.e., by sending aviation and light forces for active participation and utilizing our heavy ships, in *secure* home bases, largely as training ships. Such a course would immobilize our heavy ships, which are most certainly going to be needed either in the Atlantic or the Pacific, depending on the progress of the war.[69]

Knox duly passed the Richardson memorandum to Stark in Washington.

A few days later Richardson wrote Stark that Knox, on his visit, had invited him to Washington in early October and that his reply at the time was that he could not go "to Washington except under orders, but if Stark wanted to see" him, he supposed he would be ordered. He told Stark that he did not know "any benefit to the Navy that would accrue" from his coming to Washington, since he "had fully and frankly expressed his views to the Secretary on all points where he felt such expression might help the Navy or the Nation."

(Since Stark had Richardon's memorandum to Secretary Knox, he probably could not have agreed more with this statement.) In a post-script to a short letter he reiterated once again that he had "nothing to take up with the Department that cannot be handled by corre-spondence," but that if he were wanted in Washington he was ready to come upon his arrival in San Pedro the last part of September.[70]

Between Richardson's trip to Washington in July and Knox's visit to Hawaii in September a laboriously conceived and unprece-dented maneuver finally came to the execution phase. On September 3, 1940, the United States transferred fifty World War I type destroyers and other war materials to Britain in exchange for two bases and ninety-nine-year leases on other potential base sites, all in British pos-sessions in the western Atlantic. In the latter part of September events moved faster and faster. On September 22, Japan extracted from Vichy France an agreement for the use of three airfields, the station-ing of troops, and the rights of passage in northern Indochina. On September 24, after spirited discussion between the President, his military and cabinet advisers over a total embargo of goods to Japan (Stark and Welles were definitely against further embargo of oil), all iron and steel scrap shipments to Japan were officially stopped. The next day a new loan to China was announced. Although negotiations had been under way for weeks, the signing in Berlin on September 27 of the Tripartite Pact, a defense alliance binding Germany, Italy, and Japan together, appeared to be an answer to U.S. actions protesting Japanese moves in northern Indochina.

The Joint Planning Committee was pessimistic in a report to Stark and Marshall on the day of the Tripartite signing. They saw no as-surance that Japan would not, within the next few months, move swiftly either against the Dutch East Indies or against the Philippines or Guam, especially if the Japanese government should become in-creasingly embarrassed by embargoes on exports in the Far East, and should at the same time become convinced that, despite United States statements, it was bluffing and would back down in the face of serious challenge. If the situation in the Far East deteriorated to the point that armed opposition to Japan became necessary, even in the face of the potential threat in the Atlantic, the planners recommended that the action be limited "to minor naval surface and air forces operating from Singapore and Dutch East Indies bases, plus the interruption of Japanese shipping in the eastern Pacific."[71]

The Japanese actions in Indochina, their obduracy over the De-fense Sector problems in Shanghai, and a generally increased belliger-

81

ency prompted Admiral Hart to write Stark that "the situation seems to be rapidly changing as regards the relative importance of this command's two missions." Hart's peacetime mission of guarding American lives and interests was being overtaken by the "necessity of being 'set' in the other part of our job out here." Since the *Augusta* was so vulnerable in Shanghai and since he considered Admiral Glassford and Colonel Peck well qualified to take care of any situation on the Yangtze or in Shanghai, he planned to move his ships to Manila. At Hart's suggestion, which was readily endorsed by Ambassador Grew in Japan and the Navy Department, Secretary Hull issued a directive to his diplomatic and consular officers in China, Japan, Hong Kong, and Indochina to suggest to all American citizens in their areas that they evacuate. Through October 1940, most of the women and children and many of the businessmen and missionaries did so, in the passenger ships *Monterey* and *Mariposa* of the Matson Lines and the *Washington* of the United States Lines. Still, Hart was concerned "about leaving too many 'hostages to fortune'—in the shape of Marines and river gunboat personnel in China."[72] The getting-set phase had started—and well over a year before hostilities commenced.

On the other side of the world, decisions were being made affecting the Japanese in China. It appeared in October that Britain had weathered the threat of invasion by Germany without any further aggression by Japan against British strongholds in the Pacific. On October 4, immediately after the British Cabinet had decided to reopen the Burma Road on October 17, Churchill sent a message to Roosevelt urging him to send a sizable naval detachment to Singapore—"the bigger the better," as a display of the English-speaking naval power arrayed against Japan. Stark, Marshall, and Welles were vehemently against such a move, while Secretary Stimson urged shifting the bulk of the fleet to Singapore forthwith. Stark observed, in the meeting of the Standing Liaison Committee when the Churchill proposal was discussed, that "every day that we are able to maintain peace and still support the British is valuable time gained," while Marshall stated that "this was as unfavorable a moment as you could choose" for inviting trouble.[73] At the very time of the British proposal for an American show of force in Singapore, the admirals in the United States Navy were united in urging that the fleet be brought back to San Diego and San Pedro. The State Department, particularly Dr. Hornbeck, considered the fleet a deterrent to Japan and withdrawal after the Tripartite Pact signing would possibly indicate fear of the new Axis Union.

Admiral Richardson was summoned to Washington to participate in the discussions of the future employment of the fleet. He was most upset to find out from Knox and Stark, prior to speaking with Roosevelt, that instead of bringing the fleet to the West Coast, there was serious talk of reinforcing the Asiatic Fleet and of sending the Singapore detachment requested by the British government. On October 8, Richardson and Leahy had lunch with Roosevelt, who inquired whether sending reinforcements to the Asiatic Fleet would serve to deter Japan. Leahy thought it might have a temporary effect, but since the Asiatic Fleet might well be lost, only the least valuable combatant ships should be sent. Roosevelt did not mention sending a detachment to Singapore, but what he did suggest dismayed Richardson so much that he later asked Knox if the President was considering declaring war on Japan. If Japan was to take "drastic action" in retaliation for the reopening of the Burma Road, Roosevelt had told Knox, he was thinking of a complete embargo and the establishment of a naval patrol in two lines, one from Hawaii west to the Philippines and the other between Samoa and the Netherlands East Indies.

Suddenly this newest insight into Roosevelt's thinking meshed with the points he had covered the day before. On October 9, Richardson was told to go ahead assembling the train—support and supply vessels—for the fleet, was asked if there were enough fuel oil in Samoa for four old light cruisers, was told that a division of such ships might be sent to Mindanao in the Philippines as a gesture, and was asked for a chart showing British and French bases or possible bases for surface ships, submarines, or airplanes in the Pacific islands east of the International Date Line. Roosevelt also discussed Ghormley's liaison with the Admiralty and British desire for staff conferences. Lastly, Richardson recorded Roosevelt as having said:

> I can be convinced of the desirability of retaining the battleships on the West Coast if I can be given a good statement which will convince the American people, and the Japanese Government, that in bringing the battleships to the West Coast we are not stepping backward.[74]

Richardson tried to reason with Knox over the consequences of establishing the two lines of patrol. The fleet was not ready for such patrols, much less for war, and surely, if Japanese commerce were intercepted, war was inevitable. Knox was more sympathetic to Stimson's and Roosevelt's hard-line approaches than to excuses of unreadiness. He told Richardson on October 10 that if he did not like Roosevelt's plans, then he and Stark could draw up their own to accomplish the same purpose.[75] Richardson, the realist, did just that. With his own War Plans Officer and the officers in the War Plans Division of Stark's staff, he drew up a list of assumptions, paralleling those of Roosevelt's, of retaliatory actions by Japan against Britain should the Burma Road be reopened. A skeleton operations plan was also written redistributing forces throughout the Pacific—including the provision for a comparatively strong detachment of four cruisers, a carrier, nine destroyers, four minesweepers, and two auxiliaries—for possible dispatch to the Netherlands East Indies to be under the operational control of Commander in Chief, Asiatic Fleet. Richardson left his plan with Stark for review and submission to the Secretary of the Navy and the President.

By coincidence, while Richardson was in Washington discussing the future employment of the fleet, Secretary Knox presented Roosevelt with a long list of recommended actions necessary to prepare for war. The recommendations were not limited to those for which the Navy alone was responsible or to preparation for preparation's sake, but additionally included acts to impress the Japanese government. The memorandum showed his propensity for recommending cross-departmental actions:

> Orders have been issued for these measures to be taken at once:
> 1. Call the organized Naval and Marine Reserves.
> 2. Call Fleet Reserves, Navy and Marine, selective basis.
> 3. Lay nets and booms for drill purposes.
>
> The following steps in preparation for war can be taken to impress the Japanese with the seriousness of our preparations:
> 1. Army send reinforcement to Hawaii if contemplated.
> 2. Presidential proclamation for Maritime Commission to requisition merchant ships, in order to
> 3. Take over tankers, transports, auxiliaries, and begin to assemble Train on W. Coast.
> 4. Coast Guard transfer to Navy.
> 5. Fill up garrisons of defense battalions in 14th District outlying bases.
> 6. Presidential proclamation establishing defensive sea areas.
> 7. Withdraw nationals from China. (Inconsistent with getting merchant ships out of danger.)
> 8. Plan for evacuation of families out of Hawaii and later Panama.
> 9. Preparations regarding seizure German and Japanese merchant vessels in ports and near our coasts.
> 10. Pressure on Britain to speed leases Bermuda and Newfoundland (essential).

11. Change laws to take limit off naval and marine personnel—limit to President's discretion.
12. Prepare plans for concentration camps (Army—Justice).
13. Executive Order to call Volunteer Reserves, including communications and merchant marine reserves.
14. Withdraw Marines from North China (this means Embassy should be closed). Leave very small token force. Stop sending replacements, Marine Shanghai—let attrition operate. Consider withdrawal when currency situation permits.
15. Netherlands East Indies:—Assist in material; line up for mutual support.

The following are matters for Treasury and State:
1. Freeze credits and assets of Japan.
2. Continue to bolster Chinese credit.
3. Take such steps as may be necessary to insure Chinese currency carrying on in case Shanghai is occupied by Japan.

For consideration, but in abeyance for the moment:
1. Alert the Asiatic Station at once to get ships other than gunboats out of China. This should be the first secret step.
2. Alert the: Naval Establishment (Established security patrols, etc.)
    Military Establishment
    Merchant Marine (Clippers)
    Department of Justice—sabotage—surveillance of agents
    Panama Canal—all security measures.[76]

Roosevelt's answer the next day was short and to the point. It was the answer of a commander in chief up for reelection who could not be as aggressive as his service secretaries proposed.

In relations to Secret Memorandum of October ninth, covering measures to be taken in preparation for war, I approve the first three. Please do not put any of the others into effect without speaking to me about them. F.D.R.[77]

Upon his return to the West Coast Richardson wrote to Hart giving him the history of the Washington visit and the evolution of his substitute plan, after citing the "impracticability" of the original Roosevelt concept of the two patrol lines. Richardson pointed out that his plan was similar to the old *Orange Plan* except that the fleet was restricted from going any further than mid-Pacific because of the Atlantic situation, that there would be no Army units involved, and that the United States Fleet would have the use of the facilities at Singapore. In the event that the assumptions were not realized prior to January 1, 1941, or the decision had not been made prior to that time to send the advanced detachment to the Asiatic Fleet, a train would be assembled and a full scale exercise would be made against Christmas Island, near the equator due south of Hawaii. Coincidental with the exercise the Asiatic Fleet would be reinforced so that Japan would realize the United States' determination and capability to protect its national interests.[78] At the time of his October 16 letter to Hart, Richardson had not heard from Washington of the status of his plan, nor would he hear. Roosevelt, and his more aggressive advisers, were apparently satisfied with other contemporary actions. The Army had decided to send two squadrons of pursuit airplanes to the Philippines, and the Navy planned to base ten additional submarines for the Asiatic Fleet in Manila Bay, Australia had agreed to make fifty additional planes available for the defense of Singapore.[79]

Richardson waited a few more days after writing to Hart and, having received no further information, sent Stark a long analysis of "War Plans-Status and readiness of in view of the current international situation." He set the tenor of the seriousness of his letter in the first paragraph. He felt that it was

> . . . his solemn duty to present, for the Chief of Naval Operations, certain facts and conclusions in order that there may be no doubt in the minds of higher authority as to his convictions in regard to the present situation especially in the Pacific.[80]

He reviewed the differences he found in the thinking in Washington between his July and October trips, after which he analyzed the *Orange Plan* and its supporting United States Fleet War Plans. None of them were current or realistic in the present international situation. Next he reviewed the *Rainbow* series plans. The only two plans he had, *Rainbows 1* and *2*, were inapplicable; the former pertained only to the Western Hemisphere and the latter, which Richardson had in draft form only, concerned sustaining the democratic powers in the Pacific. According to Richardson there existed a vital necessity for a new directive, possibly *Rainbow 3*, "based on present realities, national objectives and commitments as far as these are known or can be predicted at the present time," and there should be "coordination of plans developed with National Policy and steps to be taken to implement that policy." He had no intention or desire "to evade his legitimate responsibilities" nor was anything in his letter to be so construed. He realized fully that "no plan can foresee or provide for every possible situation, and that adjustments and re-estimates must be made to fit the actual situation presented." Yet, at the same time, he "most strongly believed" that he "must be better informed than he [had been] as to the Department's plans and intentions if he [was] to perform his full duty."[81]

Richardson would not receive a *Rainbow 3* plan or an answer to his complaints about not being sufficiently informed until the latter part of December, almost two months later. When he did hear from Stark again, it was after Roosevelt's reelection. On November 12, Stark wrote to both Richardson and Hart about the genesis of his detailed analysis of future courses of action. At that time his "broad estimate" was in Roosevelt's hands. Both fleet commanders would have to wait for details of the yet-to-be-identified *Plan Dog*. In the meantime, Stark promised both a *Rainbow 3* plan "in a few days," even though the Army war planners had stopped work on *Rainbows 2* and *3* on May 23. Stark reaffirmed to Richardson his certainty that the United States would enter the war. He wrote:

> ...you know I have felt right along that it is only a matter of time before we get in [though I can not say this out loud]. The chief question that concerns us is *where* we get in, and *whom* we will fight—and "tomorrow" or perhaps "today" is what I am working towards.
>
> You have received the despatch directing the sending of submarines to Manila. There are no plans at present to send anything more in that direction. But present conditions are far from static, the Japanese appear to be making preparation for a definite move of some kind, and the answer we will give, if any, to the steps they may take in the future can not be predicted at this time.[82]

To Hart's letter Stark added the importance of "laying, with the British and possibly the Dutch, a framework for a future plan of cooperation, should we be forced into the war." This followed the words of caution which were to be the stumbling block to anything constructive in discussions on the Far East through the next year: "The Navy can, of course, make no political commitments. Therefore we can make no specific military plans for an allied war."[83]

Nevertheless, discussions with the British were the order of the day. Hull had favored, and advocated to Lord Lothian, "technical talks" between the military leaders of the United States and Britain. Roosevelt had a special observer in Rear Admiral Ghormley for liaison with the Admiralty, which, with Churchill, had been pushing hard for closer cooperation, especially in the Far East. Rejection of the proposal for the United States to send a strong detachment to Singapore did not dampen the British drive for "staff conversations." Rumors in October of important conversations to be held in Washington concerning the Far East were first confirmed by the White House, as a warning to Japan, then, for political reasons, denied because Roosevelt was being accused in the campaign of making secret commitments to Britain. Ghormley was instructed to exchange information but to make no commitments, implied or otherwise, concerning possible United States participation in the Far East.

After the election, new impetus for conversations came from two different directions. Lord Lothian, upon his return from London, saw Hull on November 25 and again raised the question "of conferences between the naval experts of [the] two Governments with respect to what each would or might do in case of military outbreaks on the part of Japan."[84] Additionally, Stark's *Plan Dog,* which had not been accepted yet by the President, War or State Departments, ended with the paragraph:

> Accordingly, I make the recommendation that, as a preliminary to possible entry of the United States into the conflict, the United States Army and Navy at once undertake secret staff talks on technical matters with the British military and naval authorities in London, with Canadian military authorities in Washington, and with British and Dutch authorities in Singapore and Batavia. The purpose would be to reach agreements and lay down plans for promoting unity of allied effort should the United States find it necessary to enter the war under any of the alternative eventualities considered in this memorandum.*

With presidential approval, Stark sent a personal invitation to Admiral of the Fleet Sir Dudley Pound on November 30 to send accredited representatives to Washington before Christmas if possible. The exchange of preliminary information and the development of position papers by each side delayed the meeting until January 1941. The basis of the American position in January would be Stark's *Plan Dog.*

Late in November, Stark asked Richardson for a more detailed analysis of defense requirements for the protection of the fleet in Pearl Harbor. The last two replies received to similar inquiries made to Admiral Bloch, Commandant, Fourteenth Naval District, were "not very definite" and Stark needed more ammunition to get the War Department to put more effort into the buildup of defense against carrier air attack. Stark admitted that the highly successful British carrier raid on November 11 against the Italian fleet anchored at Taranto prompted his concern for the safety of the fleet at Pearl Harbor. That

* For *Plan Dog* see Appendix A.

concern had "to do both with possible activities on the part of Japanese residents of Hawaii and with the possibilities of attack coming from overseas. By far the most profitable object of sudden attack in Hawaiian waters would be the Fleet units based in that area."[85] Richardson's preliminary answer, written before he returned to Pearl Harbor from the West Coast, was that torpedo nets, proposed by Stark, within the harbor were neither necessary nor practicable, that he would take up the matter of protection with Admiral Bloch, and that he would issue a plan for tighter security measures when he arrived at Pearl Harbor.

In mid-December Richardson received, by officer messenger from Stark, four advanced copies of *Navy Basic War Plan—Rainbow No. 3*. By a letter of December 17, Stark defended both *Rainbow 3* and his past cooperation with Richardson. *Rainbow 3* was "designed to provide against the most imminent and difficult war situation which may confront the United States in the near future . . . where the principal portion of the national effort is directed westward." Richardson's task relative to the new plan was quite clear:

> It is, therefore requested that the Commander in Chief prepare as soon as practicable the operating plans for a war envisaged by *Rainbow No. 3*.[86]

Stark did mention that there were "under study . . . by the naval and army officials . . . plans based on assumptions requiring the exertion of the principal portion of the national effort to the eastward (*Rainbow No. 5*) and also a plan, somewhat similar to *Rainbow No. 1*, involving the defense of the entire Western Hemisphere against attack from both the east and the west (*Rainbow No. 4*)." He considered the three plans "adequate to guide mobilization, initial deployment, and initial operations under all contingencies which [were] foreseeable."

He then chided Richardson a bit about the *Orange Plan*. He believed it was unnecessary to comment upon the applicability of the *Orange Plan*, "as that Plan was drawn up to guide the prosecution of a war under circumstances which do not now exist." He asserted that he had kept the fleet commander in chief "advised as to all matters within his own knowledge which related to current national policy and pending national decisions," and that his past practice would be continued in the future. Richardson was reminded that "the changing world military situation will continue to affect policy, and thus will influence plans for the war operation of the naval forces." It was "impracticable to draw up and to issue new Navy Basic War Plans when merely minor changes in policy occur." A few days later Stark wrote a long letter in which he discussed the assembly of a train for the fleet and the exercise at Christmas Island which Richardson had proposed to Hart. He ended that letter on his by then usual ominous note:

> There is little that I can add which is not repetition, but I shall repeat just the same that every 24 hours past is just one day nearer to actual hostilities and that your flag officers and captains should be completely in the frame of mind that we will be in the fighting business most any time, and purely as a guess on my own part, I would say at any time after the next 90 days. Our heads and our hearts and every ounce of energy that we have should be devoted exclusively to the business of war and keeping fit—and I don't mean maybe.
>
> It may come anytime.[87]

In neither letter did Stark mention his *Plan Dog* to which he had referred in passing in his November 12 letter. *Rainbow 3* was Richardson's guidance.

As 1940 drew to a close, the situation since the previous January had changed considerably. Stark, who had forecast something breaking quickly and without warning in the Far East in January, did not know in December where the United States would commence fighting but predicted that it would be fighting soon. His attention, nevertheless, was concentrated on helping Britain in the Atlantic. In China, the United States Navy's confrontations with the Imperial Japanese Navy had been less acrimonious and less frequent than in previous years. As the year ended with Hart "getting set" for other contingencies, with the British and the French military forces, the American dependents and American combatant ships withdrawn, relations were quiescent. To be sure, the whole Far East was not so. Japanese forces, jockeying for position in Indochina, posed new threats to Singapore and the Netherlands East Indies and reinforced the fears of future aggression by having formally joined the Tripartite Pact. The United States explored ways to cooperate with China, Britain, and the Netherlands to counteract the Japanese moves; the noose of economic sanctions, having been finally fashioned, was drawing slowly but fatally around Japan.

Richardson, who had balked at his fleet being held at Pearl Harbor for the politically reasoned deterrent effect, had lost each of his persuasive attempts to get it to the West Coast bases so that he might better prepare it for the inevitable war. The year ended with him preparing war plans for actions in the western Pacific based on a hastily completed *Rainbow 3* plan which would be cancelled in just eight more months.

In Washington, alarm at the highly successful German blitzkrieg had triggered multiple decisions. American aid to Britain had increased in volume and acceptability after the first threats of invasion had passed. Mid-year also saw the start of the two-ocean navy, the swearing in of two new aggressive service secretaries, Knox and Stimson, and a decision by Roosevelt to run for a third term.

The year ended with the stage set for discussions in Washington and the Far East with the British and possibly Dutch military leaders to cooperate more closely in the Atlantic and the Pacific against potentially common enemies. The incentive for talks in both areas was from the Chief of Naval Operations and the basis for the United States position would be of naval origin.

CHAPTER 6

Japan's Growing Need
For Petroleum

> It is highly probable that the aircraft which attacked Pearl Harbor and the carriers which transported them across the Pacific operated on American fuel.[1]

Two of the major prerequisites to any war machine are steel and petroleum and for both commodities Japan, since its modernization, depended heavily upon imports. Approximately 80 percent of Japan's crude oil and refined stocks in the early 1930s was imported from the United States, and from those imports Japan had accumulated a reserve for war. The war machine put into motion against China in 1937 required vast amounts of aviation gasoline and lubricants, fuel oil for ships, gasoline for land vehicles, and the various forms of oil used in the civilian economy to support the war. Yet by 1939 the carefully nurtured reserve had grown to a maximum of fifty-five million barrels.[2] If all oil imports were cut off, the reserve would last less than two years at the 1939 rate of consumption. However, the unexpected tempo of the war in China and the failure to bring that war to an early end threatened to cut into the precious reserve. Only an increased volume of imports would allow the reserve to be maintained, and, of course, to build it up despite the increased usage required an even larger volume of imports.

Reports of startling Japanese demands for accelerated imports reached the State Department in June and July 1940. The recent fall of France and the Battle of Britain were very much the major topics of concern in Washington. Did the increased demands for oil portend a Japanese move to the south or were they part of a build-up of a larger reserve for a long war in the Pacific?

Before Secretary Hull departed for a conference in Havana on

July 19, he rejected suggestions that he advocate to the President cutting oil exports to Japan to their normal volume.[3] Mr. Hull probably remembered Ambassador Grew's words of warning to President Roosevelt the year before "that if we cut off Japanese supplies of oil and that if Japan then finds that she cannot obtain sufficient oil from other commercial sources to ensure national security, she will in all probability send her fleet down to take the Dutch East Indies."[4]

On the day Hull left for Havana, Roosevelt conferred with Stimson, Knox, and Welles on a proposal passed to him by Secretary of the Treasury Henry Morgenthau, Jr. The proposal had been suggested in part by Lord Lothian, the British ambassador, who had discussed the matter with Stimson, Knox, Morgenthau, and the Australian minister, Richard Casey, at a dinner party the previous evening. The plan proposed by Lothian was for the United States, on the grounds of national defense, to stop all exports of oil. Britain would then get all its oil from the Caribbean area, arranging with the Dutch government in the meantime to destroy the oil wells in the Indies. Finally, the British would concentrate bombing attacks on the synthetic oil plants in Germany. "Where then, and how, would Japan and Germany get oil for war?"[5] Welles objected to the Morgenthau endorsement of the Lothian proposal and to embargoes against Japan in general because he believed that they would cause Japan to make war on Britain.

As a result of the July 19 meeting, Welles entered into a series of consultations with the President and Admiral Stark. A ban on oil might force the Japanese to make a decision about going into the Dutch East Indies and Welles doubted that the American people were ready to support a counter military move. He thought he had impressed Roosevelt with his argument,[6] and from later evidence he most probably had the support of Stark in his persuasive efforts.

Some cabinet members were much more prone to take a firm stand against Japan. The "hard line element" of Morgenthau, Stimson, and Knox actually succeeded in getting the President to sign a proclamation on July 25, 1940, to establish export controls over all kinds of oil and scrap metals. Welles and his worried state department subordinates were disturbed on learning of that move, because they feared that the embargo would "provoke a crisis with Japan sooner or later, and probably sooner." Welles argued his case again and managed to persuade Roosevelt to issue a State Department version of a control proclamation "to make clear the proclamation of July 25." That version applied export controls only to "aviation motor fuels and lubricants and No. 1 heavy melting iron and steel scrap."[7] The export controls desired by the hard-liners were thereby emasculated. Not until a year later were the strict controls to be evoked.

The term "aviation motor fuel" was further defined in the Presidential Proclamation of July 26, 1940 as "High octane gasolines, hydrocarbons, and hydrocarbon mixtures which, with the addition of tetraethyl lead up to a total content of 3 c.c. per gallon will exceed 87 octane number, or any material from which by commercial distillation there can be separated more than 3 per cent of such gasoline, hydrocarbon, or hydrocarbon mixture."[8] The question of circumventing the restriction on petroleum exports based on octane level became the center of controversy between those who viewed the proclamation as the minimum move in the right direction toward "tight" control and those who viewed the proclamation as a guide to maximum limits of control against Japan.

Many naval officers wanted the export controls rigidly enforced by applying restrictions to *all* fuels which could be made to serve as aviation fuel through the use of additives with or without further distillation. The section of the Navy Department best informed on efforts to circumvent the octane limits and most anxious to restrict the Japanese efforts to increase their reserve was the Office of Naval Intelligence.

The Director of Naval Intelligence, Rear Admiral Walter Stratton Anderson, informed the Chief of Naval Operations that through reliable sources his agents had information "regarding negotiations being carried on between the Associated Oil Company, Standard Oil Company of California and Japanese oil interests which appeared to be aimed at circumventing the export on aviation gasoline." Japanese importers were able "to obtain not only Kettleman fuel oil [a partially refined oil] but a special blend of crude from Kettleman rated at 89 octane." The American oil companies concerned were near agreement with the Japanese interests "to supply this special 89 octane crude against outstanding large orders for 97 octane, 92 hi-octane and 87 octane fuel." By suitable leading of this special blend with ethyl, practically all Japanese requirements for high octane fuel could be met regardless of export control. Whether or not this "special blend" was a commercial grade, or a blend developed for the purpose of satisfying Japanese requirements, was not known to the intelligence agents at that time.[9] It was highly significant to them, however, that by using a special blend of *crude* oil, which was not restricted, the Japanese could meet their gasoline needs. Since ship bunker fuel was not restricted, Japan could meet all its petroleum requirements.

Records do not indicate what, if anything, Admiral Stark did or thought about the specific information on circumvention, but four days later the Director of Naval Intelligence wrote directly to the Secretary of the Navy with *a carbon copy to the Chief of Naval Operations and the naval aide to the President.* After reviewing the circumvention techniques being worked out by certain American oil companies with the Japanese, Admiral Anderson pointed out how the desired degree of embargo against Japan could be made air-tight and such schemes of circumvention be defeated. First, it was necessary for the proper governmental authorities, presumably the State and Treasury Departments, to set forth exactly what degree of embargo they desired to enforce. Then, qualified commercial oil experts could assist in the implementation of that policy by writing the necessary rules with the proper technical specifications to make the policy really binding. Admiral Anderson added that while the navy was not charged with the primary responsibility in connection with the enforcement of any embargo, such an embargo was definitely of Navy interest, and "it is believed the Departments charged with enforcing the embargo would welcome suggestions from the Navy in the premises."[10]

The memorandum from Admiral Anderson was dually significant. First, it stated a position for the Navy, namely, that the embargo of oil was of interest to the Navy, which was ready to give suggestions on how better to enforce that embargo. The feeling expressed by the Director of Naval Intelligence was not shared by the Chief of Naval Operations which probably accounts for the direct correspondence with the Secretary. It was quite "legal" for Admiral Anderson so to correspond, but it was not the accepted procedure. The second significance of the memorandum concerns its treatment after Secretary Knox received it. Not only was Knox in agreement with the suggestions contained in the subject memorandum, he wanted to share them with the leader of the "hard line" group, Secretary Morgenthau. On Admiral Anderson's memorandum he penciled a note to James Forrestal, then under secretary of the navy, telling him to "take this up with Henry Morgenthau early next week" and to "ask Admiral Anderson for a copy of [the] letter he has on this subject and give that to H.M. also."[11] Obviously, part of the navy favored tight controls.

One of the first indications of the feelings of the Chief of Naval Operations on the subject of embargo of oil to Japan was contained in a letter of September 24, 1940, to Admiral Richardson, Commander in Chief, United States Fleet. The previous day, Stark had spent over three hours in the State Department, of which two hours were spent in the morning with Hull, Welles, and Hornbeck and an hour in the afternoon with Welles alone. In those meetings Stark strongly opposed an embargo on fuel oil to Japan. He left feeling that Welles was "in complete agreement" with him and that Hull had raised the issue to have a thorough discussion on the subject.[12] Stark was in the camp of Welles and certainly not that of Morgenthau.

If Stark did not like the look of things on September 24, he would like them less three days later. On September 27, the Tripartite Pact between Japan, Germany, and Italy was signed, increasing the chance that the United States would eventually fight Japan. A clash was possible if the United States—in support of Britain against her opponent, Germany—encountered the Japanese in support of Germany against Britain. Fear that the new formal alliance was a prelude to a Japanese move against Singapore or the East Indies prompted many discussions in Washington. Within the State Department, one faction, including Hornbeck, stood for further use at once of American economic power as a deterrent, while Hamilton and his associates in the Far Eastern Division advised otherwise—unless the United States was prepared for war. Morgenthau, Stimson and Secretary of the Interior, Harold L. Ickes, who was also petroleum administrator for national defense, wanted to lower the octane levels of exports, and in the Navy, though Knox still seemed inclined to use pressure, "the admirals from Stark down were saying the Navy was not ready for war."[13]

Meanwhile the Dutch were asking the State Department to refrain from actions which would increase Japanese pressure against the Indies. Stimson's suggestion of sending a flying squadron of warships to the Indies to deter Japanese actions was strongly opposed by Admirals Stark and Richardson. Stark and General Marshall recognized that a conflict with Japan in the near future was altogether probable, but they insisted that the United States was as yet unprepared for hostilities in the Pacific and that, in any event, it was more in the American interests to arm against Hitler and support Britain than to devote a major effort against Japan.[14]

A naval intelligence report on November 2 showed that, despite the licensing of exports since July, aviation gasoline shipments to Japan jumped to a new height two months later. Department of Commerce figures[15] for exports to Japan read:

	Barrels	
	Aviation Gas	Other Gas
July	40,938	119,277
August	8,540	283,550
September	115,051	434,284

When the intelligence agents questioned the Division of Controls (State Department) about the big increase they were informed that while the figures were accurate they were based "upon the presumption that any gasoline suitable for use or actually used in aeroplanes is *aviation gasoline*" and that the controls office used a stricter definition in terms of octane count. Officials there did admit that a very large proportion of the gasoline exported to Japan was actually used in planes and was stepped up by "boosters" to high octane count. Personnel in the Division of Controls also stated that the question was essentially political insofar as they were under instructions to follow "a lenient policy designed to appease Japan and relieve the Netherlands East Indies of pressure."[16]

Under the circumstances the State Department had little choice. The Navy was reluctant to deploy forces to the Far East and was not ready to fight Japan. Tight restrictions might force Japan to take the alternate source of supply. Lenient policy might buy time to prepare for war. It was against this background that Admiral Stark evolved his *Plan Dog*, which proposed American military support of Britain to defeat Germany and if forced to fight in the Pacific against Japan, to fight a defensive war using economic restrictions to limit the Japanese. Economic measures were to be used in a war, not to start one. Stark looked upon the embargo of oil to Japan as an unnecessary risk of war—he wanted no war until Germany was defeated.

While Stark was working out his *Plan Dog* memorandum, the British were active in attempting to get the cooperation of the United States against Japan. Lord Lothian on November 1 asked the American government to join Britain in limiting the total exports of all essential goods to Japan to only "normal" amounts."[17] Later in the month the question of restricting oil exports boiled up again. On November 20, the British sent Admiral Stark a long memorandum entitled *Japanese Oil Situation,* which reviewed in detail their intelligence on the matter. The key to the figures in the papers relative to the reserve of Japanese oil were based on the United States Navy's estimate of consumption for the last three years. The British were of the opinion, based on their war experience, that the estimate of consumption was too high and that in fact the Japanese were not as hard-pressed for oil as the U.S. Navy thought. They further proposed "that the only reliable means of dealing with the very undesirable situation inherent in further accumulation of stocks by the Japanese would be by joint policy designed to curtail Japanese chartering of foreign flag tankers." Their policy was not to cut Japan off from supplies but to cooperate with the U.S. government in restricting, by the least provocative means, Japanese imports of oil from continuing at a rate for which there was no commercial justification.[18]

The offer had merit but Hull insisted that any action which might provoke the Japanese was unwise unless the British and American forces in the Far East were stronger. Stark, who wanted to concentrate on winning the Atlantic war first, was undoubtedly influenced by Richardson's constant plea for more trained personnel and support ships. Richardson considered the fleet, in its existing state of readiness, to be unprepared for war. In Washington he had argued as strongly as he could for returning it to the West Coast, where it could prepare for war and be provided an adequate train of support. Hull and Admiral Stark, to whom the British proposals were primarily directed, let them rest. Stark had already proposed joint discussions with the British to arrive at a better basis of possible future operations together.

Although the British government "accepted the decision" of Hull and Stark,[19] there was another attempt to get consideration on their memorandum, *Japanese Oil Situation.* A copy of the paper was given to Rear Admiral Ghormley, the special naval observer in London, who forwarded it to the Chief of Naval Operations. In his forwarding letter Ghormley asked his chief to note that the proposals "contained herein were presented to the State Department on November 20th, 1940, but no reply from State Department has yet been received." Ghormley suggested to Stark that in view of conditions in the Far East the British proposals "be given careful consideration as a possible deterrent to Japan becoming engaged in war at this time."[20] Ghormley did not know, of course, that the proposals had been carefully considered by Hull and Stark and shelved.

Discussions within the Cabinet and the State Department through the following months concentrated on freezing Japan's American assets and placing further restrictions on oil. In the meantime, Japanese imports of gasoline and crude oils from which aviation gasoline could be obtained continued to increase. State Department estimates in April 1941 were that the Japanese would receive from the United States and the Dutch East Indies over twelve million barrels during that year or three times the normal amount.

Despite Admiral Stark's feeling on the embargo of oil, Japanese practices in the procurement of oil on the West Coast could not continue without comment by the Navy to the State Department. In accordance with recognized international procedures the Japanese government obtained from the State Department permission for each

Japanese naval ship to visit United States ports. The State Department personnel always advised the Navy Department and requested comment. In April Secretary Knox informed Hull that the Navy Department had no objection to a proposed Japanese ship visit, but called attention to the recent frequency of Japanese naval visits. A total of twelve Japanese naval vessels had obtained cargoes of oil from the United States within a period of six months, five of those within sixty days. Certain of the vessels listed as naval vessels had made previous similar trips in their original status as commercial vessels. It appeared more than probable that their naval status had been devised to bestow upon them, and upon their obvious purposes, a degree of immunity which commercial vessels could scarcely command. Secretary Knox suggested that the frequency of such visits was "to say the least, unusual" and "that some restrictive policy would be a timely precaution to prevent the abuse of international courtesy."[21]

The fact that the frequency of the visits had increased to one every ten days[22] through February and March was disturbing enough, but the abuse of designating commercial vessels as naval vessels was more than the naval intelligence division cared to tolerate. The courtesies of the port allowed too much freedom to the crew for the many facets of espionage work, and to accord commercial vessels the honors due to men-of-war was highly unpalatable. On the recommendation of the Director of Naval Intelligence, Secretary Knox informed Secretary Hull on May 23 that oil cargo ships posing as Japanese men-of-war need not be accorded "the privileges, immunities and courtesies which would be accorded with pleasure to any recognized ship of the Japanese Navy." The case in point was the *Kokuyo Maru* which had last visited San Francisco in a commercial status and now requested the courtesy given a man-of-war on a proposed visit to Los Angeles. What really incensed the Navy was that, in answer to the question of the commanding officer's identity, the Japanese had replied that the senior officer aboard was a naval inspector with no indication that the ship was under his command. Under these circumstances the State Department was told that the *Kokuyo Maru* could enter Los Angeles as a commercial vessel, but if the Japanese insisted on the courtesies of a "bona-fide man-of-war, the Navy Department does not consider such requests as legitimate and recommends that in this case, and all subsequent similar cases, the Japanese Government be informed that the visit is not convenient."[23]

The Navy would not have to concern itself about Japanese naval tankers for many more months. On June 20, 1941, due to an actual domestic scarcity on the East Coast and as a move against the Axis powers, oil exports from the East Coast were restricted to the British Empire, the British forces in Egypt, and the Western Hemisphere. Arguments among cabinet members over restricting oil exports from both coasts resulted in Secretary Ickes threatening to resign. Stark and Welles had again delayed cutting off oil to Japan. In July the tempo quickened. Japan was poised to acquire additional bases in Indochina. On Roosevelt's direction, Acting Secretary of State Welles informed British Ambassador Halifax that "if Japan now took any overt step through force or through the exercise of pressure to conquer or to acquire alien territories in the Far East, the Government of the United States would immediately impose various embargoes, both economic and financial."[24] The showdown on the embargo question grew near.

Among those with whom Roosevelt conferred on the oil embargo was Admiral Stark. Stark described his feelings to Welles in a letter afterwards. In mid-July Roosevelt had asked Stark for his reaction to an embargo on a number of commodities to Japan, and was given the same answer as before, but in addition, Stark said he would have the War Plans Division make "a quick study." The study was finished on July 21 and sent to the President. A copy was also sent to Hull, and Stark discussed the study with Wells.[25]

The *Study of the Effect of an Embargo of Trade between the United States and Japan* was prepared under the direction of Rear Admiral Richmond K. Turner. It reflected the belief that shutting off the American supply of petroleum would lead promptly to an invasion of the Netherlands East Indies. Although probable, this was not necessarily a certain and immediate result, because Japan, it was reasoned, had oil stocks for about eighteen months' war operations. If there were to be export restrictions on oil by the United States, they should be accompanied by similar restrictions by the British and Dutch. However, the results of a total embargo would be a severe psychological reaction against the United States and an intensification of determination of those in power in Japan to continue their present course. And then the words of prophecy:

> Further, it seems certain that, if Japan should then take military action against the British and Dutch, she would also include military action against the Philippines, which would immediately involve us in a Pacific war ... An embargo would probably result in a fairly early attack by Japan on Malaya and the Netherlands East Indies, and possibly would involve the United States in early war in the Pacific....

Recommendation: That trade with Japan not be embargoed at this time.[26]

On the copy of Admiral Turner's study, which was sent to Roosevelt, Stark wrote, "I concur in general. Is this the kind of picture you wanted?"[27] The President did not appear to have heeded the evaluations of Turner and Stark. His actions in ordering a freeze of Japanese assets on July 25 after the Japanese entered southern Indochina showed that he was less worried about immediate Japanese reaction against the United States than were his military advisers. As long as Britain stood, he thought, the Japanese would not enter the war, because they did not want to fight the British Empire and the United States together.[28]

The Navy, through the period of embargo considerations, was divided. The Secretary, and certain officers below the senior admirals, were for tight controls or even complete embargo. The Chief of Naval Operations, who had the advantage of personal contact with the President and who agreed with Sumner Welles, opposed actions which could result in war with Japan. For exactly one year they were able to influence Roosevelt against taking a harder stand. To the very end Stark held his position; he was so wrapped up in the problems of the Atlantic that he veered away from any action which would commit his limited number of ships to the Far East against Japan. Stark accepted the risk of allowing one very potential enemy to build up huge petroleum reserves in order to keep peace in one ocean while defeating an enemy considered more dangerous in another ocean.

CHAPTER 7

Allied Naval Strategy in the Pacific

The staff talks between British and American military planners in Washington in January 1941 had deep historical roots, since several of those instrumental in promoting the event had had experience in Anglo-American relations dating from World War I. Early in 1917, the First Lord of the Admiralty, Winston Churchill, had discussed with the United States ambassador, Walter Hines Page, the possibilities of a visit to London by an American admiral. Ultimately, Rear Admiral William S. Sims, president of the Naval War College, was sent as a United States naval observer to the Admiralty. His flag secretary, during his tour as the senior American naval officer in European waters was Lieutenant Commander Harold Raynesford Stark. Stark had brought his command, a flotilla of torpedo boats, from the Asiatic Station to work with the British forces in the Mediterranean Sea and English Channel.

Almost simultaneously with Churchill's return to power in May 1940 he made his request for American destroyers and his suggestion that the United States Fleet use Singapore as an advanced naval base. Temporarily failing to get satisfaction on his request for destroyers and having his suggestion on Singapore positively rejected, Churchill on June 15 appointed a special committee headed by Admiral Sir Sidney Bailey to improve relations with the United States. Admiral Bailey had retired in 1939 but was recalled to duty in the Admiralty for "miscellaneous and special assignments." The Bailey Committee's function was to review the form of American aid to be sought, the possible areas of British and American operations and the two fleets' responsibilities in those areas, the preferred policy of cooperation, and the techniques of imparting information to United States authorities.

Five days later the U.S. Naval Attache, Captain Alan G. Kirk, was advised that informal conversations between British and American staffs either in London or Washington were to be proposed. The Bailey Committee held meetings from June 20 to September 8, 1940, examining "each of the major technical aspects of future naval cooperation." It recommended at the July 15 meeting that cooperation with American naval authorities should conform closely to the 1917–1918 precedent.[1]

The pressure for naval cooperation was also exerted through the regular diplomatic channels. Lord Lothian, the British ambassador in Washington, recalling the World War I services of Admiral Sims, suggested to President Roosevelt in June 1940 the sending of another senior American admiral. Roosevelt liked the idea and discussed it with Secretary of the Navy Frank Knox and Admiral Stark. On July 12, they proposed Rear Admiral Robert Lee Ghormley, the Assistant Chief of Naval Operations and former head of the War Plans Division, who was already fully informed on the past conversations. Roosevelt, while briefing Ghormley prior to his departure for London, informed him that he "still was not convinced that the United States would be forced to intervene as a belligerent in the war against the European Axis, or would be forced to fight Japan in the Pacific to prevent continued Japanese expansion."[2] In addition to Ghormley, Roosevelt decided to send for a shorter period of time an Army representative, General George V. Strong. A third member was selected to represent the air arm, Major General Delos C. Emmons.

The trio arrived in London August 15 and were joined by the U.S. Naval Attache, Captain Kirk, and the U.S. Military Attache, Colonel Raymond E. Lee. The meetings with the British which ensued were referred to as "The Anglo-American Standardization of Arms Committee" although the discussions covered many matters of joint planning and possible cooperation, particularly on the part of the two fleets. The American delegation repeatedly stressed that they were present as individuals for discussion and recommendations, but this did not deter the British from "fielding their first military team" or from speaking with complete candor. In the British group were Admiral of the Fleet Sir Dudley Pound, First Sea Lord; General Sir John Dill, Chief of the Imperial General Staff; and Air Chief Marshall Sir Cyril L. N. Newall, Chief of the Air Staff. It was Sir Cyril Newall who gave the American visitors the crux of British strategic thinking at the time. Their plans for the future certainly relied on the continued economic and industrial cooperation of the United States in ever-increasing volume, but no account had been taken of the probability of active cooperation by the United States, since this was clearly a matter of high political policy. The economic and industrial cooperation of the United States were fundamental to their strategy.

Discussion relative to the Far East pointed up the fact that the earlier British assumptions were admittedly invalid relative to possible Japanese action. First, it had been assumed that the threat to British interests would be seaborne; second, that a fleet could be sent to the Far East. The Japanese now threatened to expand through the southeast in such a way as to make land invasion of Malaya possible; and the British were obviously in no position to send a fleet to the Far East. At this juncture, important as Singapore and Malaya were, they could not be supported at the cost of security in the Atlantic or the Mediterranean. The British position impressed the American delegation then and was to prove an area of disagreement later.

Generals Strong and Emmons continued on in London through the height of the German air attack which was to have defeated Britain. Impressed by the British coolness and determination under heavy attack, they returned to Washington the last part of September confident that Britain would stand—at least for the immediate future. Admiral Ghormley stayed on in London as a special naval observer.

Admiral Ghormley conferred almost daily with the Bailey Committee. The committee, on the assumption that the U.S. naval strength would be concentrated in the Pacific, had recommended that strong forces be moved into the Southwest Pacific and China Sea, in order to restrain Japanese movements to the south, and particularly into the Netherlands East Indies. Admiral Ghormley, in commenting on this recommendation, reviewed the problems that would be involved for the United States Navy in moving such detachments across the Pacific. He pointed out that the First Sea Lord and other officers of the naval staff had themselves suggested that the Royal Navy was not sufficiently strong in the Atlantic. Assistance from the United States Navy would probably be required in the Atlantic, in addition to whatever action might be taken in the Pacific. Admiral Ghormley referred to the existing strength of the U.S. Navy in the Atlantic. A large proportion of these naval forces would probably be needed to cooperate with the British in the Atlantic although this would depend upon developments in the relations with Japan and on the attitude which the administration and public opinion might take, should the United States enter the war.[3]

The revised text of the Bailey Committee reports were sent by Admiral Ghormley to Admiral Stark, with a record of the discussions which had been proceeding since September 17. Stark, in a dispatch of October 2, suggested that the naval attache return to Washington to be available for consultation there while these proposals were under consideration. Admiral Richardson, Commander in Chief, United States Fleet, was in Washington conferring on what to do with the fleet in the Pacific when Kirk received his orders to proceed to Washington for discussions in December concerning cooperation with the Admiralty. On October 14, 1940, after the United States had turned down once again the suggestion to send a strong detachment to Singapore, Lord Lothian presented Roosevelt with a proposal from Churchill for staff conversations on a "comprehensive basis." On October 16 in London Admiral Pound spoke to the same purpose in conversations with Ghormley. The Churchill proposal to deter the Japanese from taking counteractions to the reopening of the Burma Road was first confirmed by the White House, then, because of its political ramifications, denied. On October 27, Lord Lothian's memorandum was returned without action or further comment. Roosevelt had to win an election first before there could be even secret talks with the British strategists.

The temporary reluctance to conduct conversations with the British military leaders because of political liabilities and, concomitantly, Roosevelt's procrastination on reaching an agreement with his own military advisers on a national policy prompted Stark to try his hand at writing an estimate of the world situation. The initial purpose of this naval effort on November 4 was to arrive "at a decision as to the National Objective in order to facilitate naval preparation." Much of the strategic thought in the estimate came from Captain Richmond Kelly Turner, who had become head of the War Plans Division less than a month before. Turner had come from the staff of the Naval War College where, in April of that year, discussions of the world situation had led to certain conclusions which now became key elements in the November study in Washington—priority given to the defeat of Germany, aid to the democracies to hasten the defeat of Germany, and an initial defensive posture relative to Japan.[4] Stark's first rough notes were reviewed, debated, and revised by a group of his staff officers, most of whom would be renowned admirals in the future. In addition to Turner, Captain Royal Eason Ingersoll and Commander Charles Maynard Cooke, Jr., War Plans Division officer, and Commanders Forrest Percival Sherman and Oscar Charles Badger worked "day and night, Saturdays and Sundays, for about ten consecutive days"[5] on the paper.

The product of their joint effort, submitted as a memorandum from the CNO to Secretary Knox on November 12, was undoubtedly one of the most important policy papers, if not the most important one, in the immediate pre-war years. It would ultimately become the basis for the American position in conversations with the British, would become the United States national war policy and the basis for *Rainbow 5*.

Initially, Stark analyzed the various ways by which the United States might become involved in the war. Shortly thereafter, he stated of the national objectives as he saw them:

> ... preservation of the territorial, economic, and ideological integrity of the United States, plus that of the remainder of the Western Hemisphere; the prevention of the disruption of the British Empire, with all that such a consummation implies; and the diminution of the offensive military power of Japan, with a view to the retention of our economic and political interests in the Far East.[6]

He rationalized why it was in the United States' interest to "prevent the disruption of the British Empire" and especially to ensure that the British Isles remained intact. The British Isles, the "Heart of the Empire," must remain intact as the "geographical positions from which successful land action can later be launched" against Germany. Second only to the British Isles in strategic importance were Egypt, and Gibraltar, combined with west and northwest Africa.

Various possible options of support to the British and Dutch forces in the Pacific were also discussed in depth, along with a thorough analysis of the shortcomings of the existing *Orange Plan*. The crux of the recommended policy in the Pacific was "a limited war against Japan" reducing her offensive power chiefly through economic blockade. To accomplish that blockade the

> ... allied strategy would comprise holding the Malay Barrier, denying access to other sources of supply in Malaysia, severing her lines of communication with the Western Hemisphere, and raiding communications to the Mid-Pacific, the Philippines, China, and Indo-China.[7]

The defensive strategy also called for reinforcement of army strength in Hawaii and Alaska, the establishment of naval bases in the Fiji, Samoan, and Gilbert islands and possibly reinforcing the Philippines with aircraft. Stark did not believe that "the British and Dutch alone could hold Malay Barrier without direct military assistance by the United States." He was convinced that "they would need in addition to the Asiatic Fleet further reenforcement by ships and aircraft drawn from the Fleet in Hawaii, and possibly even troops." All the Pacific options were weighed against their impact on Atlantic operations. Shifting the discussion back to the Atlantic, Stark reasoned that naval assistance alone would not *"assure* final victory for Great Britain," but that additionally it would be necessary "to send large air and land forces to Europe or Africa, or both, and to participate strongly in this land offensive."[8] Ironically, it was naval strategists who were advocating large U.S. land armies to defeat Germany.

Stark next presented most succinctly the necessity for deciding upon a national policy.

> With war in prospect, I believe our every effort should be directed toward the *prosecution of a national* policy with *mutually supporting diplomatic and military aspects,* and having as its guiding feature a determination that any intervention we may undertake shall be such as will ultimately best *promote our own national interests.* We should seek the best answer to the question: "Where should we fight the war, and for what objective?" With the answer to this question to guide me, I can make a more logical plan, can more appropriately distribute the naval forces, can better coordinate the future material preparation of the Navy, and can more usefully advise as to whether or not proposed diplomatic measures can adequately be supported by available naval strength.[9]

Having stated the urgency for a national policy decision, Stark presented four possible plans which could be considered feasible for the United States: (A) Western Hemisphere defense only; (B) full offensive against Japan and strictly defensive in the Atlantic; (C) the strongest possible military assistance both to the British in Europe and to the British, Dutch, and Chinese in the Far East; and (D) "eventual strong offensive in the Atlantic as an ally of the British and a defensive in the Pacific." This latter plan was the recommended course of action. Since, in the phonetic alphabet in use at the time, "D" was "Dog," the plan became known as *Plan Dog.*

Copies of *Plan Dog* were sent to General Marshall and Admirals Richardson and Ghormley. Through Ghormley a copy was shown informally to the Admiralty and Churchill. Long before Stark's recommendations were approved as the United States' position by Roosevelt or accepted by the United States Army, Churchill had, within his own circle of advisers, completely endorsed *Plan Dog.* On November 22, Churchill told his senior military officers:

> In my view Admiral Stark is right, and *Plan Dog* is strategically sound, and also most highly adapted to our interests. We should therefore, so far as opportunity serves, in every way contribute to strengthen

the policy Admiral Stark, and should not use arguments inconsistent
with it. . . .

I am much encouraged by the American naval view.[10]

The closing paragraph of *Plan Dog* certainly must have hit a re-
sponsive chord with the British staff. For months they had been pushing for conversations with their American counterparts. Stark's last
recommendation was for immediate secret staff talks on technical
matters with both the military and naval authorities—in London or
Washington with the British, in Washington with the Canadians, and
in Singapore or Batavia with the British and Dutch.

The proposed position for the United States as advanced by Admiral Stark was not completely acceptable to the other factions in the
decision-making scheme. The Army's War Plans Division staff generally
agreed with the emphasis of *Plan Dog* on British survival and the
necessity of American assistance to that end; however, they were most
definite in their stand of "making no commitments in the Far East."
Plan Dog, with the Army comments, was sent to Roosevelt on November 13. Receiving no answer, Stark and Marshall on November 18
directed the Joint Planning Committee to apply itself to drafting a
national policy acceptable to the Army and Navy which would meet
presidential approval. On November 29, General Marshall informed
Admiral Stark that the Army still could not accept the strategic concept of the war or the opinion set forth in the plan relative to the proposals concerning the Malay Barrier. Army planners thought United
States war plans should be based on the immediate goals of Britain's
survival, Germany's defeat, and concentration of "our power to operate effectively, decisively if possible, in the principal theater—the
Atlantic." As far as Malaysia was concerned, they thought the United
States should avoid dispersing its forces into that theater; however, it
should assist the British in reinforcing their naval forces in the Far
East by relieving them of naval obligations in the Atlantic. This
would provide a more homogeneous force for Malaysia and would, in
effect, concentrate rather than disperse American naval power.

Stark's answer to Marshall on the same day, November 29,
showed something of his pique with his Army associates and a veiled
indication of presidential omnipresent influence in strategy. He replied, "Should we become engaged in the war described in *Rainbow 3,*
it will not be through my doings, but because those in higher authority have decided that it is to our best national interest to accept
such a war."[11] In the same memorandum he also said, "I consider it

essential that we know a great deal more about British ideas than we have yet been able to glean."

Roosevelt in no way committed himself to the theory of strategy outlined in *Plan Dog* and whatever he said to Stark about his plan did not become a matter of record.[12] He did authorize conversations between representatives of the American and British staffs to explore the problems raised by Stark. Stark instructed Ghormley, whose exploratory conversations in London had reached the limit of their usefulness, to arrange with the British staffs for serious conversations to begin in Washington early the next year. Since Stark regarded the British ideas of American naval deployment in the Pacific as unacceptable, he told Ghormley to inform the Admiralty that anyone they sent to Washington "should have instructions to discuss concepts based on equality of considerations for both the United States and British Commonwealth, and to explore realistically the various fields of war cooperation." Impatient for an answer, Stark personally requested the First Sea Lord, Admiral of the Fleet Sir Dudley Pound, on November 30, to send accredited representatives to Washington before Christmas if that were possible. In reply to the initial invitation Admiral Ghormley, on December 2, announced the names of the British staff who were to come to Washington in January. Admiral Pound, in answering Stark's letter, assured the Chief of Naval Operations that the ideas already expressed by the Admiralty were not to be regarded as "an unalterable basis" of discussion.

The announcement of the British acceptance of the invitation to converse in Washington lent urgency to the determination of an agreed-upon military policy. The Joint Planning Committee reported to the Joint Board on December 21 on its study and offered a tentative draft of a joint memorandum to the President from the Secretaries of State, War, and Navy. Not unexpectedly, it emphasized the priority of operations in the Atlantic. The *Plan Dog* influence showed in the assertion that, although United States interests in the Far East were important, it was incorrect to consider them as important as the integrity of the Western Hemisphere, or as important as preventing the defeat of the British Commonwealth. The issues in the Orient would largely be decided in Europe. The final proposed recommendations were a rapid increase in military and naval strength, concomitant with not provoking an attack by any other power and not willingly engaging in any war with Japan. If forced into a war with Japan, Pacific operations should be restricted to permit use of forces for a major offensive in the Atlantic. Finally, no important Allied decision should be accepted without a clear understanding "as to common objectives, as to contingents to be provided, as to operations planned, and as to command arrangements."[13]

Secretary Hull declined to approve the proposed recommendations since he doubted the propriety of his joining in recommendations to the President concerning technical military statements. Out of the conference over the State Department's acceptance of the policy, a long-overdue change in the upper echelon liaison became effective. Hull suggested, and it was agreed, that the three secretaries would meet each Tuesday on national defense matters, thus superseding the Liaison Committee of Sumner Welles and the military representatives.

The written record does not show the rationale leading to the event, but it is reasonable to assume that the calling of the three secretaries, the Chief of Naval Operations, and the Chief of Staff to the White House on January 16 was prompted by the immediately past discussions on national and military policy. Also, the President, as recorded by General Marshall the next day, had in mind the possibilities of sudden and simultaneous action on the part of Germany and Japan against the United States. He felt that there was one chance in five of such an eventuality, and that it might culminate any day. He devoted himself principally to a discussion of the United States' attitude in the Far East towards Japan and to the matter of curtailment of American shipments of war supplies to Britain. He thought that, in the event of hostile action by Germany and Japan, Churchill should be notified immediately that this would not curtail the supply of material to Britain. The final directive from the President was that the United States would stand on the defensive in the Pacific with the fleet based on Hawaii; that the Commander in Chief, Asiatic Fleet, would have discretionary authority as to how long he could remain based in the Philippines and as to his direction of withdrawal —to the east or to Singapore; that there would be no naval reinforcement of the Philippines; that the Navy should have under consideration the possibility of bombing attacks against Japanese cities; that the Army should not be committed to any aggressive action until it was fully prepared to undertake it; that every effort be made to continue the supply of material to Britain and to disappoint Hitler's principal objective of involving the United States in a war at that particular time.[14]

Meanwhile the Joint Planning Committee, at the suggestion of Admiral Turner, had been directed on December 11 to draw up instructions for the United States Army and Navy representatives for holding conversations with the British staff due to arrive the next month. The report was submitted to the Joint Board initially on January 13, 1941, and after additional work again on January 21. After criticizing most of the recent leadership in Britain, the basic report gave a general evaluation of probable British proposals. The joint planners asserted that the United States was capable of safeguarding the North American continent, and probably the Western Hemisphere, whether allied with Britain or not, and it could not afford to entrust its national future to British direction. Military planners unanimously agreed that Britain could not defeat Germany unless the United States provided direct military assistance to a far greater degree than had been given so far and that, even then, success against the Axis was not assured. They expected that proposals of the British representatives would have been drawn up with chief regard for the support of the British Commonwealth and protection of their postwar commercial and military interests. The United States likewise should safeguard its own eventual interests. To avoid commitment by the President, the joint planners recommended that neither he nor any member of his cabinet should officially receive the British officers, but that they be informally received by the under secretary of state, and the service chiefs. [15]

The enclosure to the basic report on the forthcoming conversations contained agenda items and a clear statement of United States intentions. It was approved verbatim by the military chiefs and forwarded to Roosevelt via the service secretaries. On January 26, he sent a memorandum to the Secretary of the Navy with minor changes recommended. He thought the procedure was "all right." Taking a page out of the book of President Woodrow Wilson, under whom he had served as an assistant secretary of the Navy, Roosevelt preferred to use the term "associates" rather than "allies" in reference to possible future relationships between the United States and Britain. The planners had used a clause, "should the United States decide to resort to war." Roosevelt changed "decide" to "be compelled." His only other change was to modify the assistance to be given in the Mediterranean to read "navally."[16]

The purpose of the conversations with the British, as finally agreed upon, was "to determine the best methods by which the armed forces of the United States and the British Commonwealth [could] defeat Germany and the powers allied with her, should the United States be compelled to resort to war." The national position of the United States closely paralleled *Plan Dog*. It was to "defend the Western

Hemisphere, aid the British Commonwealth against Germany; and oppose by diplomatic means any extension of Japanese rule over additional territory." Additionally, the two countries should "endeavor to keep Japan from entering the war or attacking the Dutch," but should Japan enter the war, "the United States operations in the mid-Pacific and the Far East would be conducted in such a manner as to facilitate the exertion of its principal military effort in the Atlantic or navally in the Mediterranean."[17]

The selected agenda items with which the conversations were to be concerned were indicative of the keen appreciation of possible political repercussions from any agreement. The descriptive term applied to the conversations (by Captain Ingersoll in London in January 1938 and Stark in *Plan Dog*) was "on technical matters," and the connotation of "technical" was a very restrictive "military." Considerations, the nature of which required obvious decisions by the heads of government, were "political" and consequently ruled out of the purview of the military planners. Although joint military plans, *per se,* have political significance when executed or made public, as in a threat to use same, joint preliminary planning may be readily accomplished in a strictly "military" sense. Under certain stated assumptions, *with no political decisions required,* military representatives may draw up quite intricate disposition plans, command arrangements, tasks assignments, etc. Such were the rules to be followed in the joint talks with the British. As added warranties to guarantee the maintenance of the "military" status, no member of the government was to be present and no cabinet official would formally receive the visitors. (Originally Sumner Welles, under secretary of state, was to have informally welcomed the group, but neither he nor any other government official actually was present at the first meeting.) Though the military services were each represented by senior officers, they were not the highest in any case, so the requirement for approval by higher authority was tacitly understood throughout the talks. The American military chiefs absented themselves after the initial meeting.

The flexibility enjoyed by the military planners in this case was unique. In essence, they could make plans which were not binding on either side and yet were detailed enough to be the basis for effective cooperation when approved by their respective political superiors. The planners likewise were not bound in the scope of their conversations to a rigid policy position which would have been inherent if the participants included political representatives or the senior military leaders.

During the interim period between the announcement on December 2, 1940, of the British intention to come to Washington and their departure from Britain, neither Admiral Ghormley nor Brigadier General Raymond Lee, the United States military attache in London, was able to get any advance information on the British position. The British explanation was logical and simple—it would jeopardize the security of their war plans to give the information at that time. The long list of questions posed by Ghormley and Lee solicited information desired by their respective services' war plans division in Washington. The list included questions on British strength and capabilities in the different areas of the world, on the relative importance of those areas in their strategic thinking, and what their proposed courses of action would be under certain conditions. The questions were answered in detail and made available to the Americans after the party left Britain.

On January 29, 1941, Chief of Naval Operations Stark and Army Chief of Staff Marshall welcomed the British delegation in a room set aside for the meetings in the Main Navy Building in Washington. The United States representatives were:

Major General S. D. Embick, Army representative on the Permanent Joint Board Defense (Canada-United States)

Brigadier General Sherman Miles, acting Assistant Chief of Staff, G-2

Brigadier General L. T. Gerow, head of the Army War Plans Division

Colonel J. T. McNarney, an air officer

Rear Admiral R. L. Ghormley, special observer in London

Rear Admiral R. K. Turner, head of Navy War Plans Division

Captain A. G. Kirk, assistant to Rear Admiral Turner and former naval attache in London

Lieutenant Colonel O. T. Pfeiffer, U.S. Marine Corps

The British representatives were:

Rear Admiral R. H. Bellairs, head of the British delegation

Rear Admiral V. H. Danckwerts

Major General E. L. Morris

Air Force Marshall J. C. Slessor, of the British Purchasing Commission in Washington

Captain A. W. Clarke, assistant naval attache in Washington

The Secretariat included:

Lieutenant Colonel W. P. Scobey, U.S. Army

Commander L. R. McDowell, U.S. Navy

Lieutenant Colonel A. T. Cornwall-Jones, British Army[18]

113

The American military leaders presented their position, which had been approved by the President, and then stressed the urgency for secrecy, especially in the light of the proposed Lend-Lease Act which was then being discussed in Congress. The British replied that they had come as a corporate body representing the British chiefs of staff, that they had complete freedom to discuss the general strategic position and to consider dispositions in the event the United States should enter the war.[19] In their opening talk the British gave a clear summation of their views and three propositions of general strategic policy:

> The European theatre is the vital theatre where a decision must first be sought.
>
> The general policy should therefore be to defeat Germany and Italy first, and then deal with Japan.
>
> The security of the Far Eastern position, including Australia and New Zealand, is essential to the cohesion of the British Commonwealth and to the maintenance of its war effort. Singapore is the key to the defence of these interests and its retention must be assured.[20]

The first two propositions were in direct accord with American feelings; the retention of Singapore certainly was not. The British repeatedly had told American representatives since the June 1940 visit of Lieutenant Commander Hampton of the Admiralty that they were unable to send major forces to the Far East. Their proposition amounted to an open invitation for the United States to defend Singapore. The policy to retain Singapore in the face of mounting Japanese power and British maneuverings to gain American acceptance of the idea became formidable obstacles upon which the meetings almost foundered. The British saw Singapore as more than just a military base. For political, economic, and psychological reasons it was a symbol of British Commonwealth unity and security in the Far East. Thus, for many reasons, it was part of British strategic thinking, and they never were to give up trying to make it part of British-American strategic plans.

Churchill's message on May 15, 1940 might be considered one starting point in the Singapore controversy, though to be sure Singapore had been discussed with Captain Ingersoll in January 1938. Roosevelt had wisely dodged the offer "to use Singapore in any way convenient." As a compromise the United States Fleet had been ordered to remain at Pearl Harbor shortly thereafter. On October 4, Churchill again wrote to Roosevelt mentioning the possibility of war with Japan over the re-opening of the Burma Road and the fact that

Japan had joined the Tripartite Pact. He asked at that time if it were possible to send "an American squadron, the bigger the better, to pay a friendly visit to Singapore." As a further suggestion, Churchill thought the occasion of the visit could be used for "technical discussion of naval and military problems in those and Philippine waters, and the Dutch might be invited to join."[21] Admiral Stark opposed the suggestions and even the reinforcement of the Asiatic Fleet because of the situation in the Atlantic. Roosevelt once again agreed with his naval advisers.

With such a past history of British proposals on Singapore, it was not surprising that the American planners would be wary of similar proposals at the Washington meetings. At the sixth Plenary Meeting on February 10, 1941, the situation in the Far East was the chief subject discussed. The British again emphasized their concern over the future status of Singapore. They urged that the United States should take early action both to keep Japan out of the war and to assure the defense of Singapore against a Japanese attack.[22] The proposal at this time was that the United States should send four heavy cruisers, an aircraft carrier, planes, and submarines to Singapore. The next day the British presented a detailed paper: *The Far East—Appreciation by the U. K. Delegation.* At the same time that the paper was being presented to the American military participants, Lord Halifax, the new British ambassador, was communicating its substance to Secretary of State Hull.[23]

The British paper pictured Singapore as a symbol of British ability and determination to protect the dominions and colonies and their trade with Britain. The loss of Singapore would greatly weaken the power of political leaders in Australia, New Zealand, India, and China who believed in the value of British friendship. The British representatives admitted that even if Singapore was lost, Australia and New Zealand could be held and the Japanese kept out of the Indian Ocean; the British insisted, however, that Singapore was a necessary "card of re-entry" when the European war should have taken a turn for the better. Without the base at Singapore, a successful attack against the Japanese would have to be launched across thousands of miles of ocean, either from India or Australia. In short, the British stand on Singapore was based "not only upon purely strategic foundations, but on political, economic and sentimental considerations which, even if not literally vital on a strictly academic view, are of such fundamental importance to the British Commonwealth that they must always be taken into serious account."[24] What the British delegation could not say specifically and what was obvious to the Americans was that the prestige of the British Empire in the Far East and at home was at stake.

The seriousness with which the British held to the Singapore position is shown by two key statements in the subject paper:

(a) The security of the Far Eastern position, including Australia and New Zealand, is essential to the maintenance of the war effort of the Associated Powers. Singapore is the key to the defense of these interests and its retention must be assured.

(b) If Singapore were in serious danger of capture, and the United States still withheld their aid, we should be prepared to send a Fleet to the Far East, even if to do so would compromise or sacrifice our position in the Mediterranean.[25]

The loss of Singapore, in the opinion of the British chiefs of staff, "would be a disaster of the first magnitude, second only to the loss of the British Isles."[26]

On February 13, U.S. Army and Navy representatives met to discuss the British paper. Rear Admiral Turner reviewed the background of the British proposals that had begun two and a half years before when "the President and Secretary of State more or less committed the United States Fleet to actions in conjunction with the British forces in the Far East." He observed that when Ingersoll was in London, in January 1938, the British proposed that the "United States send their whole fleet to Singapore and that the then combined United States and British forces should start a campaign against the Japanese." The British two years later were unable to send a strong force to the Far East, "but still would like the United States to send their whole fleet, together with a large United States Army, to engage against the Japanese." It was not until the last staff conversations that "they modified their requests for reenforcements to a force of four heavy cruisers, aircraft and submarines." Despite Stark's caution to Pound before the talks started and Pound's response that the British ideas were not to be regarded as "unalterable," it was now apparent to the American delegation

(a) That a concerted drive was being made by the British to influence the United States into accepting the British point of view in reference to the Far East situation.

(b) That the United Kingdom, while accepting the United States' Staff Committee's decision not to send the Pacific Fleet to the Far East, continues to push their requests for United States' commitments in that theater.

Major General Embick suggested that it was the duty of the United States delegation, as military advisers to the President, to present to him sound military opinion with reference to the Far East strategic situation with a suggested course of action.[27]

At this juncture the American delegation became quite perturbed upon learning of the Halifax-Hull discussion of the British military paper on the Far East. To have their own Secretary of State learn from a foreign diplomat about the controversial Singapore question was embarrassing, for the Americans had rigidly adhered to the "military" nature of the talks by not informing the State Department of the nature or progress of the joint meetings. To have the same unilaterally originated paper used in preliminary military talks discussed at the highest diplomatic levels violated a cardinal premise upon which the conversations were to take place. A protest was officially registered with the British delegation that the action appeared to the Americans to be an attempt to secure political pressure to influence their decision on Singapore.

One should remember, before condemning the British action, that the British military group in Washington was the best source of military information and strategy the British ambassador had in the country and, conversely, the ambassador was the highest government representative in the area to whom the military could refer. The exchange of information between the British representatives in Washington was certainly understandable; the use to which the ambassador put information so gained was the crux of the objection.

The British delegation replied to the protest and their answer was discussed by the Navy section of the United States staff delegation on February 20. Rear Admiral Ghormley stated that he thought their reply had clarified "the situation to the point wherein the plenary conversations could be resumed." Rear Admiral Turner wanted to take a much harder line. He wanted assurances that no United Kingdom delegation papers would be sent to the State Department and that, in addition, none of the United Kingdom delegation points developed in the course of conversations should be presented orally to the State Department through diplomatic channels. Staff conversations were to have been "on a purely military plane," and when concluded would become the basis "for sound military decisions representing, in the considered judgment of the combined membership, the best measures to be undertaken for the successful prosecution of the war." Until such joint decisions were reached, the presentation by British diplomats to the State Department of any matter under discussion tended to induce the latter to arrive at incorrect conclusions which would be difficult to change, since the United States delegation was not furnishing the State Department with its own views.[28]

Although the United States Navy representatives, especially Turner, thought that the British delegation was not playing the game fairly, further open conflict over the Singapore question ceased in the Washington conversations after presentation of *The United States Military Position in the Far East* on February 19. The Americans admitted that the loss of symbolic Singapore would be a serious blow, but it did not follow that serious blows always lead to final disaster. The common basis of American-British strategy was the security of the British Isles and control of the North Atlantic. Rather bluntly the British were told that they would have to do the best they could in protecting their interests elsewhere. The United States contribution was to eliminate the German threat to the British Isles and the North Atlantic.

Admiral Stark, who had been kept informed of the various stages of the discussions, felt that the whole question of policy to be followed by the United States in the Far East should be submitted to the President. In view of the disagreements of the United States and British delegations as to the strategic concepts which should govern any plan for combined action in the Far East, it seemed necessary to him that in any policy discussions between the State Department and the British ambassador, or between the President and the Prime Minister, the views of the American naval staff should be clearly understood.[29]

It soon became apparent that Admiral Stark's views on the importance of defeating Germany first continued to enjoy Roosevelt's approval. The *Plan Dog* concept was the touchstone of the "position" paper given to the British on February 19, and the "President informed the Chief of Naval Operations and the Chief of Staff of his approval of the position adopted by the American Delegation in the Staff Conference." He further agreed that this position was in conformity with the Stark memorandom of November 12 (*Plan Dog*).[30]

Singapore had become a dead issue in the American-British conversations (ABC). The final report, called *ABC-1*,[31] was finished on March 27, 1941. The basic report reiterated the general policy positions of the two governments, dealing almost exclusively with the Atlantic conflict. The two key paragraphs pertaining to Japan are significant. The first mentioned neither Japan nor Singapore, though the actions of the former and the importance of the latter had recently been argued.

The security of the United Kingdom must be maintained in all circumstances. Similarly, the United Kingdom, the Dominions, and India must maintain dispositions which, in all eventualities, will provide for the ultimate security of the British Commonwealth. A cardinal feature of British strategic policy is the *retention of a position in the Far East* such as will ensure the cohesion and security of the British Commonwealth and the maintenance of its war effort.[32] (Emphasis supplied.)

The second paragraph was the only subdivision of ten which mentioned Japan under a heading: "Plans for the Military operations of the Associated Powers will likewise be governed by the following:"

(d) Even if Japan were not initially to enter the war on the side of the Axis Powers, it would still be necessary for the Associated Powers to deploy their forces in a manner to guard against eventual Japanese intervention. If Japan does enter the war, the Military strategy in the Far East will be defensive. The United States does not intend to add to its present Military strength in the Far East but will employ the United States Pacific Fleet offensively in the manner best calculated to weaken Japanese economic power, and to *support* the defense of the Malay barrier *by diverting Japanese strength away from Malaysia*. The United States intends so to augment its forces in the Atlantic and Mediterranean areas that the British Commonwealth will be in a position to release the necessary forces for the Far East.[33] (Emphasis supplied.)

Annex 3 to *ABC-1* was a United States-British Commonwealth Joint Basic War Plan. Forces and tasks were assigned by areas and by countries. Under tasks assigned American naval forces in the Pacific were:

(a) Support the forces of the Associated Powers in the Far East by diverting enemy strength away from the Malay Barrier through the denial and capture of positions in the Marshalls, and through raids on enemy communications and positions.

(b) Destroy Axis sea communications by capturing or destroying vessels trading directly with the enemy.

(c) Protect the sea communications of the Associated Powers within the Pacific Area.

(d) Support British naval forces in the area south of the Equator, as far west as Longitude 155° East.

(e) Protect the territory of the Associated Powers within the Pacific Area, and prevent the extension of enemy Military power into the Western Hemisphere, by destroying hostile expeditions and by supporting land and air forces in denying the enemy the use of land positions in that Hemisphere.

(f)   Prepare to capture and establish control over the Caroline and Marshall Island area.[34]

In the Far East Area the American naval tasks were generally the same as in the Pacific Area—raids, destroying communications, and attacking vessels. A "Special Command Relationships" section was included which would promote more plans and disagreements in the months ahead. The pertinent parts were:

30.   The defense of the territories of the Associated Powers in the Far East Area will be the responsibility of the respective Commanders of the Military forces concerned. These Commanders will make such arrangements for mutual support as may be practicable and appropriate.

31.   In the Far East Area the responsibility for the strategic direction of naval forces of the Associated Powers, except of naval forces engaged in supporting the defense of the Philippines, will be assumed by the British Commander in Chief, China. The Commander in Chief, United States Asiatic Fleet, will be responsible for the direction of naval forces engaged in supporting the defense of the Philippines.

32.   The British Naval Commander in Chief, China, is also charged with responsibility for the strategic direction of the naval forces of the Associated Powers operating in the Australia and New Zealand Area.[35]

The guide lines for conversations between the British and American commanders in chief in the Far East have been stated here. How they were followed will be discussed in the next chapter.

The associations of the British and American navies had reached a high point in World War I when the United States supported Britain in the defeat of Germany. Certainly another high point was the agreements reached in *ABC-1*. Discussions had covered strategic concepts, objectives, and the exchange of information on forces to meet those objectives. A basic war plan had been produced and general tasks assigned primarily to defeat Germany using American forces, should the United States be "compelled to resort to war." The problems in the Pacific were not so neatly resolved. The thinking there was defensive, with each government responsible for the defense of its own territories. Despite the positiveness of the American position on the Singapore question in February and the fact that there would be no reinforcement of the Asiatic Fleet, latitude was still given for discussions on mutual support between the on-scene commanders in chief.

The evolution of cooperation in the Pacific between the British and Americans was not complete with *ABC-1*, but it had reached a "point of no return." The United States was irrevocably tied to Britain in two oceans: in the Atlantic, to defeat a European enemy; in the Pacific to stand defensively against an Asiatic enemy. In both, the use of the U.S. Navy was most important, and in the Pacific beyond Hawaii it was the only American force ready for use. *ABC-1* immediately became the basis for United States War Plan *Rainbow 5* and the matrix against which future agreements in Singapore would be compared and rejected.

CHAPTER 8

American-British-Dutch Defense Plans

The general guidelines for Anglo-American cooperation in the Pacific and Far Eastern areas were cautiously agreed upon as part of the *ABC* conversations in Washington in March 1941. After the near-catastrophic schism in the discussions over the issue of Singapore, the participants had settled on words which in and of themselves left no doubt that the United States would not commit forces from its Pacific Fleet to defend Far Eastern territories—either territories belonging to others or even its own Philippine Islands.

> The United States does not intend to add to its present Military strength in the Far East but will employ the United States Pacific Fleet offensively in the manner best calculated to weaken Japanese economic power, and to support the defense of the Malay barrier by diverting Japanese strength away from Malaysia.[1]

Later there appeared the words: "The defense of the territories of the Associated Powers in the Far East Area [was] the responsibility of the respective commander of the military forces concerned." Immediately following these words of finality was the caveat that these "commanders will make such arrangements for mutual support as may be practicable and appropriate." Put in proper historical perspective, these few words advocating arrangements for mutual support in the Far East told the story of an elusive goal spanning years before their *ABC* enunciation and continuing to within hours of the long-dreaded and finally executed Japanese attack.

As early as the fall of 1936 when Admiral Yarnell assumed duty as Commander in Chief, Asiatic Fleet, he observed that the British officers were concerned over the United States withdrawing "protection from that gateway to Singapore and India" by granting independence to the Philippines and leaving them to their political fate. Senior British officers in the Far East at that time thought that the "Japanese menace could only be met with British-American cooperation and that the Japanese projected 'southward expansion policy' could be prevented by a strong naval base in the Philippines plus the Singapore base."[2] Yarnell made his impact on future American thinking relative to the Far East when in September 1939, he reasoned with Admiral Stark, the Chief of Naval Operations that since the United States would never build a "first class naval base in the Philippines" it should never engage Japan singlehandedly. "Great Britain, France and the Netherlands are vitally interested and should take part." Yarnell was not given the authority, nor did he seek it, to reach agreements with the other European powers to contain an advance by Japan south of China. Those tenuous agreements that were reached were achieved, not in the Far East, but in London in January 1938 as a result of Captain Ingersoll's visit with the Admiralty. The agreement to cooperate with naval forces was cast aside in 1939 when Germany threatened Europe.

In February 1940, Admiral Stark quoted Yarnell when he passed his words of advice across the Pacific to Yarnell's successor, Admiral Hart. Hart was told that the United States should never start "anything in the Western Pacific unless the principally interested powers (United States-French-British-Dutch) act in concert." Nevertheless, Stark thought the "possibility of getting such concerted action" to be improbable due to the "unpredictable state of affairs in Europe." Despite the improbability of cooperation Stark's planners were considering the use of Hong Kong, Singapore, North Borneo, or French or Dutch possessions in concerted actions, but they were not sure any of them would be available.[3]

Uncertainty in February 1940, over the availability of bases in the Far East was nothing compared to the uncertainty of Japanese actions vis-à-vis the Netherlands East Indies after Germany occupied the Netherlands in May. To a slightly lesser degree there was uncertainty over Japanese reaction to the embargoes imposed by the United States in July. There was genuine fear, which became stronger with each week in the early fall of 1940, that Japan would move swiftly against the Netherlands East Indies or the Philippines and Guam or against all of them. In September the Joint Planning Committee recommended to the Chief of Naval Operations and the Chief of Staff that if the United States were confronted with the necessity of armed opposition to Japan, the effort should "be limited to the employment of minor naval surface and air forces operating from Singapore and Dutch East Indies bases, plus the interruption of Japanese shipping in the eastern Pacific."[4]

In line with the thoughts in Washington on cooperative action in the Far East against the Japanese threat, Admiral Hart sent his assistant chief of staff, Commander Frank Pugh Thomas, to Singapore for preliminary talks with the British military commanders in October. Thomas returned to Manila—where Hart had the bulk of the Asiatic Fleet—with a copy of the British Far Eastern War Plan. In time the plan was forwarded to Washington where Stark commented that it showed the usual British wishful thinking.

Meanwhile from London came another report of British wishful thinking. Rear Admiral Ghormley, the special naval observer, who was in daily contact with the Bailey Committee and other admiralty members, reported the British to be expectant of active American participation in the war now that Roosevelt had been reelected. They talked about the defense of the Malay Barrier and an "alliance between themselves, us, and the Dutch, without much thought as to what the effect would be in Europe."[5]

Stark, who relayed the information from Ghormley to Hart, had no idea whether the British would immediately fight if the Dutch alone, or the United States, alone, were attacked by the Japanese. Furthermore, although he believed the Dutch colonial authorities would resist an attempt to capture their islands, he questioned whether they would fight if only the Philippines, or only Singapore, were attacked. Hart was told that the Navy could make no political commitments, consequently, he could make no specific military plans for an allied war. However, Hart could perform a useful service "by laying with the British and possibly the Dutch, a framework for a future plan of cooperation," should the United States be forced into the war. Stark doubted that the Dutch would talk freely with Hart, but if they would, he should explore the fields of "command arrangements, general objectives, general plan of cooperative action, including the approximate naval and military deployment."[6]

Stark's letter to Hart, written on November 12, contained the first indication of optimism over immediate Japanese actions. Stark believed that Japan would avoid hostilities with the United States and it was doubtful at that time that she wished to fight the British and the Dutch. However, if a war developed between Japan and an alliance of the United States, Britain, and the Netherlands, Stark's version of the allied objective was economic starvation and the holding of a blockade along the Malay Barrier. (This was written the same day *Plan Dog* was finished.) Then followed a definite promise of assistance to Hart which would be positively reversed four months later in the *ABC* conversations:

> One thing (and this is for your ears alone) you can depend upon is that we would support you, probably by sending a naval reenforcement to you at Soerabaja or Singapore, and by other means.[7]

Hart was also told that the Navy's part of *Rainbow 3* was nearing completion and would be sent "within a short time." That was the plan which called for securing control of the western Pacific as rapidly as possible. Stark planned to send *Rainbow 3* to Hart via one of the naval attaches recently approved for Singapore, Ceylon, and three ports in the Netherlands East Indies: Soerabaja (Surabaja) and Batavia (Djakarta) in Java and Balikpapan in Borneo.

A month later Stark forwarded two copies of *Rainbow 3* to Hart stressing the "possible eventuality" of war with Germany, Japan, and Italy and directing that high priority be given to operating plans and the preparation of vessels, aircraft, and personnel. One of the assumptions of the plan was that the United States would fight the war, having Britain and the Netherlands Colonial Authorities as allies. Staff conversations with the British had already been scheduled to commence in Washington the next month, yet Stark considered that the only useful staff conversations concerning an allied operating plan and command arrangements in the Far East would be those which the Commander in Chief, Asiatic Fleet, might be able to hold with the British and Dutch supreme war commanders in that area. Again he stated his belief that Hart might be able to hold such conversations with the British, but he had considerable doubt "as to the extent of the conversations which may become possible with the Dutch, owing to their fear of repercussions in Japan." He authorized Hart to conduct staff conversations with the British and Dutch supreme commanders, with the specific understanding that he was in no way to commit the United States government to any particular political or military decisions, and that the purpose of the staff conversations was solely to facilitate joint operations should "war eventuate under the approximate conditions shown in the assumptions of *Rainbow 3*." Hart was further cautioned to conduct his discussions in secret, taking particular care not to permit the Japanese to learn of the efforts to establish contact with the Dutch.[8]

Captain William Reynolds Purnell, chief of staff to Admiral Hart, had attended a British-Dutch meeting in Singapore in December when Stark's letter to Hart arrived, directing more talks with the Dutch. From January 10 to 14, Purnell conferred with Vice Admiral C. E. L. Helfrich and his staff in Batavia on possible joint defensive actions against the Japanese southward movements. The Dutch feared an attack by Japan and were highly desirous of any support. That support did not appear to be forthcoming from the British authorities in Singapore whose interest, one Dutch committeeman caustically remarked, dwindled as the scene moved eastward from Singapore.[9] Captain Purnell asked what steps the Dutch would take in case the Japanese attacked Singapore, and was told that the British and Netherlands had not given each other guarantees of mutual help. The Singapore conferences had made a proposal to the two governments, that if the Japanese moved in force south of the 6° North parallel, the British and Netherlands East Indies forces would be free to attack them without further declaration of war. The Netherlands government had rejected the proposal and the decision of the British government was unknown.

Captain Purnell was asked two major questions: first, what action would the United States take in case of a Japanese attack against the Netherlands East Indies coming through the Sulu Sea, and second, what would the United States do about the protection of shipping from the East Indies to the West Coast of the United States in case of a Japanese-N.E.I. war, the United States remaining neutral? To the first query Captain Purnell replied that the United States would guarantee the neutrality of the Philippines to the extent of attacking with all forces available, would notify Japan as well as all other nations of serious breaches of neutrality, and would probably maintain a benevolent neutrality toward the Dutch and British. To the second question he replied that he thought a war zone would be prescribed and that conditions would be the same as existed then in European waters. As an entirely personal view he stated that he believed the United States would take the necessary step to protect shipping, or to secure the materials, if the loss of the materials would seriously hamper United States production. When asked if he thought the United States would go to war with Japan if she attacked the Netherlands East Indies, he stated, emphasizing it was his own personal view, he thought she would.[10] The Netherlands authorities reciprocated by furnishing Purnell with detailed information on their naval and air strengths, and the status of their facilities, ports, bases, and storage areas.

In mid-February, when the question of defending Singapore was warming up the American and British staff conversations in Washington, another British-Dutch meeting in Singapore was announced to begin on February 22. Stark directed Hart to have his representative participate with the other two powers' representatives in order to agree on a joint plan of operations for the United States, British, and Dutch forces, but without making any political commitments. Any agreements were to be subject to Hart's and Stark's approval. Rules to be followed by the Asiatic Fleet representative were to "include provisions for a common acceptance of equality of political, economic and military control and be based on the use of only the forces now" in the Asiatic Fleet. Strategic plans adopted were to be fully realistic, and to this end the United States representative was told to express Stark's "view that British and Dutch strategic arrangements which depend for their efficacy upon intervention by the United States would not be sound, since there is doubt that Congress would declare war in case of Japanese aggression against powers other than the United States." Stark acknowledged that his instruction put Hart in "a difficult position but more definite instructions" could not be given to him.[11]

Two weeks later Admiral Hart reported to the Chief of Naval Operations the disappointing results of this latest attempt to develop a definite agreement without American guarantees of cooperation. That which the naval leaders sought and did not get was a strategic plan of operations against the Japanese in which the United States would participate if it should be "compelled to resort to war" against Japan—something similar to *ABC-1* in the Atlantic relative to Germany.

Specifically, the purpose of the conference was to agree upon an Anglo-Dutch-Australian plan—the first step. Present were separate representatives of the army, navy and air arms for Britain and Australia and of the army and navy for the Netherlands. Certain agreements were reached for cooperative action subject to the approval of their respective governments, but according to Captain Purnell, the United States representative, they "didn't really get down to cases enough . . . They *all*, except for some Dutch promises, have altogether a defensive attitude on water as well as on shore. . . . Their navies are now intended primarily for guarding their own ship lanes—not at all for going after the enemy's . . ." Yet Purnell was convinced that the British and Dutch *local* navies, but not the Australian-New Zealand navies, would do whatever the United States asked if they felt their own sea supply and reinforcement lines were reasonably secure and if the United States made a definite commitment toward participation. That commitment of course could not be given, and the disappointment expressed by Admiral Hart and reechoed in Washington would prove to be the rule rather than the exception relative to other Singapore talks. At the end of Hart's letter, which transmitted the latest Purnell report, he asked Stark to think over the advisability of the Asiatic Fleet's making "a Netherlands East Indies cruise just as a matter of peacetime course, something that has been done in former years."[12]

Admiral Hart's letter reporting the lack of progress being made in the Far East planning scheme arrived as the *ABC-1* plan was nearing completion. The Far East agreements had been sought to complement the Washington talks, and the unfavorable report prompted Stark to attempt corrective action. Copies of Hart's letter were sent to the President and the Secretary of State in the belief that a word from each of them "may do much toward getting the British, the Dutch, the Australians and the New Zealanders together." Stark assured Roosevelt that the Navy would do what it could toward this end. In the same memorandum Stark endorsed Hart's idea for the Netherlands East Indies cruise, provided it was properly timed. He liked the idea, because it was "the most positive move" the Asiatic Fleet could make; it was in line with United States war plans, so if war were to break, the Navy "would be sitting with [its] surface ships where [it] wanted them." Stark mentioned that sometime ago Hart had asked permission to pay a visit to Hong Kong with his flagship, and like the present proposal, Stark thought it was a good move. That visit was vetoed in deferrence to the objections of the State Department, as was this last one.[13]

The agreements in the *ABC-1 Report* were reached with the full approval of Admiral Stark and General Marshall, who, though not in attendance at the meetings, kept currently informed on the staff conversations. As a result of the accord with the British in Washington, the Joint Planning Committee was given a new directive for the preparation of the joint basic plan, *Rainbow 5*, "based upon the report of the United States British Staff Conversations, dated 27 March 1941 (*ABC-1*) and upon the Canadian-United States Basic Defense Plan No. 2 (*ABC-22*)." Stark and Marshall took steps immediately to implement the *ABC-1* agreement by arranging for detailed planning within the War and Navy Department staff and commands to conform to the agreement. Instructions were also sent to Major General

George Grunert, commanding general of the Philippine Department, and Admiral Hart—the two senior United States officers in the Far East—"to complete arrangements with the British and Dutch Commands for a Far Eastern Staff Conference at Singapore at as early a date as possible."[14]

On April 2, General Marshall sent by courier a complete copy of the *ABC-1* report to Grunert to permit advance planning with Commander in Chief, Asiatic Fleet, and Commandant Sixteenth Naval District. Grunert was specifically ordered not "to discuss" the matter with the British and Dutch commands. On April 4, the restriction not "to discuss" was revoked by a message from Marshall that a conference had been called in Singapore.[15]

A parallel message from Admiral Stark to Admiral Hart was sent on April 5 announcing a staff conversation in Singapore on April 18 composed of representatives from the United States, Australia, New Zealand, the United Kingdom, and the Netherlands East Indies. Its purpose was to prepare plans for the conduct of military operations in the Far East in accordance with *ABC-1*. Hart was directed to arrange transportation not only for his own representative but for the representative of General Grunert, but neither were to leave Manila until they had had time to study the *ABC-1* which was scheduled to arrive by courier by April 14. Special attention was invited to paragraph 31 of Annex 3. As previously stipulated, any agreements reached were subject to Stark's approval.[16]

Paragraph 31 of Annex 3 to *ABC-1* became, as Stark suspected, a seed of discord. It read:

> 31. In the Far East Area the responsibility for the strategic direction of naval forces of the Associated Powers, except of naval forces engaged in supporting the defense of the Philippines, will be assumed by the British Commander in Chief, China. The Commander in Chief, United States Asiatic Fleet, will be responsible for the direction of naval forces engaged in supporting the defense of the Philippines.[17]

The conference in Singapore lasted from April 21 to 27 with the United States represented by Captain Purnell, who by now was a familiar person at Far East conferences; Colonel A. C. McBridge, Assistant Chief of Staff, United States Military Forces, Philippines; Captain Archer Meredith Ruland Allen, the United States naval observer at Singapore; and his army counterpart, Lieutenant Colonel F. G. Brink. The British representatives were the ranking British officers in the Far East: Air Chief Marshall Sir Robert Brooke-Popham, Commander in Chief, Far East, and Vice Admiral Sir Geoffrey Layton, Commander in Chief, China. The ensuing ADB (American, Dutch, and British) agreement reflected a decidedly British position, possibly due to the influence of the much more senior British officers. The official *ADB Report* was not received in Washington until June 9; however, the British Military Mission in Washington received from London a telegraphic summary of the report and circulated it to the American delegation on May 6.[18]

The information in the summary on the recommended defense of the Philippines was the first major fault with the report. It prompted the American military chiefs to inform the British military mission of their reaction without waiting for the complete report. Commander Lewis Richard McDowell, American secretary for collaboration to the British Joint Staff Mission, was instructed to inform the British mission in Washington that the United States intended to adhere to its earlier decision not to reinforce the Philippines except in minor particulars, such as the addition of several minesweepers and a few torpedo boats. The American military chiefs also believed that the principal value of the position and strength of the United States forces in the Philippines was in the fact that their defeat would require a considerable effort by Japan and might well cause a delay in the development of an attack against Singapore and the Netherlands East Indies. A Japanese attack in the Philippines might thus offer opportunities to the Associated powers to inflict losses on Japanese naval forces, and to improve their own dispositions for the defense of the Malay Barrier. The Chief of Staff and the Chief of Naval Operations did not agree that Hong Kong was likely to be altogether a strategic liability, rather than an asset. They considered that Hong Kong, like the Philippines, might contain or delay Japanese forces which would otherwise be employed in a more decisive theater. As to the document itself:

> ... the Chief of Naval Operations and the Chief of Staff regret that they must reject this paper in its entirety, as either being contrary to the commitments of *ABC-1,* or as relating to matters which are the sole concern of the British Government.[19]

The dissatisfaction over the *ADB Report* registered in June with the British military mission in Washington was just a preview of a longer, stronger, and more detailed denunciation a month later, after the American military staffs had had time to study the full report. A joint letter from the Chief of Naval Operations and the Army Chief of Staff directed the special naval and military observers in London to inform the British chiefs of staff that the United States was unable to approve the *ADB Report* for "several major, as well as numerous minor particulars." The major objections may be summarized as follows:

(a) Statements requiring political decisions were included in the report; specifically: that an attack on one of the Associated powers would be considered an attack on the other powers (paragraphs 6 and 8); counterattacks on Japan would be recommended in the event of certain listed Japanese actions (para. 26); a call for increased assistance to China (para. 78).

(b) The creation of a new intermediate command was not envisaged in *ABC-1* The "Eastern Theater" and Commander in Chief, Far Eastern Fleet, had not been planned in *ABC-1*. The United States had agreed to British naval strategic direction of naval forces not engaged in the defense of the Philippines. There had been no agreement to the use of United States forces by the British outside the Far East area.

(c) The strategic importance of the Netherlands East Indies was not appreciated.

(d) After the arguments over the importance of the defense of Singapore during the *ABC-1* conversations and as a concession to British insistence in the final writing of the report, the following was included as part of paragraph 11(b): A permanent feature of British strategic Policy is the retention of a position in the Far East such as will insure the cohesion and security of the British Commonwealth and the maintenance of its war effort.[20]

In addition, paragraph 4 of the *ADB Report* had listed as the most important interests in the Far East: (a) the security of sea communications and (b) the security of Singapore. Yet, in spite of the importance, repeatedly stressed by the British, of the Malay Barrier to the security of Singapore and the whole Far East, only three of forty-eight British ships in the Far East were assigned to operate in the vicinity of the Malay Barrier. No British vessels whatsoever were committed to the naval defense of the barrier against Japanese naval forces advancing southward, nor to offensive operations designed to close the barrier to the passage of Japanese raiders. All British naval forces were assigned to escort and patrol work, most of them at great distances from the position which the British chiefs of staff had asserted to be "vital." It was pointed out that the naval defense of this position was entrusted, by the *ADB Report,* solely to United States and Dutch forces. Since the eventual dispatch of a strong British fleet to the Far East

131

was considered problematical, the Chief of Naval Operations and the Chief of Staff advised the British chiefs of staff that, until such time as a plan was evolved whereby British naval forces could take a predominant part in the defense of the British position in the Far East area, they would be constrained to withdraw their agreement to permit the United States Asiatic Fleet to operate under British strategic direction in that area. The incongruity between the British position in Washington that Singapore was *sine qua non* to their Far Eastern security and the British position in Singapore of assigning none of their ships directly to support that theory was undoubtedly the major provocation for American rejection of the *ADB Report*.

    (e)   The assignment of United States naval aviation units to British control was in violatiin of paragraph 14(f) of *ABC-1*.

    (f)   There was no strategic plan in the *ADB Report*. Although American and Dutch forces had clearly defined tasks, those tasks assigned the British could "be approximately deduced only from the deployment proposed in Appendix 1."

The report was completely unacceptable to the American military chiefs. This instant failure, immediately following the concordance of strategic considerations in *ABC-1*, and the history of past failures to get the Far Eastern military commanders of the Associated powers to agree on a strategic plan of action against the Japanese, induced the Chief of Naval Operations and the Chief of Staff to suggest that if further conferences were to be held in Singapore for drawing up an operating plan for the Associated powers, that an agenda to guide the deliberations be agreed upon in advance.[21]

Before another Singapore meeting could be scheduled or the need arise for an agenda, the British chiefs of staff attempted, after the Atlantic Conference, to salvage the *ADB Report* by bringing it in line with *ABC-1*. During that conference between Roosevelt and Churchill in August their respective military leaders had gotten together to discuss the shortcomings of the *ADB Report*. Despite the British efforts on October 3 the revised report, designated *ADB-2*, was rejected by the Americans. The British mission in Washington was informed that the United States staff had given very careful study to the Admiralty's proposals for a new Far East area agreement, and whereas the proposals of *ADB-2* had met some of the American objections, the fundamental defects had not been eliminated. In fact, Admiral Turner thought that it not only was not an advance on the original report, but that it actually represented "a retrograde step."

132

Although neither the United States Army nor the Navy had reached a final decision, at the time they were inclined to believe that, until a really practicable combined plan could be evolved for the Far East area, it would be better to continue working under an agreement for coordination of effort by the system of mutual cooperation. The various commanders in the Far East were exchanging ideas and establishing technical procedures required for cooperation. Therefore, failure to issue a plan for unified command would not greatly retard progress. They felt quite strongly that the defense of the Malay Barrier was primarily a concern of the British and Dutch. Turner's suggestion was that the British chiefs of staff in London give this matter their earnest attention, and endeavor to prepare an effective campaign plan that would "have real teeth in it."[22]

Admiral Turner, in his letter rejecting *ADB-2*, mentioned to the British representative that "the military situation out there has changed considerably since last Spring, and will change more after the United States reenforcements, now planned, arrive in the Philippines." It was more than just planned reinforcements that changed the desperate strand of pessimism found in 1939 to 1940 to a fiber of hopefulness and, finally, restrained optimism. The dynamic personality of General Douglas MacArthur, recently recalled to active duty in command of United States Army Forces in the Far East; the mobilization and intensive training of native Philippine troops; the enthusiasm for the offensive power in the newly proven B-17 bombers which were to be flown to the Philippines in increasing numbers; and additional patrol planes, submarines, and torpedo boats for naval use in the Philippines all gave substance to the belief that within a few months the Philippines could be defended against a Japanese attack regardless of other agreements in the area.

While the United States was accelerating efforts to defend the Philippines, the British were re-examining their plans for defense of their interests in the Far East. Ghormley in London told Stark by dispatch on October 25 of a most important decision made by the British.

Admiral Tom Phillips, former vice chief, naval staff, was going at once direct to the Far East in *Prince of Wales* as Commander in Chief, Eastern Fleet, accompanied by Rear Admiral Arthur Francis Eric Pallister as chief of staff and additional staff officers. United States progress with *Rainbow 5* implementation and early repairs to British ships had enabled the Admiralty to plan an early dispatch of battleships to the Eastern Fleet, eventually to bring the total there to six;

however, they had only eight destroyers available of which four were modern.

The Admiralty felt that *ADB* was dead and that *ABC-1* was sound, and that what was needed was "a strategical operating plan" which could be drawn up in London or Washington but, better yet, in the Far East. Such a plan might require the use of Manila as an advance base for *ADB* naval forces and the development of adequate air routes throughout the area for concentrating of air forces. The Admiralty believed the disadvantages of the proximity of Manila to Formosa and possible effective air attacks had been disproved in the European theater. It was apparent that the British were taking prompt steps to meet the Japanese threat by sending able officers to the theater of possible operations, by desiring to make sound strategic plans, and by reinforcing their naval forces in the Far East. Those forces, however, were deficient in destroyers, submarines, and strategically located secure bases.[23]

Ghormley's informal message to Stark was soon followed by an official letter from the First Sea Lord, Admiral Pound. Reiterating the gist of Ghormley's message, Pound stated that he considered that neither *ADB-1* nor *ADB-2* met the new conditions caused by a change of government in Japan. (General Tojo had become prime minister and home minister on October 17 while retaining his post as minister of war.) Pound suggested that the need for a conference to draw up strategic operating plans for the Far East based "afresh on *ABC-1*" had become urgent. If Stark agreed in principle to the abandoning of further discussions on *ADB-1* and *ADB-2,* and to holding a fresh conference on the basis of *ABC-1,* they could then proceed to discuss the agenda.[24]

Admiral Stark replied the next day, November 6, through Ghormley. He agreed that the United Kingdom and the United States should act promptly on Pound's idea. He then gave a hasty review of what the United States was doing in the Far East. The Army was reinforcing both land and air forces as rapidly as practicable and was training the Philippine Army intensively. The Navy was reinforcing the Asiatic Fleet with twelve modern submarines, eight of which had departed Hawaii on October 24 and the remainder on November 4. Six motor torpedo boats had been delivered to Manila and six more might be sent. Stark then shifted to a discussion of strategy. He believed that *ADB* should not be revived since *ABC-1* was an adequate major directive, which "should be implemented by a sound strategical operating plan drawn up between British, Dutch and United States Navies and between British and Dutch Air Forces and U.S. Army Air Forces." Admirals Hart and Layton had agreed on the framework of various plans, but they had been unrealistic because Admiral Layton was practically without naval forces. Due to the intricacies of the problem, it seemed preferable to Stark for the United States and United Kingdom naval forces and the three air elements in the Far East to coordinate their operations through cooperation and not by unity of command.[25]

Stark approved the British move in creating a new position, Commander in Chief, Eastern Fleet, now that capital ships were being sent to the area and suggested that the British consolidate their naval forces under one flag officer. In answer to a query on the use of Manila by combined naval forces, Stark replied that Luzon was suitable for light naval forces and air elements but limited facilities and supplies precluded use by heavy forces. The United States was willing to assign eight destroyers to supplement the British capital ship force "if the United States is then at war with Japan."[26]

Five days later, on November 11, the United States Chiefs of Staff suggested to the Admiralty via the military mission in Washington the holding of new conferences in Manila. The three senior officers who could reach a strategic agreement, Vice Admiral Phillips, Admiral Hart, and General MacArthur, would attend.

Admiral Phillips visited Manila on December 4 to 6, but he was forced to terminate his visit without reaching an agreement. His abrupt departure was due to an unexpected incident: the British sighting of a large Japanese force proceeding toward Malaya. Phillips hurried back to his flagship, the *Prince of Wales* at Singapore, and together with the battle cruiser *Repulse,* moved to intercept the Japanese landing parties. Without protective air cover both ships were quickly sunk by Japanese land-based aircraft. The loss of the only allied battleship and battle cruiser west of Hawaii was staggering, but to British-American·cooperation the loss of Admiral Phillips was just as great. In the opening hours of the game it was he who had talked with Captain Ingersoll in London about American cooperation—in the very area where he gave his life shortly after an eleventh-hour effort to reach an agreement with the Americans.

The period of pre-war conferences was over. The attempts to derive a plan of action against the Japanese expansion had failed, one after the other. The reasons for the failures were many. From an American point of view, the countries involved were too concerned with their own interests, commerce, and position. National jealousies were very much in evidence. But before criticism becomes oppressively heavy, let it be remembered that the delegates were military men whose agreements had to pass the approval of their respective governments. Early British-Dutch proposals were vetoed by their respective governments. Restrictions placed on them before a conference limited their scope of agreement. The United States naval representatives were given reasonable scope, considering the grand strategy of defensive war in the Pacific and, until the last phase, the position of not reinforcing the Asiatic Fleet. Consequently, the American representatives had little to offer the collective force *until* the United States was at war. To the planners in the Far East this nebulous support was not enough. Whether that support, if definitely promised and used collectively with other Associated powers, would have withstood the Japanese will never be known, for the plans of action which were often conceived but never born could never be tested.

CHAPTER 9

U.S. Naval
Deterrent Strategy

As January 1941 unfolded, the tense international situation became ominously charged with suspense. British and American planners discussed and revised their respective positions in preparation for the joint staff conversations later that month in Washington. Final touches were put to the proposed Lend-Lease Act, which was to provide Britain with the war material to fight Germany and Italy. Fighting had commenced in the previous month in Indochina between French forces and Japan's new ally, Siam (Thailand), over a border dispute in the Mekong River basin. The planning staffs of the Asiatic Fleet and U.S. Fleet had just commenced work on their respective complementing plans to support *Rainbow 3* which each staff had received late in December. Before the month was over Japan would have caused new consternation by her actions both in Indochina and the Netherlands East Indies and by the verbal outbursts of her foreign minister, Matsuoka.

Immediately upon his return to Hawaii in December 1940, Richardson conferred with Rear Admiral Bloch, Commandant, Fourteenth Naval District, and Lieutenant General Herron, Commanding General Hawaiian Department, "concerning the security of the Fleet and the present ability of the local defense forces to meet surprise attacks." The three agreed that an attack on the base at Pearl Harbor would undoubtedly be brought by carriers. Such attacks would have to be repulsed either by locating and destroying the carriers prior to their launching their planes or "by driving off attacking bombers with anti-aircraft guns and fighters." The naval component of the Hawaiian defense forces did not have the material means for either option. It had no long-range reconnaissance aircraft to find an approaching enemy and no fighter aircraft or anti-aircraft batteries for use against an air attack. Sole reliance was on Army defense forces and what could be spared by fleet units when they were in port. The Army forces were pathetically inadequate and obsolete—59 B-18 bombers, 36 pursuit planes, 26 fixed and 44 mobile three-inch guns. Bloch estimated that "at least 500 guns of adequate size and range would be required for the efficient defense of the Hawaiian area." In his endorsement of Bloch's evaluations Richardson agreed that until the Army could build up its forces, air defense forces would have to be augmented by fleet units in port, but continuous readiness of carrier aircraft and shipboard antiaircraft batteries was not contemplated.[1]

Richardson, in a letter to Stark, also reiterated his earlier view on the impracticality of placing torpedo baffles or nets "within the harbor to protect the ships moored therein against torpedo plane attacks." Because of the requirements for heavy ships to move freely and for patrol aircraft to land and take off, Richardson considered these passive measures too restrictive. Then, in his report to Stark, Richardson added a tragically inaccurate forecast:

> Considering this and the improbability of such an attack under present conditions and the unlikelihood of an enemy being able to advance carriers sufficiently near in wartime in the face of active Fleet operations, it is not considered necessary to lay such nets.[2]

Before Stark had received the report from Richardson on Pearl Harbor defense shortcomings, he informed Richardson on January 5 —by message in a special code held only by the two of them—that Richardson would be relieved on February 1, 1941, by Rear Admiral Husband Edward Kimmel, then Commander, Cruiser Force. Additionally, on February 1 the United States Fleet would be reorganized into the Atlantic, Pacific, and Asiatic Fleets, with the Asiatic Fleet continuing without reinforcements. Rear Admiral Ernest Joseph King would become Commander in Chief, Atlantic Fleet, on February 1 while Kimmel's command would be called the Pacific Fleet.

The news that he would have less than a month in his assignment must have been quite disturbing to Richardson, especially since just the previous October, Stark and Rear Admiral Chester W. Nimitz, Chief of the Bureau of Navigation (which then controlled personnel assignments) had told Richardson that in their belief he would remain in his command for two years.[3] Later when Richardson reported to the Secretary of the Navy in Washington for duty on the General

Board, he was told what he suspected—that when he had argued against Roosevelt's ideas of patrol lines to intercept Japanese shipping, he had "hurt the President's feelings."[4]

While Richardson prepared to turn over his command to Kimmel, Secretary of State Hull in Washington on January 15, speaking before the House Committee on Foreign Affairs in support of the Lend-Lease legislation, condemned Japan's actions against other Asian countries. He pointed out that it had been clear for some time that Japan had broad and ambitious plans to be the dominant power in the western Pacific, and that her leaders were openly declaring their determination to achieve and maintain that position by force of arms. Hull's observation of the "New Order" was:

> ... it should be manifest to every person that such a program for the subjugation and ruthless exploitation by one country of nearly one half of the population of the world is a matter of immense significance, importance, and concern to every other nation wherever located.[5]

The next day, January 16, almost as if to affirm Hull's statement, Japan made new demands on the Netherlands East Indies which, if completely accepted, would have made them an economic pawn of Japan. Included in the demands were requests for stipulated quantities of war materials, permission for Japanese exploration of oil and minerals, increased immigration, permission for Japanese fishing and commercial vessels to operate in territorial waters, and the right to use closed ports. The plucky Dutch stalled for time and then rebutted the demands as they had similar ones the preceding October.

On January 18, the Japanese military commander in Indochina demanded that the Vichy French forces, which had just soundly defeated the Thai attempts to seize French territory, conclude an armistice. This further Japanese intrusion into the affairs of the French in southern Indochina argued badly for the French and also for the British, for it was obvious that if Japan moved into southern Indochina she would be much closer to overland approaches to the bastion at the end of the Malay peninsula—Singapore. Admiral Leahy, ambassador to Vichy France, reported in late January that Japan was using her ally Germany to exert pressure on the Vichy government. Japan demanded that she be the mediator between Thailand and France and the French were in no position but to accept.

On January 21, Richardson was informed of a meeting five days earlier between Roosevelt and the Secretaries of State, War, and Navy, the service chiefs. The primary purpose of the meeting was a final discussion of the United States position for the *ABC* talks but out of it evolved a general policy directive from the President:

> That we would stand on the defensive in the Pacific with the fleet based on Hawaii; that the Commander of the Asiatic Fleet would have discretionary authority as to how long he could remain based in the Philippines and as to his direction of withdrawal—to the East or to Singapore; that there would be no naval reinforcement of the Philippines; that the Navy should have under consideration the possibility of bombing attacks against Japanese cities.

> That the Navy should be prepared to convoy shipping in the Atlantic to England, and to maintain a patrol off-shore from Maine to the Virginia Capes.

> That the Army should not be committed to any aggressive action until it was fully prepared to undertake it; that our military course must be conservative until our strength had developed; that it was assumed we could provide forces sufficiently trained to assist to a moderate degree in backing up friendly Latin-American governments against Nazi inspired fifth column movements.

> That we should make every effort to go on the basis of continuing the supply of material to Great Britain, primarily in order to disappoint what he thought would be Hitler's principal objective in involving us in a war at this particular time, and also to buck up England.[6]

Richardson construed this information, which was quite specific that the Navy would be employed *defensively* in the Pacific, as overturning the basic assumptions of *Rainbow 3* which called for *offensive* operations in the western Pacific. He told Stark that in view of the fact that the major effort was to be exerted in the Atlantic and, even if Japan entered the war or committed overt acts against United States interests or territory, the attitude in the Pacific would be primarily defensive, and priority would be given to the preparation of plans supporting *Plan Dog* rather than *Rainbow 3*. His tentative assumptions upon which future plans would be predicated included the following: that the United States was at war with Germany and Italy (Roosevelt had said that there was a one-in-five chance of simultaneous war with Germany and Italy any day.); that units of the Pacific Fleet might be detached and sent to the Atlantic on short notice; and that

> Japanese attacks may be expected against shipping, outlying possessions or naval units. Surprise raids on Pearl Harbor, or attempts to block the channel, are possible.[7]

Richardson stressed again that the Pacific Fleet, in the list of tasks assigned to it, was "severely handicapped by the existence of certain marked deficiencies in the existing local defense forces and equipment both Army and Navy." After listing the inadequate antiaircraft guns and the obsolete and weak defense aircraft strength, Richardson fired his parting salvo:

> It is considered imperative that immediate measures be undertaken to correct the critical deficiencies enumerated above. It is further believed that these measures should take priority over the needs of continental districts, the training program, and material aid to Great Britain.[8]

(Richardson's sequence of priority would be followed exactly in reverse in 1941.) In his long letter to Stark, Richardson pointed out that it "had been prepared in collaboration with the prospective Commander-in-Chief, U.S. Pacific Fleet, Rear Admiral H. E. Kimmel, U.S.N." and that it represented Kimmel's, as well as his own, views.[9]

In the meantime, Stark had written to Kimmel on January 13 to congratulate him on being selected Commander in Chief, Pacific Fleet, and to share with Kimmel his gloomy forecasts. Kimmel was told that he had "enormous responsibility on [his] shoulders in one of the most critical periods in our history, and where the Navy more than any other branch of the Government [was] likely to have to bear the brunt." In Stark's "humble opinion" the United States might "wake up any day with some mines deposited" on its "front door steps or with some of [its] ships bombed" and find itself "in another undeclared war, the ramifications of which call for our strongest and sanest imagination and plans."[10]

But Stark told Kimmel that he did not want to become involved in the Pacific, although he fully realized that the United States might become involved in the Pacific and in the Atlantic at the same time. Then followed a compliment that concomitantly, in view of the recently past relations with Richardson, could be interpreted as a slap at Richardson: "I am thankful that I have your calm judgment, your imagination, your courage, your guts, and your head, at the seagoing end. Also your CAN DO—rather than *can't*."[11] (Emphasis Stark's.)

From the Asiatic Fleet came reports of yet another Japanese challenge to American actions registered, as in previous incidents, through diplomatic channels. On January 14, the *Mindanao* overtook and passed a Japanese destroyer off the south China coast near Canton. The Japanese consul general in Canton, acting on instructions from local Japanese naval authorities, had registered a verbal protest against the American ship passing too close and photographing a Japanese naval vessel. The Japanese naval authorities demanded an apology, the immediate surrender of the film, and assurances that there would be no recurrences. The commander, South China Patrol, considered the Japanese demands unjustified and requested instructions from the Commander in Chief Asiatic Fleet, Admiral Hart, who agreed and directed Rear Admiral Glassford in Shanghai to call on Admiral Shimada, the commander in chief of Japanese naval forces in China. Glassford was to inform him that Admiral Hart "was amazed that the Japanese naval authorities at Canton should make such demands and that he personally had witnessed the photographing of his own flagship by persons on Japanese men-of-war, notably HIJM *Idzumo,* the Japanese flagship, and that he never dreamed of protesting such action." Glassford, unable to see Shimada, did deliver Hart's message to Rear Admiral Tetsuri Kobayashi in Shanghai. Hart's positive action was evidently effective because within several days the Japanese naval authorities withdrew their demands, thereby laying that issue to rest.[12]

Despite the peaceful settlement of an isolated incident by the naval commanders in the Far East, the Japanese news media showed a marked increase in tensions and anti-American and anti-British statements. Lashing back at Hull's congressional testimony criticizing Japan, Matsuoka on January 26 said:

> Japan must dominate the Western Pacific, not for the sake of Japan, but for the sake of humanity. Japan must demand America's reconsideration of her attitude and if she does not listen, there is slim hope for friendly relations between Japan and the United States.[13]

Two days later Ambassador Grew passed to the State Department an excerpt of a sword-rattling speech by Admiral Nobucasa Suetsugu in which he appealed to the Japanese people in North America to serve Japan "in your various positions," and asserted that Japan was ready to fight the United States if it insisted upon misunderstanding Japan. Stark relayed this information to his key commanders, Hart, Kimmel, Bloch, and King with a terse comment: "Take it for what it is worth."[14]

Stark might have attached more significance to the Grew report if he had known at the time that Admirals Suetsugu and Shiratori, with full support and encouragement from the German ambassador, General Eugen Ott, were arguing vehemently in Tokyo for a surprise attack on Singapore. Foreign Minister Matsuoka agreed with the activists. If Britain were dealt a crippling blow in the Far East, American aid to her in Europe might be diverted, or even more hopefully, the futility of aiding Britain might deter the United States from entering the war.

Through the United States naval attache's office in London the British Admiralty passed a few of the "straws in the wind" which indicated to them that the Japanese were "apparently planning a large scale offensive, presumably against Indo-China, the Malay Peninsula or the Dutch East Indies no doubt to be coordinated with an attack on Great Britain approximately February 10."[15] There was nothing concrete—just rumors and indications such as the cancellation of Japanese ship sailings, arms shipments to Thailand, and of course the vilifying speeches from Tokyo. The British chiefs of staff genuinely feared that the pending offensive against them in Southeast Asia would be synchronized with a German offensive against them in the Balkans and eastern Mediterranean. If such an eventuality developed, Britain would be unable to send reinforcements to aid in the defense of Singapore.

Before the British ambassador, Lord Halifax, could approach Secretary Hull or Churchill could communicate another appeal to Roosevelt, the top American leadership met in the White House to discuss the situation in the Far East. The two-hour meeting was triggered by the report from London, but in the meeting everything from Iceland to Indochina was discussed. Stark, Marshall, and Secretaries Hull, Knox and Stimson presented their respective views. Stark's position, preserved as a memorandum to Roosevelt on February 5, was the one which, with Stimson's support, was accepted by the President.

Stark partially defused the urgency of the threat to Singapore by the Japanese actions in pointing out that the dispatches from the naval attache's office in London were a "re-hash of the story by Douglas Robertson in the *New York Times* of February 2d." Stark had been watching the situation "with extreme care" and saw "no present reason for alarm." The Navy staff knew in advance that "the Japanese were sending some ships to Thailand and Indochina to enforce cessation of hostilities between those states." Since the armistice negotiations, which had commenced on the Japanese light cruiser *Natori,* had been moved to Tokyo, Stark reasoned that the negotiations were "likely to be rather long-drawn out" and the Japanese demands "far-reaching." In addition, there were not enough land forces to occupy "Indo-China, Thailand, for attacking Singapore, and for keeping a force ready to use against the Philippines." Nor were there enough

143

transports available. Stark questioned Japan's "readiness to attack the British before June," although he allowed that his belief was subject to revision.[16]

In his reasoned analysis, Stark thought that Japan desired to move against "the British, the Dutch, and the United States in succession, and not take on more than one at a time." For the time being she did not want to fight the United States at all, in order that she "could continue her imports of materials useful for war and for her general economy." If she got a favorable opportunity she might move against Malaya and possibly Burma, hoping the Dutch would not intervene. In fact, Stark thought that Japan might conquer the Netherlands East Indies "primarily by economic and political penetration." He also thought that Japan would wait and see what success Germany had in conquering the British Isles. If Germany succeeded, Japan would move; if Germany failed, Japan would wait for a "more favorable opportunity before advancing beyond Indo-China." She was playing for a secure advance without too great an expenditure of military energy.[17]

Despite subsequent urgings by Lord Halifax to Hull and a message from Churchill to Roosevelt reiterating the fear that Japan would take action against Singapore or perhaps raid New Zealand or Australia, Roosevelt decided to go along with Stark's advice. The threat to Singapore was definitely assessed differently on each side of the Atlantic, as had been shown by the two national sides in the *ABC* conversations. On the American side there was concern that any deterring action against the Japanese might jeopardize the passage of the Lend-Lease Act which was being debated in Congress at the time. On the issue of strategy neither Stark nor, for the time being, Roosevelt, wanted to risk forcing Japan to take offensive action which would detract from concentrating United States support in the Atlantic—*Plan Dog* strategy.

Secretary Hull was not immune to the British idea, strongly supported by Dr. Hornbeck, of naval ship visits to deter the Japanese southward expansion. On February 10, Stark argued for an hour and a half in the White House against an idea set forth by Hull to send ships to the Far East on a visit in order to deter Japan. This time it looked as if Roosevelt might order a large detachment of three or four cruisers, a carrier, and a division of destroyers to make a cruise to the Philippines, perhaps going down through the Phoenix and Gilbert Islands or the Fiji Islands. In the past talks had centered about similar cruises to Australia, Singapore, and the Netherlands

East Indies. In a memorandum to the President the next day Stark
stated again his objections to splitting his Pacific forces. A small force
would not deter Japan, Hart had no facilities for such a sizeable force,
and in fact, was "up against it for facilities" to care for what he had.
In case of sudden attack, such a force might be lost and if they returned it would "certainly look like turning tail and running." There
was a chance that further moves against Japan would precipitate hostilities rather than prevent them. The main effort was against Germany. Besides there was a risk in showing Japan that the United
States had any interests in the Gilbert, Solomon, or Fiji islands. Stark
was afraid the Japanese, who had better amphibious capability according to him, would occupy them before the United States could.[18]

Stark wrote to Kimmel on February 10 about his struggle to keep
from sending ships to the Far East. In the same letter he stated that
he was continuing to urge Marshall to reinforce the defenses of Oahu
in order to protect the fleet in Pearl Harbor. He had been successful
in getting the Army to send eighty-one fighter aircraft to Oahu and
in expediting their delivery by providing aircraft carriers to transport
them to Hawaii. Stark had also been struggling every time "he got in
the White House, which [was] rather frequent, for additional men."
He felt that he "could go on the Hill this minute and get all the men"
he wanted if he "could just get the green light from the White
House."[19] For some unknown reason throughout the naval expansion
program in 1941, Stark had to fight each step of the way to get more
personnel for the ·Navy. The obduracy was in the White House and
not in Congress.

In mid-February Roosevelt received the new ambassador from
Japan, Admiral Kichisaburo Nomura. Nomura had twice refused the
assignment, but finally, after having been assured by the senior Japanese Army and Navy officers that he would be supported in seeking a
rapprochement with the United States, he accepted the post. He had
been foreign minister from September 1939 to January 1940, and early
in his career had been a naval attache in Washington where he was
well known and respected by United States naval officers. Roosevelt,
in his first meeting with Nomura on February 14, emphasized that
the United States wanted peace and not war. However, he also pointed
out that incidents like the sinking of the *Maine* (the *casus belli* in the
Spanish-American War, 1898) could arouse the American people to
insist upon war despite presidential leadership. With tongue in cheek
Roosevelt said the *Panay* sinking had been smoothed over before a
wave of indignation had swept the country and Nomura should in-

form his country that American leadership now was trying to keep things quiet. If opinions in Tokyo were divided over war with the United States, Roosevelt was leaving the door open for talks.

Despite pleas from the British ambassador, Lord Halifax, the foreign minister, Sir Anthony Eden, and Churchill for positive actions or at least words by the United States, the February crisis passed without increased American involvement in the Far East, militarily. Matsuoka backed down in his bellicose language and assured Britain that Japan had no designs on Singapore or the Netherlands East Indies. A number of actions had given Matsuoka pause to reconsider his future moves. Eden had told the Japanese ambassador in London, Mamoru Shigemitsu, that Britain would fight in the Far East before she would sacrifice her possessions to Japan or allow Japan to control the people of the Far East alone. Additionally, Britain let it be known in Tokyo that she intended to mine the east coast of Malaya. The Dutch recalled their ships in Japanese and Chinese waters. The United States Congress authorized the reinforcement of Guam and, in the long-term future, the most telling action taken was an extension of economic controls relative to Japan. In January, 1941, license control was invoked over the export of copper, brass and bronze, zinc, nickel, and potash. Steel scrap and petroleum of more than 89 octane were already on the list. The embargo of brass and bronze, particularly, hurt Japan since she had a reserve stock equal to about a year's imports. Later during the war she experienced a shortage in the metals. Almost each week after the January order, there was control of another commodity needed in war production—lead, jute, burlap, phosphate, carbon black, cork, and all animal and vegetable fat.[20] Hull, and especially Stark, persuaded Roosevelt not to impose a complete embargo on petroleum products for fear that Japan would immediately take the Netherlands East Indies to satisfy her requirements. Hull did agree, however, and Roosevelt did act to impose restrictions on the export of metal drums, containers, and storage tanks (exported in component parts for easy assembly), and oil drilling and refining equipment. By March American-owned tankers, even those flying foreign flags, were taken off the oil shuttle service to Japan.

The end result of the collective action was a reassessment by Matsuoka, shown in a speech on February 21, that Japan would take no action that would cause the United States or Britain any concern. Three days later Ambassador Shigemitsu assured Churchill personally in righteous innocence that Japan would not attack Singapore or Australia or gain a foothold in the Netherlands East Indies. For the time being the appeals of Nazi Germany to attack Singapore would be ignored and Britain and the United States would have many more months before the war would finally come to the Pacific area.

On February 15, Stark sent another letter to Kimmel which would figure in latter-day investigations. Richardson, in a January letter concurred in by Kimmel, had expressed doubts about the advisability of torpedo protection baffles in Pearl Harbor. Stark, whose information on torpedo development should have been superior to that available to the fleet commanders, stated that the Navy Department had considered the installation of anti-torpedo baffles within Pearl Harbor for protection against torpedo plane attacks, and concluded that

> ... the relatively shallow depth of water limits the need for anti-torpedo nets in Pearl Harbor. In addition the congestion and the necessity for maneuvering room limit the practicability of the present type of baffles.[21]

Since the water depth in Pearl Harbor was thirty feet or less except in the dredged channels where it was generally forty feet, Stark's evaluation, which coincided exactly with that of Richardson and Kimmel, was readily acceptable to the latter.

On February 18, Kimmel wrote Stark a long letter containing even more "nuggets" of thought which would take on much more significance before the year was over. Acknowledging the fighter aircraft which the Army was getting in Hawaii, Kimmel pointed out, as Richardson and Bloch had done earlier, that it was of the highest importance to send as many bombers and antiaircraft guns to "Oahu as the Army establishment can support with the greatest effort." Kimmel had just had a couple of meetings with Herron's successor, Major General Walter C. Short, who had taken command on February 7. He found him "fully alive to the situation and highly cooperative," but he recommended that Stark "keep continuous pressure on this question of Army reinforcement of Oahu."[22]

As the first phase of establishing Marine garrisons on the outlying islands protecting the approaches to Hawaii, Kimmel had just sent a Marine defense battalion to Midway Island, 1,100 miles northwest of Oahu. Since the train vessels, which Richardson had asked for and which Kimmel would never receive, did not exist in February, the Marines had been transported by Cruiser Division 8, Destroyer Division 11, and the *Antares*, a cargo ship.

In response to the information about a detachment being sent to Manila or elsewhere as a show of force, Kimmel said he would "study, prepare plans and be ready for a quick decision in case orders" were received. He told Stark such a move was "most ill-advised," since his destroyer and cruiser strength was already limited and a carrier could "ill be spared" if the fleet had "to carry out other proposed plans."[23]

As the naval expansion program picked up speed, more and more qualified officers and enlisted men were ordered out of the Pacific Fleet to newly constructed ships, to train new personnel, or to assist in the production of weapons, ships, and aircraft. Three categories of officers in particular were being stripped from the fleet and ordered to the mainland stations and the resulting degradation of the experienced level concerned Kimmel. He had just received a long list of officers who had postgraduate training in ordnance, and who were being ordered out of the fleet. Almost all these officers occupied important command, gunnery, and staff positions. Kimmel wanted the "opportunity to comment on the detachment in each case of officers with ordnance experience, prior to final action." He would not get his desire. Qualified engineering officers were nearly as critical and going the same route from the fleet. Experienced aviators were the third category. Kimmel stated that he realized that some aviators were needed "to train new personnel and to produce the material." However, since he was losing experienced aviators and not getting new aircraft to modernize the fleet, he had the "distinct impression that the Bureau of Aeronautics [was] primarily concerned with the expansion program and that the supply of planes and personnel to man the Fleet [was taking] a secondary place."[24]

In reviewing the war plans situation, Kimmel pointed out that his staff was working on *Plan Dog* and *Rainbow 3*. Until Stark had told him otherwise in mid-February, Kimmel had agreed with his predecessor, Richardson, that *Plan Dog* appeared to demand a higher priority. He assured Stark that *Rainbow 3* would get first attention from then on.

In a postscript to his letter Kimmel first raised an issue which he would repeat a number of times without ever receiving full satisfaction—his being kept informed by the Washington naval staff. Shortly after Kimmel had taken command of the Pacific Fleet, Vice Admiral Wilson Brown, who had just come from Washington duty to become one of Kimmel's task force commanders, told him of some confusion in the Navy Department as to who had the responsibility of furnishing the Commander in Chief, Pacific Fleet, with information of a secret nature. Kimmel had heard that the Office of Naval Intelligence considered it to be the "function of Operations to furnish" the commander in chief with secret information and that Operations considered the responsibility to "be that of ONI." He closed his letter with the following question:

> I do not know that we have missed anything, but if there is any doubt as to whose responsibility it is to keep the Commander-in-Chief fully informed with pertinent reports on subjects that should be of interest to the Fleet, will you kindly fix that responsibility so that there will be no misunderstanding?[25]

Reiteration and elaboration of his previous correspondence to Kimmel were the substance of Stark's letter of February 25. Kimmel was told to get the "Operating Plan of *Rainbow 3* in the hands of Admiral Hart" and the Pacific Fleet subordinate commanders so that subordinate operating plans and logistic requirements could be prepared. Almost as if to answer a question on the dichotomy of emphasizing *Plan Dog* and *Rainbow 3*, Stark said: "Even if we fight this war according to '*Plan Dog*,' we have designed *Rainbow 3* that a shift to '*Dog*' . . . will [at least at first] require only minor changes in the tasks of either the Basic Plan or your Operating Plans."[26]

Kimmel was told that when he made his plans for offensive raids against Japan he should carefully study making "aircraft raids on the inflammable Japanese cities (ostensibly on military objectives), and the effect such raids might have on Japanese morale and on the diversion of their forces away from the Malay Barrier." Stark surmised that Kimmel might consider such raids "unjustified from a profit and loss viewpoint" or he might consider them very profitable. "In either case (and this is strictly SECRET) *you and I may be ordered* to make them, so it is just as well for you to have considered plans for it."[27] (Stark's emphasis.)

Again Stark brought up the subject of ships possibly being sent to the Far East. He agreed with Kimmel's view that it was unwise, but since he had written earlier in February "the subject [had] twice come up in the White House." Each of the times the subject had arisen, Stark's position had "prevailed, but the time *might* come when it will not." Stark was also very concerned over a "rising tide for action in the Far East if the Japanese go into Singapore or the Netherlands East Indies." The Navy Department recommendations not to implement *Rainbow 3* might be ignored. In that event the proposed detachment of ships from the Pacific Fleet to assist Britain in the Atlantic "would be reduced by just so much as [the United States] would send to the Asiatic" area.

Finally, Stark reported proudly that there had been "no public leak" that the conversations with the British representatives (*ABC*) were taking place in Washington. Optimistically, he hoped that the conversations would be finished in about ten days.

Ten days later, February 27, Rear Admiral Ghormley, at Stark's direction, informed Kimmel and Hart that the *ABC* meetings would be completed in two to four weeks. Upon completion of the meetings Rear Admiral Victor Hilary Danckwerts, Royal Navy, senior British naval participant, planned to fly to Singapore and possibly Australia and New Zealand via Hawaii and Manila. He wanted to talk with Kimmel and Hart after the results of the conversations in Washington. The two American admirals were told Danckwerts was very clever but honest. Admiral Ingersoll's advice to Kimmel and Hart was "to listen and talk little."[28]

On March 3, Rear Admiral Chester Nimitz, Chief of the Bureau of Navigation, answered Kimmel's concern over losing so many experienced officers and men. He spelled out in detail the problems resulting from a very rapid expansion in production facilities and in the naval force size. In the first area, personnel with technical competence were needed as inspectors and supervisors and in the second area they were needed to train the influx of new men. Production of ordnance material was falling further and further behind and if the Navy, even at existing strength, was to have the necessary ordnance supplies to carry on a war, drastic measures had to be taken. Complicating such problems were those involving lend-lease administration; "the task of procurement, inspection and delivery of enormous—almost astronomical—quantities of ordnance supplies for the British Navy and any allies which may survive to fight the Dictators." Secretary Knox had just directed Nimitz to give the Chief of the Bureau of Ordnance, Rear Admiral William Henry Purnell Blandy, "all practicable aid in the form of competent officers to assist in producing ordnance supplies." Knox and Stark knew of the personnel requirements and that they would come almost exclusively from the fleet. "The situation regarding aviators [was] not unlike that of Ordnance P.G.'s."[29] To get all the new air training stations functioning qualified aviators were a necessity. They too had to come from the fleet.

Two pieces of legislation had been initiated to help solve the need for additional personnel. A three-year Naval Academy course, commencing with the class of 1943, was proposed. The class of 1942 would be graduated in February 1942 instead of June 1942. Legislation also was in the works for a navy of 232,000 men "during normal times, with a limit of 300,000 for emergency." Stark and Nimitz had wanted to ask for a ceiling of 500,000, but Roosevelt turned them down and insisted on a year-to-year program. The projected figure for 1942 was 292,000.

While Nimitz was answering Kimmel on the personnel issues, Stark was inspecting naval bases along the Atlantic seaboard and in the Caribbean. When he returned to Washington, he too answered Kimmel's letter of February 18. He reinforced Nimitz's earlier position on the need to get ordnance, aviation, and engineering specialists from the fleet. Stark handled Kimmel's complaint that the fleet was getting its modern types of aircraft on a secondary basis by drawing on the views of the Chief of the Bureau of Aeronautics, Rear Admiral John Henry Towers.

> . . . Towers states the impression that the Bureau of Aeronautics is relegating fleet aircraft needs to a position of lower priority than the general expansion program, is in error. He says that the Bureau of Aeronautics has exerted and continues to exert every possible effort to provide the Fleet with new replacement aircraft for the old models at a rate only limited by the productive output of the contractors and diversions instituted by *specific directives to* the Bureau of Aeronautics.[30] (Stark's emphasis.)

The specific directives were well-known to Stark, Knox, and Roosevelt and they *did* give priority to British orders. Kimmel was definitely correct in his statement of secondary treatment for the very reason of the specific directives, and because of them, the fleet would still be waiting for modern aircraft on December 7, 1941.

In answer to Kimmel's question as to whether Stark would fix responsibility for keeping him informed about secret information, Stark used the same procedure of quoting one of his staff as he had done in answer to the aircraft situation. This time he referred to Captain Alan G. Kirk, the chief of naval intelligence. "Kirk informs me that ONI is fully aware of its responsibility in keeping you adequately informed concerning foreign nations, activities of these nations and disloyal elements within the United States."[31] That was a non-responsive answer. Kimmel had asked if Stark would "fix the responsibility so that there would be no misunderstanding." There was nothing to indicate that ONI had full responsibility or shared it with Stark, nor was there anything to indicate who determined what "adequately informed" meant. There was still a question of how such information affecting the Commander in Chief, Pacific Fleet, would be sent to him. If Kirk understood in February what Kimmel rightly asked, something happened before many months had passed, because Kimmel was *not* kept informed.

In Stark's lengthy reply to Kimmel's letter he identified each paragraph and addressed each issue except the one concerning war plans. For some reason that paragraph was slighted. As important as *Rainbow 3* and *Plan Dog* were to the grand strategy, to Stark, and to Kimmel, it is difficult to rationalize an obvious omission.

The month of February was an important one in the relationships within the Navy. Kimmel had taken command of a truncated Pacific Fleet. King's command in the Atlantic had come into official existence. Kimmel had had his first serious exchange with the Washington hierarchy. The month of March was marked heavily with incidents of international character. The Lend-Lease Act, passed on March 11, assured Britain that the United States would provide unlimited war material for her fight against the Axis powers. The *ABC* meeting ended on March 27 with agreements on prospective joint actions between the United States and Britain. In March also Stark lost two rounds in his sparring with the State Department naval strategists.

Hart had proposed, on March 4, a visit by ships of the Asiatic Fleet to the Netherlands East Indies. Stark had heartily endorsed the idea since it supported existing war plans to the extent that if war started there the ships would be where they were needed. Hull, undoubtedly advised by Hornbeck and Hamilton, vetoed the Hart proposal because at the time Japan and the Netherlands East Indies government were still involved in economic conversations. The diplomats did not think that that was the time or place to attempt to influence Japan. It was the time, they thought, to use naval visits for other reasons. Foreign Minister Matsuoka was on a visit to the Soviet Union and Germany in the wake of the Lend-Lease Act. Since the United States was by the act deeply involved in Britain's fight against Germany and Italy, the strategy of the English-speaking powers was not to provoke Japan but to deter her from further expansion, or more hopefully, from entering the war. In line with these thoughts Roosevelt's State Department advisers convinced him, over Stark's objections, to send a detachment of the Pacific Fleet to Australia and New Zealand for a show of force. Stark's objections were that such a weakening of the fleet in Hawaii negated the deterrence of a powerful force on the flank of any Japanese move to the south and such a visit might be extended to Singapore. That issue—not to defend Singapore with American ships—had just been thrashed out in the *ABC* talks. The major reasons for sending ships "down under" were to show unity with the English-speaking countries in the Far East and to impress Japan with the capabilities and intentions of the United States Navy.

The force sent to New Zealand, Australia, the Fiji Islands, and Tahiti consisted of the cruisers *Chicago, Portland, Savannah,* and *Brooklyn,* escorted by Destroyer Squadron 3. Roosevelt was so impressed with the idea that he thought more visits should be planned. He wanted more ships sent out "to keep them popping up here and there and keep the Japs guessing."[32] Stark had some hard maneuvering ahead of him before he could torpedo that idea.

In the latter part of March the United States dealt the Axis powers a blow and helped eventually to meet some of the critical requirements for transports to carry lend-lease material to Britain. Roosevelt directed the seizure of all German, Italian, and Danish ships in United States ports after increasing reports of sabotage. The Coast Guard, early on Sunday morning March 30, 1941, boarded and took control of thirty-five Danish ships and thirty Axis ships totaling 600,000 tons. At the same time Stark directed the Navy to take custody of four Danish ships in the Philippines. After the seizure it was discovered that twenty-five of the twenty-seven Italian ships had excessive machinery damage due to sabotage. Roosevelt asked Congress on April 10 for authority to requisition the ships. After that request became law on June 6 the Danish ships, a number of them manned by their own national crews, were put in service in the Atlantic for the lift to Britain. The timing was most opportune because in March and April Britain had lost over 1,200,000 tons of shipping to German submarines—a tonnage almost equal to the output of her shipyards for a year. The Axis ships seized were not used until after Pearl Harbor.[33]

The effectiveness of Germany's submarine warfare had certainly cast an ominous cloud over the question of Britain's survival, with primary concern being the food supply and munitions. Stark considered the situation "obviously critical" and "hopeless except as we take strong measures to save it." The submarine campaign was only part of the grim picture. By mid-April the Germans appeared almost invincible. Their Balkan campaign launched on April 6 was equally successful. In ten days Yugoslavia had been occupied and British troops in Greece were in full retreat. In North Africa German armored troops were pushing the British rapidly across Libya to the Egyptian border. The strong measures which Stark thought appropriate to take had partially been decided by Roosevelt, partially been decided in the *ABC* talks, and completely complemented his own *Plan Dog* concept. Before they were implemented, however, many other factors compounded the problems, including considerations in the Pacific and Atlantic which would have a bearing and cause delays.

As early as February, Roosevelt had considered taking over control of Greenland and Iceland, strategic North Atlantic islands belonging to Denmark. Britain had occupied the latter shortly after Germany had invaded Denmark in April 1940. Greenland, the larger island, had not been occupied and was consequently easier to take under control. On April 10, 1941, the United States announced that the Danish minister in exile in Washington had agreed with the United States, Britain, and Canada that the United States should include Greenland in her "sphere of cooperative hemispheric defense." Four days later Mr. Harry Hopkins, personal confidant and roving messenger for the President, and Under Secretary Welles began secret talks with Icelandic officials for the United States to take similar actions relative to Iceland. Marines finally landed in Iceland on July 7, eventually to relieve the British forces there. This action gave the United States another strategic base, one within 700 miles of the British Isles on the evolving convoy route across the North Atlantic.

As the protective zone was enlarged, so grew the urgency for naval forces to control it. Admiral King's Atlantic Fleet had been created as a separate command, effective February 1, 1941. On April 2, Roosevelt had talked of providing escorts for Atlantic convoys and had directed the Navy to draw up plans to attack German submarines and raiders in the western Atlantic. On April 7, a heavy detachment of the U.S. Pacific Fleet—in fact, approximately 20 percent of it—had been ordered to the Atlantic Fleet. The units designated to shift were the carrier *Yorktown;* the battleships *New Mexico, Idaho,* and *Mississippi;* the light cruisers *Brooklyn, Philadelphia, Savannah,* and *Nashville;* and Destroyer Divisions 8 and 9. Knox, Stimson, Marshall, and Stark wanted to move the bulk of the Pacific Fleet to the Atlantic then. Hull and his State Department team convinced Roosevelt that a force of sufficient strength should be kept in Hawaii to continue as a deterrent to Japanese moves to the south. As events unfolded, Roosevelt reversed his original order for the transfer of the large detachment and authorized only the carrier and a destroyer squadron to join the Atlantic Fleet.

A number of strands of the recent past came together in April to form a web of indecision. Hull's discussions with Nomura, discussions in Singapore, and Matsuoka's visit to Germany and the Soviet Union all contributed to the State Department's recommendation and Roosevelt's acceptance of the rationale for keeping the fleet in Hawaii.

Commencing with their first serious talk on March 8, Secretary Hull and Ambassador Nomura met in the latter's Hotel Carlton apartment to discuss informally how their two countries could remain at peace. They would ultimately meet some fifty times in that futile quest. Evolving from these talks was a Hull proposal for agreement based upon four abstract points, and although tacit at times, they would be the basis for discussions between the two countries until war commenced. Those four points were:

1. Respect for the territorial integrity and the sovereignty of each and all nations.
2. Support of the principle of non-interference in the internal affairs of other nations.
3. Support of the principle of equality, including equality of commercial opportunity.
4. Non-disturbance of the *status quo* in the Pacific except as the *status quo* may be altered by peaceful means.[34]

The Japanese leaders were interested in specific issues rather than abstract principles. They wanted the United States to stop its aid to China, to lift the ever-tightening economic embargo, and to allow Japan economic independence and a dominant position in the Pacific.

Nomura sent Hull's list to Tokyo on April 14, the day after the signing of the Soviet-Japanese Neutrality Act. For a month there were heated debates over Hull's thoughts within the Japanese Cabinet, since that which he proposed was so completely antithetical to the expansionist faction. Matsuoka wanted Japan to assist Germany and to move to the south now that the northern flank was reasonably secure. Lack of progress in getting favorable concessions from the Netherlands East Indies government, intelligence on what they perceived to be secret military agreements in Singapore, and the tightening economic restraints by the United States forced the more conservative elements in the Japanese government on May 14 to agree to discuss Hull's four principles. Although Hull realized that agreement to discuss could not be equated with agreement itself, he was relieved enough to endorse a partial transfer of the Pacific Fleet to the Atlantic Fleet.

In February, while the *ABC* talks were in progress in Washington, Captain William R. Purnell from Admiral Hart's staff attended a meeting in Singapore as an observer to a British, Dutch, and Australian attempt at mutual security. The results were discouraging. There were additional pressures for another meeting in April. Air Chief Marshal Sir Robert Brooke-Popham, commander in chief of

British forces in East Asia, stopped in Manila on April 3, followed by Dutch Foreign Minister E. N. Van Kleffens on April 5, to discuss with Admiral Hart and Generals MacArthur and Grunert the possibilities of United States participation in containing a Japanese advance. Immediately after the *ABC* talks Stark directed Hart to send a representative to Singapore for another meeting there. The meeting from April 21 to 27 ended with a plan for defense against Japan. When reviewed by Stark and Marshall it was rejected both in its original form and later after revisions by the British chiefs of staff.[35]

While the Japanese Cabinet debated the Hull proposals and while the military planners met in Singapore, the debate continued in Washington over moving the fleet from Hawaii. Knox, Stimson, Marshall, and Stark considered the urgency of assisting Britain in the Atlantic much more pressing than anything in the immediate future in the Pacific area. Hull still held out, waiting for an answer to his proposals from the Japanese government. Even Churchill and the British mission in Washington, were brought into the discussions. Rear Admiral Danckwerts, who stayed in Washington after the *ABC* talks as a member of the British mission, was queried by Rear Admiral Turner on April 25 about the British attitude towards the fleet transfer proposals. After having consulted with the defence committee of the British cabinet and Australian and New Zealand officials, he answered on May 8

> ... that any marked advance by the U.S. Navy in or into the Atlantic would be on the whole more likely to deter Japan from going to war than the maintenance of the present very large U.S. Fleet at Hawaii, and further that it might exercise a profound influence on the present critical situation in Spain, Turkey and Vichy France.
>
> 3. The problem for the U.S. authorities is so nicely to judge the degree of the transfer that while still retaining the deterrent effect of a strong U.S. Fleet in the Pacific, there will also be the deterrent effect of an increased U.S. Fleet in the Atlantic.
>
> 4. It is not only the strength but also the composition of the Fleet in the Pacific which will act as a deterrent, and in our view the necessary effect will not remain unless the Fleet in the Pacific consisted of not less than 6 capital ships and 2 aircraft carriers. Inclusion of the latter is considered of greatest importance.[36]

Later the British military leaders were overruled by Churchill who did agree that the bulk of the U.S. Fleet would do the most good in the Atlantic.[37] By the end of May the three battleships, four cruisers, and remaining destroyers originally ordered on April 7 were sent to the Atlantic Fleet.

In the meantime, Kimmel continued his fight for some degree of efficiency within the force he still had. On April 22, he made a strong case for some permanency in key personnel aboard his ships. The battle efficiency of the fleet and the ability to train new recruits and reserve officers both suffered from constant turnover of commanding officers, executive officers, heads of departments, and senior petty officers. Kimmel proposed a permanent nucleus for each ship. He also asked if it were not possible "to obtain legislation which will stop the discharge of qualified men and permit them to remain in their present billets?"[38] Receiving no answer to his April 22 letter, Kimmel repeated his pleas again on May 5. Most of the enlisted men in Hawaii whose enlistments were expiring were not reenlisting. The high wages of the rapidly expanding economy gearing for war production and the continued separation from families left on the West Coast were the two main reasons for the exodus from the Navy. Kimmel thought "congressional legislation of some kind" was the only solution.[39]

On May 15, when Stark finally answered Kimmel's letters to him and Nimitz on retention of personnel, he reviewed the problems as seen from the Washington vantage point. A bill had been introduced in January in the Senate to allow automatic extension of enlistments during war and national emergency. Representative Carl Vinson, chairman of the Naval Affairs Committee, would not introduce a similar bill in the House of Representatives because he was "apparently opposed to it." Part of the problem was the existing Selective Service Act, which provided that a man inducted for training for one year must be discharged at the end of that time unless Congress had declared "that the national interest [was] imperiled." The Navy could not hold men past the expiration of their enlistments until Congress had so acted. Stark was initiating legislation to the effect that should Congress declare the national interests imperiled, all regular Navy and Marine Corps enlisted men would be detained in service for the emergency and up to six months after it ended. Stark reminded Kimmel that on May 6 the Bureau of Navigation had changed its policy of ordering enlisted personnel from the fleet by name to a policy of levying requirements by designated ratings. The change helped to a degree, since it permitted those whose services could best be spared to be transferred in lieu of key personnel in the same rating. To the extent possible, the Bureau of Navigation would make every effort not to detach experienced officers where these transfers could be avoided but would ask for nominations from the forces afloat. With the change in policy, Kimmel at least was a participant, however reluctant, in the drawdown of fleet experience instead of being just a frustrated observer.

In March when the large detachment of the Pacific Fleet made the Australian cruise, Roosevelt expressed a desire that he wanted more of the same thing. His conception of the State Department's suggestion for visits was to keep the ships "popping up everywhere." Stark, who thought a "lot of State Department's suggestions and recommendations are nothing less than childish," decided to put an end to the encroachment of diplomatic strategists into his domain. He suggested a northern cruise in strength. Initially the President approved the cruise. Stark's purpose in going north was "to give the State Department a shock which might make them haul back," although he admitted later to Kimmel that the northern cruise had some good points. Stark's scheme worked as planned. He "had a broad inward smile when the State Department in effect said: 'Please, Mr. President, don't let him do it'; or words to that effect. It was a little too much for them."[40] Yet despite Stark's "victory," behind the scenes the War Plans Division made extensive preparations just in case the President said, "Go!"

The timing of the proposed cruise had been predicated on Foreign Minister Matsuoka's return to Tokyo from his visit with Germany and the Soviet Union. A few days after his return, a Pacific Fleet force of one carrier, a division of heavy cruisers, a squadron of destroyers, and a tanker would arrive in Attu in the Aleutian island chain northeast of Japan. The Soviet Union would be requested to allow several cruisers and a destroyer division to visit Petropavlovsk, a port on the Kamchatka peninsula north of Japan. Ambassador Grew, on the day of their arrival in Petropavlovsk, would inform Japan that the visit to the Soviet Union did not reflect on United States-Japanese relations. While some of the ships were in Petropavlovsk, the carrier and remaining units would stay in the Aleutians on maneuvers. After the visit they would all regroup and visit Kiska, Unalaska, and Kodiak before returning to Hawaii. If the Soviet Union refused permission for the visit to its port, the operation would be carried out with that exception. Navy planners calculated that for two weeks after Matsuoka's return the Japanese Cabinet would be in the throes of discussion over Matsuoka's agreements made on his trip. The proposed cruise to the north would take place in those two weeks.

In his detailed analysis of the probable results of the cruise to the north, Admiral Turner of the War Plans Division described what the effect would be on the younger "rabid expansionists," on the "long-range expansionists of older officers and some businessmen," and finally, on "the liberals of some officers, the diplomats and many businessmen." He reasoned that there would be a struggle among the three groups over future policy and that "the cruise might well have a hardening effect on Japanese minds; in this case the cruise would act as a sort of catalytic agent in solidifying Japanese opinion. whereas it ought to be our wish to keep it in the present confused state." Turner thought the cruise would be beneficial only in case Japan decided to go ahead with its aggressions. In that case, the cruise should be made only after it was evident that the Japanese concentrations had been initiated for further moves. "If made then, the cruise might well have a decidedly unsettling effect on Japanese plans which would cause delays and uncertainties in their execution." Turner's recommendation was that the cruise not be made at that time and that it be made in the future only if it became apparent that Japan had decided on a more aggressive policy.[41]

When Stark informed Knox about the cruise proposals, he pointed out its open threat aspects and that Japan "might become more than ever determined to stick to the Axis and proceed with the southern program." He then advised Knox on discussions with the President and Hull concerning the cruise:

> Please note that the force recommended for this demonstration is considerably greater than was suggested by the President. It is a real striking force, operating in an area well situated to cause concern to a people which might fear bombing raids. Because it is stronger, and because of the necessity for a concurrent diplomatic effort, you will doubtless (sic) wish the President to re-examine the project. When you subsequently take this up with Mr. Hull, I suggest you ask that the least possible number of persons in the State Department learn of it. You will recall that three or four times recently matters under discussion by the State and Navy Departments have promptly found their way to one or the other of two pairs of newspaper columnists. If this project be approved, we want, so far as possible, to insure no leak.[42]

The President's subsequent decision to accept the State Department's objections put an end to ships "popping up everywhere" and to the northern cruise.

By mid-May of 1941 there was genuine fear that Germany would parlay her successes in the Mediterranean area into a new push into the Atlantic. Vichy France appeared to be cooperating in every respect with the German moves and the possibilities loomed large that French colonies in North Africa and Dakar on the western coast of Africa would be used by Germany. There was also the possibility that Germany would overrun the Iberian peninsula and from there seize the Portuguese Azores Islands in the Atlantic. On May 22, Roosevelt gave Stark thirty days "to prepare and have ready an expedition of 25,000 men to sail for, and to take the Azores."[43] He also gave Marshall the task to prepare a force to go into northeastern Brazil, the bulge of that country opposite Dakar. The intransigence of President Salazar of Portugal to agree to the Azores' occupation until it was certain that Germany would attack his country; the noncommittal attitude of Brazilian President Vargas; and finally and most decisively, Hitler's choice of striking in the opposite direction against the Soviet Union relieved the pressure to occupy the Azores and to send troops to Brazil. In the meantime, Stark had ordered auxiliaries for the Azores operation to the Atlantic Fleet from Kimmel's already meager force in the Pacific. They were not returned despite the cancellation of the operation. In addition, the oceangoing units of the Coast Guard, in peacetime under control of the Treasury Department were transferred on May 7 to the Navy, primarily for duty with the Atlantic Fleet in patrol operations around Greenland and Iceland. Stark's *Plan Dog* emphasis on the Atlantic theater was obviously influencing the assignment of forces.

On May 26, Kimmel wrote a seventeen-page letter spelling out in detail his problems in trying to meet his assigned tasks with a smaller fleet deteriorating in effectiveness due to the constant drain of experienced personnel and ship transfers to the Atlantic. Almost 69 percent of the men whose enlistments were to expire between June 1 and August 31, 1941 did not intend to reenlist. In addition, the quotas on the fleets for experienced ratings were unbalanced. Of the requirements for shore stations in the next three months 73 percent would come from the Pacific Fleet. Kimmel's aircraft were obsolete and not being replaced rapidly enough, his pilots were inexperienced, and he had no support train. The Army and Navy forces in the Fourteenth Naval District were incapable of defending Pearl Harbor due to material shortages. To top off his long and bleak list he reiterated again the issue of being kept informed.[44]

Kimmel's point about being kept informed became a major issue in his later defense against charges of not properly preparing for an enemy attack on Pearl Harbor. The Navy did in fact have unusually reliable sources of information when Kimmel was asking for it. In August 1940 the highly secure Japanese diplomatic *Purple* code was broken and a machine devised to decrypt messages sent in that code. Ultimately duplicate machines were provided to Army and Navy intelligence units in Washington, an intelligence unit assigned to the Commandant, Sixteenth Naval District in Cavite, and the British Intelligence Service in London. No machine went to Hawaii. Intercepted Japanese diplomatic traffic between Tokyo, Washington, and Berlin was processed in Washington and translations were disseminated to a limited number of top decision-making recipients. Distribution tightened up after German intelligence in April and May warned Japan that the United States was reading Nomura's traffic—a certain fact. The Japanese, confident that *Purple* could not be broken, transmitted the whole story in that code.[45] Kimmel was provided with *selections* of decoded *Purple* messages through July 1941, when the decision was made in Washington that the risks of the Japanese finding out that their code had been compromised were too great for the utility of the information to Kimmel.

In addition to breaking Japan's diplomatic code, the United States also was fortunate in breaking up an espionage net. The Federal Bureau of Investigation and naval intelligence agents had uncovered espionage activities of a number of Japanese naval officers who were in the United States as language students in the spring of 1941. The State Department agreed on May 27 to their arrests. First to be picked up was Lieutenant Commander Tachibana in Los Angeles, California. On June 14, Nomura besought Hull to let Tachibana be deported immediately without trial. When Hull delayed his answer and Tachibana's trial began, the Japanese naval attache in Washington, Captain Ichiro Yokoyama, attempted through United States naval channels to get Tachibana off the hook. He called Captain Kirk, ONI, for help in getting Tachibana deported. He pointed out that as the Japanese naval attache he

> ...had been especially selected by the Imperial Japanese Navy Department...to work with the Ambassador, Admiral Nomura, in the interest of promoting cordial relations between the United States Navy and the Japanese Navy....The Japanese Navy believes that the attitude between the two Navies in this respect will have great influence on the Japanese Government in preserving peace.[45]

Yokoyama's pleas failed to impress his American acquaintances, because naval intelligence had information that, if the trial were to continue, evidence would probably show that Yokoyama was involved in the act also. It was well known to ONI that a large, well-financed, and well-staffed espionage system was being built up in the United States as rapidly as possible. Figures prominent in Japanese Espionage Service in Manchukuo and Shanghai had recently entered the United States as officers of the Japanese government. It was also known that preparations were being made by Japan to move its spy center into Mexico in the event the United States became involved in hostilities. The naval intelligence staff members were all for letting the trial continue and stopping the espionage before it grew more serious. Hull "decided to grant Nomura's request, out of consideration for him" and because his talks with Nomura were at a "crucial stage."[46] Tachibana was deported on June 21. Two more of Tachibana's fellow officers, Lieutenant Commander Okada and Lieutenant Yamada, were deported on July 5. A similar treatment was meted out to Lieutenant Commander Ezima, who was assigned to the Japanese naval inspector's office in New York City but who was primarily engaged in passing intelligence to Germany.[47]

CHAPTER 10

Economic Sanctions
Against Japan

While the United States counterintelligence agents were ferreting out the Japanese espionage agents, Congress was taking further action against Japan. On May 28, Public Law 75 was passed, extending export control provisions of the National Defense Act to all territories, dependencies, and possessions of the United States. Immediately the President applied it to the Philippines, thereby denying Japan that source for iron and chrome ores, maganese, copper, copra, and abaca fiber. In another move the President, by Executive Order on June 14, froze all German and Italian funds and, although Japan was not directly affected, the significance of the move had its impact. The facility with which the other Axis powers' funds were frozen could just as quickly and fatefully be applied to Japanese funds. By coincidence, within days of the freezing of funds, the Japanese negotiators broke off talks with the Netherlands East Indies officials. They just could not, without resorting to force of arms, coerce the Dutch into the concessions demanded. In the meantime, the activists within Roosevelt's cabinet were arguing vehemently for a complete embargo of oil to Japan. On June 20, a decision was made to restrict all oil exports from East Coast and Gulf ports except to the British Empire, British forces in Egypt, and the Western Hemisphere. Once again Stark, Welles, and Hull managed to temper the finality of total embargo and to convince the President to allow restricted shipments of petroleum from the West Coast to Japan.

After agreement among the British and American war planners on *ABC-1* in March 1941, there had been increased American participation in the Atlantic area and a more determined effort to deter Japan in the Pacific area. Yet approval of *ABC-1* and its supporting

American war plan, *Rainbow 5,* was frustratingly slow for the Army and Navy staffs. The Joint Board approved both plans on May 14, and after approval by the Secretary of Navy on May 28 and by the Secretary of War on June 2, the plans were sent to the President. Although he was informed that the British chiefs of staff had provisionally approved *ABC-1* and submitted it to their government for approval, Roosevelt on June 7 returned both plans to the Joint Board without either approval or disapproval. Through his military aide, Major General Edwin M. Watson, he explained that since the British had not yet approved the plans he would not approve them "at this time," however, "in event of war the papers would be returned to the President for his approval."[1]

Fears, so prevalent among the British and American leaders in May, that Germany would move into the Atlantic territories were partially assuaged with the German invasion of the Soviet Union on June 22. That invasion, which gave Britain a short respite in the Middle East and Atlantic, also affected the decision makers in the two major non-belligerents—the United States and Japan.

Stark wanted to seize "the psychological opportunity presented by the Russian-German clash and announce and start escorting immediately, and protecting the Western Atlantic on a large scale." Such actions he realized would almost certainly involve the United States in war, but he considered "every day of delay in our getting into the war as dangerous," and that much more delay might be fatal to Britain's survival. Stark's eagerness to aid Britain, his impatience at the lack of progress made to that end, and his solution are shown in a letter to Captain Charles Maynard Cooke, Jr., a friend and confidant who had been on Stark's staff:

> . . . I have been maintaining that only a war psychology could and would speed things up the way they should be speeded up; that strive as we would it just isn't in the nature of things to get the results in peace that we would, were we at war.
>
> The Iceland situation may produce an "incident." . . . Whether or not we will get an "incident" because of the protection we are giving Iceland and the shipping which we must send in support of Iceland and our troops, I do not know. Only Hitler can answer.[2]

While Stark considered the time ripe to rush into action in the Atlantic, on the other side of the world Matsuoka thought the golden opportunity had arrived for Japan to go to Germany's assistance. Bypassing his prime minister, Prince Konoye, Matsuoka approached the Emperor directly, urging him to take Japan into the war against the

Soviet Union. Fortunately for the Russians, who were reeling before the German onslaught, Matsuoka was alone in the Japanese Cabinet in thinking that way. Before the German attack on the Soviet Union the Japanese Army and Navy had agreed on the strategy of moving south into Indochina and, as recently as June 10, had asked Germany's assistance in getting Vichy France to grant bases in southern Indochina for prospective attacks on Singapore and the Indies. At a Cabinet meeting on June 25, Matsuoka's plan to attack the Soviet Union was overruled, because as the minister of war, General Hideki Tojo, pointed out, a quick German victory would permit Japan to take the Russian maritime provinces later without a fight. The emphasis should continue to the south. Fully realizing that their suggested actions might well provoke the United States and Britain, the ministers urged the Emperor to support a plan to get the bases in southern Indochina even if they had to resort to force of arms. At a follow-up Cabinet meeting on July 2, the Japanese war leaders decided to bring the China Incident to a close by cutting off foreign assistance to China from the south, to adopt a wait-and-see attitude toward the German-Soviet war, to continue all necessary diplomatic negotiations with Britain and the United States, and if they should break down, to be prepared for war against both powers.

The Japanese army war planners, after that meeting, accelerated their work for operations against the Netherlands East Indies, Borneo, and the Philippines. The Navy began operational training for a plan drawn up the previous January—one using low-flying aircraft, dive bombing, and tactics perfecting a shallow water torpedo. To keep up the semblance of neutrality Japan assured the Soviet Union that their Neutrality Pact of April 13, 1941 would be honored. The Kwantung Army—the Japanese Army in Manchuria—withdrew from the immediate Soviet border areas, but in meticulous planning for future contingencies, it doubled the size of the force to nearly 600,000 concentrated at interior points.

For three weeks after Germany invaded the Soviet Union, arguments raged within the Japanese Cabinet. Matsuoka insisted on support for Germany and no negotiations with the United States, whereas the military leaders wanted negotiations continued until their objectives in Indochina had been secured and the outcome of the German-Soviet war was more clear. Finally, the whole Cabinet resigned in order to get rid of Matsuoka. Two days later a new cabinet was formed with the same members except that Matsuoka had been replaced by Admiral Teijiro Toyoda as foreign minister.

It was soon apparent that nothing but a personality had changed as far as foreign relations were concerned. By *Magic,* the system that broke the *Purple* code, the United States readily learned that Berlin and Rome were assured that Japan would continue with the Tripartite Pact and would continue with her plans to go into Indochina. Germany was asked again on July 19 to support the ultimatum given Vichy France by Matsuoka to get the requested bases.

While the Japanese leaders planned their short- and long-range strategies, American leaders planned countermeasures. Admiral Turner, director of the Navy War Plans Division, with the advantage of *Magic* analysis of intercepted Japanese diplomatic messages, advised Stark that Japan would "occupy important points in Indo-China" and "would adopt an opportunistic attitude toward the Siberian Maritime Provinces." Indications of Japan's preparation for war were the taking over of "many ships suitable for use as transports and the withdrawing of all others from the Atlantic." Turner recommended closing the Panama Canal and continued aid to China as actions which "may have a considerable effect on Japanese decisions." The degree of tension that existed in July is readily apparent from Turner's other recommendations to Stark:

> ... Since it is inexcusable for military forces to be surprised for an attack, even if the chances for such attack appear small, it is recommended that steps be taken to place our Army and Navy forces in the Far East in an alert status, to be achieved so far as practicable within about the next two weeks. Specifically, it is recommended that the Chief of Naval Operations and the Chief of Staff issue concurrent orders to United States forces in the Philippines to:
>
> (a) Establish underwater defenses by the laying of mines, nets and booms;
> (b) Deploy their forces, and maintain them in an alert condition, for Japanese attack against the Philippines;
> (c) Place into effect measures for full cooperation between the Army and the Navy.... It is not recommended that troops and river gunboats be withdrawn from China at this time.[3]

In anticipation of further retaliatory action, Turner also completed a *Study of the Effect of an Embargo of Trade between the United States and Japan.* His conclusions were that an embargo would "probably result in a fairly early attack by Japan on Malaya and the Netherlands East Indies, and possibly would involve the United States in early war in the Pacific." His strong recommendation, completely supported by Stark, was that trade with Japan not be embargoed at that time.[4]

166

While Turner was developing his position papers relative to Japan, a Japanese admiral in Washington was having his share of problems relative to the United States. Admiral Nomura, the Japanese ambassador, was very disturbed by Matsuoka's demands on Vichy France and was convinced that they would lead to war with the United States. He informed the senior Japanese naval officials in Tokyo of the dangerous situation and asked that he be allowed to resign and return home. On July 15, Admiral Oikawa, minister for the Navy, and Admiral Nagano, chief of the naval general staff persuaded him to remain at his post. On July 13, Nomura traveled to White Sulphur Springs, Virginia, to converse with the ailing Secretary Hull. Nomura wanted to justify his country's actions in Indochina by explaining Japan's needs for raw materials and desire to prevent encirclement. Hull refused to see him, because he thought Nomura "had nothing new to offer."[5] Stymied in his attempts to communicate with Hull, Nomura turned to his naval contacts. He tried on Sunday, July 20, to see Stark and then Ingersoll, the assistant chief of naval operations. Finding neither at home, he next went to his old friend, Admiral Turner. It was quite natural that Turner would be on Nomura's list, because next to his association with Admiral William Veazie Pratt, a former chief of naval operations, he had probably been closer to Turner than to any other United States naval officer. Turner had commanded the *Astoria,* which had carried the ashes of the Japanese ambassador to Japan in April 1939 and he had been to Japan four times. When Nomura came to Washington as ambassador he asked Turner to meet him for a long conversation. In the course of that conversation on March 13, Nomura had outlined his assignment—to keep peace between the two countries. In mid-July he despaired of being able to do anything more and, since Hull would not see him, his last desperate hope was the possible intercession by his American naval friends directly with the President.

In an unusually frank discussion with Turner, Nomura admitted that Japan's economic position was bad and getting worse. He complained about United States pilots serving in Chiang Kai-shek's air force and American improvements to the Burma Road, China's last link with the outside world except through the Soviet Union. He asserted that it was "essential that Japan have uninterrupted access to necessary raw materials, particularly iron ore and iron products, oil, rubber, cotton and food." Then, in a show of trust, he told Turner that "within the next few days Japan expects to occupy French Indo-China." He anticipated "that the United States would take further action against Japan, either economically or militarily, as soon as Japanese troops were known to be occupying French Indo-China." Although he did not say so directly, he gave Turner the impression that Japan contemplated no further move to the south for the time being. Turner pointed out that anything that affected the "future security of the United Kingdom, in any part of the world, was of interest to the United States from the defensive viewpoint." The occupation of Indochina by Japan was particularly important for the defense of the United States, since that would threaten the British position in Singapore and the Dutch position in the Netherlands East Indies. Should Singapore and the Indies "pass out of their present control, a very severe blow would be struck at the integrity of the defense of the British Isles, and these Isles might well then be overcome by the Germans." Turner continued with the declaration "that Japan really [had] very little to fear from American, British or Dutch activities in the Far East."[6]

Having talked with Turner and seeing that there was little that he could do, Nomura decided to take a short vacation in Maine. Hull, still in White Sulphur Springs, had some second thoughts about his treatment of Nomura. He telephoned Welles to make one more attempt with Nomura to point out the gravity of Japan's going into southern Indochina. Nomura, having been intercepted in New York City, returned to Washington and again turned to his American naval friends. Prior to seeing Welles he spent two hours with Stark on July 23, explaining that Japan needed the rice, tin, rubber, and other materials in Indochina. He pleaded with Stark to get him an appointment with Roosevelt as soon as possible. After Nomura left Stark's office for his session with Welles, Stark talked with Roosevelt and did arrange a meeting with Nomura the next day. While Stark was talking with Roosevelt, Nomura was being told by Welles that there was no more need for continuing the conversations with Hull, because of Japan's persistent actions of aggression. From his arrival as ambassador to the break on July 23, there had been twenty-six meetings between the two diplomats. Now Nomura was told that his country's actions negated any basis for future meetings.

The next day, July 24, Stark, Welles, and Nomura met with Roosevelt, who offered to do what he could to neutralize Indochina, in the same way that Switzerland was considered neutral, and to help Japan obtain her raw materials. He gave a hint that the United States might embargo oil and emphasized again why oil had been allowed to be exported to Japan. If Japan tried to get oil from the Netherlands East Indies by force, the Dutch and British would undoubtedly resist and since the United States was assisting Britain, a serious situation would immediately result. Roosevelt's offer to neutralize Indochina, which emasculated the self-serving charge of encirclement of Japan, was all but ignored. Nomura promptly reported back that a diplomatic break was a strong possibility and economic sanctions were certain to follow. Neither Nomura nor the Japanese government anticipated the degree of American reaction to the completion of the Indochina seizure.

At the same time Stark was trying as persuasively as he could to convince Roosevelt not to embargo oil to Japan, he was fighting equally hard to get approval for an increase in the level of authorized naval personnel. He was pleased to report to Kimmel on July 24 that Roosevelt had just "okayed a figure of 553,000 enlisted men and 105,000 marines." The next step was to increase recruiting so as to replace those men not reenlisting and to fill the newly authorized quotas.[7]

During the next few days decisions were announced which had been delayed by debates for a number of months previously; they had the full support of those who advocated a tough line with Japan, and they were the type from which it would not be easy to retreat. The lines were drawn by the United States initially in the hope of deterring Japan from further aggression in the Pacific so that Britain would continue to obtain from her Pacific colonies and Allies the necessary war materials to fight Germany; so that the United States could concentrate her meager naval strength in helping the British in the Atlantic; and so that China, which had managed to survive merciless devastation, could continue to fight and exist. Later the decisions made by the United States on July 25 and 26, 1941 became the basis for more serious operations. For Japan, they lead to an attack on the United States as the only hope of holding on to her recently expanded empire. For the United States, the July decisions created a new defensive posture in the Philippines, a hardening of attitude toward Japan and Germany, and the consequent corollary—a more positive support for Britain, China, and the Soviet Union.

That the United States would take *some* action after July 24 was almost a certainty. At the very time of Nomura's meeting on July 24 with Roosevelt, Stark, and Welles, the Japanese Army was moving into southern Indochina in force. On July 25, against the unrelenting advice of Stark and Turner, Roosevelt decided to "freeze" (require a license for all business transactions) all Japanese assets in the United States. This of course included a complete embargo on petroleum, which had been so assiduously avoided in the past. The embargo of oil and associated actions were the warning to Japan to desist from further aggression and to consider seriously her future moves.

Stark and Marshall, in a joint dispatch on July 25 to their major subordinate commanders in Panama, Hawaii, the Philippines, Asiatic, and Atlantic Fleets, warned that the United States would impose economic sanctions on Japan on July 26 at 1400 Greenwich civil time. The United States did not intend to seize Japanese merchant shipping in American ports nor order American shipping "to depart from or not enter ports controlled by Japan." Stark and Marshall did "not anticipate immediate hostile reactions by Japan through the use of military means" but the commanders were furnished information on the embargo so that they might "take appropriate precautionary measures against possible eventualities."[8]

The next day, July 26, 1941, was probably the most significant day in Japanese-American relations prior to the Pearl Harbor attack, because all ensuing conversations revolved about modifying the consequences of the decisions made that day. On July 26, Roosevelt issued the Executive Order implementing his decision to freeze the Japanese finances in the United States. In rapid order Britain, the Dominions, Burma, and the Netherlands followed suit with similar freezing orders. Additionally, a new Army command was announced on July 26— the United States Army Forces in the Far East under Lieutenant General Douglas MacArthur. For months MacArthur, who had been military adviser to the Commonwealth Governor of the Philippines since his retirement in 1935, had been corresponding secretly with Secretary of the Army Stimson, Roosevelt, and Marshall. His recall to active duty, the creation of a new Army command, and the calling to active training duty of the Philippine Army caught most of the Army and all the Navy war planners in Washington by surprise. Shortly after the July 26 announcements, the Japanese government was informed that the Panama Canal would be closed indefinitely for repairs.

During the same week new emphasis was given to the appointment of Brigadier General John Magruder, former military attache to China, as a special military adviser to Chiang Kai-shek. By early August his official status had been defined by the War and State Departments and he began his role of helping the Chinese government obtain and use effectively American lend-lease material. At the same time, and again having to do with China, additional encouragement was given to pilots and ground crews in the United States Army,

Navy, and Marine aviation units to leave military service and join General Claire Chennault's Flying Tigers as civilians fighting for China against Japan. An unpublicized Executive Order of April 15, 1941 permitted such moves. By late September 1941, 100 American pilots and 180 ground crewmen were flying and maintaining the 100 P-40 fighter aircraft provided China through Lend-Lease.

An interesting coincidence to the July 26 events in Washington originated in Kimmel's letter of the same date to Stark. He commenced with another plea to be kept advised of Navy Department policies and decisions and "the changes in policies and decisions to meet changes in the international situation." He cited as an example that since the German attack on the Soviet Union he had

> ...received no official information as to the U.S. attitude towards Russian participation in the war, particularly as to the degree of cooperation, if any, in the Pacific, between the U.S. and Russia if and when we become active participants. Present plans do not include Russia and do not provide for coordinated action, joint use of bases, joint communication systems and the like. The new situation opens up possibilities for us which should be fully explored and full advantage taken of any opportunities for mutual support.[9]

Kimmel then asked Stark a number of questions as to what British and American reactions would be under various circumstances if Japan attacked the Soviet Union. In an analysis of the Far Eastern situation, which paralleled the thinking of Stark, Marshall, and Turner, Kimmel wrote:

> Depending upon the progress of hostilities, the Russian situation appears to offer an opportunity for the strengthening of our Far Eastern defenses, particularly Guam and the Philippines. Certainly, no matter how the fighting goes, Japan's attention will be partially diverted from the China and Southern adventures by either
> 1. diversion of forces for attack on Russia or
> 2. necessity for providing for Russian attack on her.
> It is conceivable that the greater the German success on the Eastern front, the more Russia will be pushed toward Asia, with consequent increased danger to Japan's "New Order" for that area. In my opinion we should push our development of Guam and accelerate our bolstering of the Philippines. The Russo-Axis war may give us more time.[10]

Thereafter followed four pages of priority items which Kimmel considered important enough to require immediate attention in preparation for a Pacific war. First on his list were the light converted destroyer transports taken from his command for the earlier planned Azores invasion in the Atlantic.

> These vessels were originally conceived and developed for a *Pacific* campaign. They are especially suitable for use in attacks on atolls and may be the only means of readily attacking those positions. While by no means discounting their usefulness in the Atlantic, the need for them in the Pacific is paramount. If at all possible, they should be returned to this ocean *at once*.[11] (Emphasis Kimmel's.)

In addition Kimmel listed increasing requirements for ammunition, aviation support, training, and base development.

The freezing order of July 26 in its official language did not indicate a complete embargo, although the British and American press interpreted it to mean so. The Dutch, who were in the most precarious position and the leading condidate for further Japanese aggression, tried to find out in Washington on July 27 and again on July 29, without success, what the United States would do if the Indies were attacked by Japan. Meanwhile in negotiations with Japan, the Netherlands East Indies government on July 28 announced the requirement for special permits for all exports, cash on all transactions, and no further exports of tin and rubber. In Washington it was decided to leave the door open for some trade at the 1935–36 level with appropriate licensing. Cotton and food could still be sold to Japan. Since excuses were always to be found not to do so, licenses were never granted and the embargo in fact was complete.

On July 25, the same day Roosevelt decided to impose economic sanctions on Japan, Stark wrote Kimmel a short note about an item he had forgotten in the previous day's letter: the possibility that Kimmel might be called upon "to send a carrier load of planes to one of the Asiatic Russian ports." Stark did not know for sure if it would actually happen, but since Roosevelt had told him to be prepared for it, he wanted to alert Kimmel to the possibility.[12]

Kimmel's answer on July 30 was totally opposed to such an idea. He reiterated his own deficiencies in aircraft and his opposition to using one of his three carriers as a transport. He then reminded Stark that the "most logical method of effecting delivery" was to fly the aircraft via Alaska and Eastern Siberian airfields. He reasoned that if the planes were sent to Asiatic Russian ports Japan would surely find out about the operation and that it would be "tantamount to initiation of a Japanese-American War." Kimmel felt the minimum escort and covering force for a carrier transport was the entire Pacific Fleet and if Japanese air or naval combatant forces were encountered, they should be attacked at once "rather than wait for them to gain an initial advantage through destroying any part of [his] own fighting strength." His final salvo on the idea was:

> ...If for reasons of political expediency, it has been determined to force Japan to fire the first shot, let us choose a method that will be more advantageous to ourselves. Certainly an operation such as that proposed is far less likely to bluff Japan into acquiescence or inactivity than it is to disturb her to the point of hostile use of bombs, torpedoes and guns.[13]

Also on July 30, the other fleet commander in the Pacific, Hart, was reviewing the Far Eastern situation for Stark. He forecast that Japan would move into Thailand since the occupation of Indochina had "been so quick and easy." Japanese occupancy of the harbors and waters around Singapore made "things look considerably different" there "from a naval standpoint." Hart had just received from Admiral Layton, Royal Navy, at Singapore, a tentative plan for joint naval defensive operations against Japan. Layton had asked for further information on Hart's Asiatic Fleet, and for comments and agreements on the tentative plan. Hart provided the requested information, but he could not agree to the plan. The reasons he gave Layton were that he had been informed unofficially that the Navy Department had disapproved the *ADB Plan* and that the disapproval was due to "the failure to take proper measures to deny the 'Malaya Barrier'...." Hart told Layton that *ADB Plans* would have a chance of working if the British "did not allocate so many ships to dispersed duties over the Indian Ocean, Australian and New Zealand waters."[14]

Hart's comments on recent changes in the Philippines were at once colorful, very personal, and parochial:

> People in these islands are all agog about MacArthur's assumption of command and, although everything is serene on the surface, there is considerable underneath-the-surface seething, in Army circles. But I do not see that this change is going to make much of any difference in *Naval* affairs, on this Station. I do rather expect that, as soon as my friend Douglas gets to it, he will raise the point that we should use all of my forces primarily in defense of Luzon; such is in line with the thesis under which he has talked and acted for some time, and he *may* be consistent! I apprehend no difficulty of our own, in handling any situation incident to this change in Army command, because I doubt that my old friend Douglas will combat me very much, for some time at least. I am hopeful about the effect of his taking over in *one* respect at

least;—That he will have the guts and sufficient draft of water to put the local U.S. Army air service on the reservation, and buck them up. From all I can learn about those boys, things are not as they should be. They have a fair equipment of planes, but when it comes to their use in war, there is a great deal to be done.[15]

American announcements on July 26 definitely did shock the Japanese leaders. Nomura, who had tried his very best to forestall the drastic American reactions, had failed. He was not a professional diplomat and he acknowledged his shortcomings once again to Admiral Toyoda, the foreign minister, on August 4.

I deeply fear lest I should make a miscalculation at this moment, and besides, there is a limit to my ability...I am unable to perceive the delicate shades of the policy of the Government, and am quite at a loss what to do.[16]

Nomura asked for a senior member of the diplomatic staff, specifically Soburo Kurusu, to assist him. Kurusu, who had married his American secretary and who was completely fluent in English with the extra qualification of having had earlier duty in Washington, would not arrive until mid-November.

In Tokyo, joint conferences of the Cabinet and the military leaders took place on July 29 and 30 and on August 2 and 4 to decide what to do relative to the United States. A compromise proposal to present was finally hammered out on August 4. Roosevelt's neutralization proposal for Indochina was summarily rejected. The Japanese Army, lead by General Hideki Tojo, minister of war, was adamant toward any suggestion that its freedom of action be limited. The rabid elements of the Army and Navy wanted immediate war with the United States. Admiral Osami Nagano, chief of naval general staff, was opposed not only to war at any time, but also to Japan's continuing with the Tripartite Pact association, which he perceived as the major stumbling block in reaching an understanding with the United States. Although other admirals supported him, Nagano's views were clearly in the minority. Japanese naval officers were most concerned about oil reserves, which they estimated at less than a two-year supply. Likewise, they were concerned about the vulnerability of lines of communications if Japan attacked the Netherlands East Indies without first eliminating the potential threat from Singapore, the Philippine Islands, and even Hawaii. Should Japan succeed in neutralizing these threats, it was still highly probable that the Dutch would destroy their oil wells and it could take upwards of eighteen months to two years to get them operational again. To the Japanese naval planners it was a closely calculated risk. Prince Konoye, the prime minister, threatened to resign if the military hierarchy could not reach agreement. The Japanese Army's position prevailed and the split between the two services continued behind the scenes until the final decision, in October, to carry out the attack against Britain and the United States.

The proposal agreed upon in the August 4 joint conference "was designed to be the key to reopening the Japanese-American conversations" which Hull had broken off on July 23. Konoye listed the gist of the proposals in his memoirs as follows:

1. Japan has no intention of sending troops further than French Indo-China, and will withdraw them from French Indo-China after the settlement of the China Incident.
2. Japan will guarantee the neutrality of the Philippines.
3. America will remove her armaments in the Southwest Pacific.
4. America will cooperate in Japan's obtaining resources in the Netherlands East Indies.
5. America will act as intermediary in the direct negotiations between Japan and China, and will recognize Japan's special position in French Indo-China, even after the withdrawal of troops.[17]

Instructions were sent with the proposal to Nomura on August 5. The race with time had begun. For Japan each day of delay in breaking out of the economic vise meant a fractionally weaker position. Oil was used daily without hope of its being replaced. Each day lessened the chances of a military victory against the United States, Britain, and the Netherlands East Indies, whose representatives were known to be planning in Singapore. (Japanese intelligence apparently did not learn of the repeated failures to reach an agreement in the American-Dutch-British conversations.) The two obvious courses of action open to Japan were either negotiations to reach a rapprochement with the United States or an early war against the United States and her allies. For the United States each day of delay allowed an incremental increase in defensive strength in the Far East, making the chances of a Japanese victory all the more unlikely.

Konoye was torn between the prospects of waging a war, the outcome of which was in question, and the success of reaching an agreement based on a proposal sent to Nomura on August 5. Friendly relations with the United States would buy time—time to delay a hopeless war, to build up synthetic oil supplies, and perhaps to find a basis to convince the United States to accept a new role for Japan in the western Pacific. Without waiting for an answer to the August 4 proposal, he tried a new tack, a personal meeting with Roosevelt. He presented his new plan to the war and navy ministers on the evening of August 4. Basically, Konoye was not sure that Germany could win against Britain, the United States, and the Soviet Union, He was apparently willing to break the Tripartite Pact for American concessions to a "Greater East Asia Co-Prosperity Sphere." The Japanese Navy agreed at once and was optimistic for the outcome. Tojo answered in writing so that there would be no mistake about the army's position. Tojo thought such a meeting would weaken the diplomatic relations of Japan since those relations were based on the Tripartite Pact, would cause considerable "domestic stir" and that the meeting would most probably fail. However, if Konoye insisted and did try to convince Roosevelt to see things in Japan's favor and then failed, he was not to resign but "to assume leadership in the war against America."[18]

After conferring and receiving agreement from the emperor, Konoye sent Nomura the necessary instructions on August 7 to arrange the meeting with Roosevelt. The timing could not have been worse for the Japanese diplomats. Nomura saw Hull on August 8. On that day Hull had the United States' response to the first August 4 proposal. He told Nomura that Japan had not responded to the United States' offer to neutralize Indochina and that he held out no hope for an agreement. Discussions with Roosevelt about meeting with Konoye were also out of the question for the time being because Roosevelt had left Washington for a meeting with Churchill.

Since early in 1941 Roosevelt had wanted a personal meeting with Churchill. The German occupation with the fighting in the Soviet Union took enough pressure off Britain to allow Churchill to make the trip across the Atlantic. Roosevelt, in the heavy cruiser *Augusta,* and Churchill in the new battleship *Prince of Wales,* met off Argentia, Newfoundland, on August 9 where they discussed overall strategy, Japanese aggression, and lend-lease procurement problems. Each brought with him senior military officers to discuss informally their mutual problems. In the American party were Admirals Stark, Marshall, King, and Turner, General Henry H. Arnold, U.S. Army Air Corps, Commander Forrest Sherman, and Lieutenant Colonel Charles W. Bundy, U.S. Army. The latter two officers were from their respective service War Plans Divisions. The British group included five senior officers from the Admiralty, two from their War Office, and one from the Ministry of Air.

Unlike the harmony between Roosevelt and Churchill which produced an agreement that Roosevelt would give a strong warning to

Japan immediately upon his return to Washington, the military agreements were few and far between. The Americans did agree to take on
escort duty of all merchant shipping as far as Iceland. This allowed
the Royal Navy to move fifty escort ships from the western Atlantic to
other areas where they were sorely needed. Admiralty representatives
tried again as in the *ABC-1* conversations to get an American commitment relative to Singapore. Stark, speaking for the United States delegation, rejected the idea and also a reworked version of the already
vetoed *ADB-1 Plan* which emanated from Singapore. Likewise, the
United States Army did not look with favor on the British planners
recommending the use of American troops for duty in North Afrca.

Welles flew back from Argentia bearing the strongly worded
warning agreed upon with Churchill. Hull, who was to arrange a
meeting between Roosevelt and Nomura upon the former's return,
toned down the warning:

> ... the United States Government will be forced to take immediately
> any and all steps of whatsoever character it deems necessary in its own
> security notwithstanding the possibility that such further steps on its
> part may result in conflict between the two countries.[19]

to the less threatening:

> ... the Government of the United States will be compelled to take
> immediately any and all steps which it may deem necessary toward
> safeguarding the legitimate rights and interests of the United States
> and American nationals and toward insuring the safety and security of
> the United States.[20]

Roosevelt, upon his return to Washington, approved Hull's
changes and agreed with him to make an attempt to break the impasse
with Japan by offering to reinstitute the suspended conversations. In
a meeting with Nomura the same day the President told him that the
United States' opposition to Japan's present course was well-known.
It was up to Japan to change, if the two countries were to have
friendly relations. Nomura then presented Konoye's proposal to meet
with Roosevelt mid-way between the two countries to "sit down and
talk out ... the difficulties in a peaceful spirit." Without responding
directly to the proposal Roosevelt gave the Hull version of the warning message. Allowing a few minutes for the warning to register,
Roosevelt followed up with Hull's second message, which ended with
the conditions:

> In case the Japanese Government feels that Japan desires and is in
> position to suspend its expansionist activities, to readjust its position,

and to embark upon a peaceful program for the Pacific along the lines of the program and principles to which the United States is committed, the Government of the United States would be prepared to consider resumption of the informal exploratory conversations ... it would be helpful if the Japanese Government would be so good as to furnish a clearer statement than has yet been furnished as to its present attitude and plans, just as this Government has repeatedly outlined to the Japanese Government its attitude and plans.[21]

Nomura reported that Roosevelt was in high spirits throughout the conference and that it was he who suggested a meeting in mid-October in Juneau, Alaska.[22] In Tokyo at the very same time, Admiral Toyoda spent two and a half hours defending Japan's course of action to Grew, pleading for the economic strangulation to be lifted, and urging the meeting between Roosevelt and Konoye. Grew thought the foreign minister was sincere and, since the Emperor also had approved the meeting, Grew thought there was hope that much good would come from it.

While the diplomats in Tokyo and Washington weighed the prospects of the proposed Konoye-Roosevelt meeting, decisions in August affected United States military forces and future posture throughout the Far East. There was a noticeable change in policy relative to the Philippines after MacArthur's command had been formed. Requests which had been made earlier by General Grunert of the Philippine Department, had either been ignored or answered with a token amount. For example, in the winter of 1940–1941 Grunert requested 500 Reserve officers to mobilize and train ten Philippine divisions, but received only 75. MacArthur was assured in his first week of duty that he would receive the remaining 425 Reserves and "specialists, individuals and organizations required" by him. A few days later Marshall promised to send twenty-five 75-mm guns in September, another twenty-five in October, antiaircraft artillery, a company of tanks, and ammunition. In mid-August Marshall's promise had increased to fifty-four tanks. Also in August the decision was made to provide as a deterrent force as many B-17 long-range bombers as could be spared. The race was clearly on in the Philippine Islands to reinforce as quickly as possible in order "to deter or minimize Japanese aggression."[23]

In China a much different situation was developing in August 1941 relative to the United States Marines there. Unlike the optimistic buildup in the Philippines, in China there was an ominous inevitability of defeat or retreat. On August 16, Ambassador Gauss in Chungking telegraphed Hull that he did not believe U.S. Marines should be withdrawn from China "unless and until it becomes evident that relations with Japan have deteriorated to the point where a rupture appears inevitable." If the Marines were to be withdrawn, Gauss recommended that provisions be made to remove all American citizens who did not want to remain at their own risk. He did not want to see the United States "scuttle prematurely," and he admitted that in his isolation he was not in a position to judge when the proper time was to withdraw. When the Marines were withdrawn Gauss thought the situation in Shanghai would "deteriorate rapidly whether or not hostilities between the United States and Japan ensue, and the position of Americans in China generally will be affected."[24]

Admiral Glassford, Commander, Yangtze River Patrol, and Colonel Samuel L. Howard, Commander, Fourth Marines, recommended—with the concurrence of Consul General Lockhart in Shanghai and Admiral Hart in Manila—that the U.S. Marines be withdrawn, this affected 162 at Peiping, 16 at Chinwangtao, 111 at Tientsin, and approximately 900 at Shanghai. Glassford based his recommendation for withdrawal on his conviction that "despite Japanese Navy opposition, the Japanese Army will not long be restrained from taking over the International Settlement," that because of general deterioration in the local situation, increasing demands were being made on the Fourth Marines to support the International Settlement police, which increased all the more the chances of a confrontation with the Japanese army.[25] Glassford was also concerned about the disposition of the five remaining river gunboats specially built for Yangtze duty and not structurally suitable for voyages at sea. *Tutuila,* already at Chungking, was later turned over to the Chinese through lend-lease; the *Luzon* and *Oahu* managed to sail to Manila in November; the *Wake* acted as a radio relay station in Shanghai until she was captured on December 8; the *Monocacy* was scuttled in the mouth of the Yangtze.

On August 28, Hart wrote a long letter to Stark spelling out his reasons for recommending the withdrawal of Marines and gunboats. He could see no "single military advantage" in keeping them in China, because "in the event of war with Japan they would be quickly contained and destroyed, probably without being able to inflict even a comparable loss on the enemy." After conceding that he might have overlooked a reason against withdrawing which would constitute a "serious tactical error in the realm of international politics and diplomacy," Hart analyzed four factors relative to withdrawal:

1. Protection of lives and property of United States nationals.

Hart stressed that United States forces gave protecion against mob action, banditry, and unorganized lawless violence, not against *organized* armed forces of a recognized authority. With concentration of Japanese troops in the cities, the threat of unorganized lawlessness was gone.

2. Loss of national prestige. Hart wrote:

> It is only in the event that we wish to create the fiction of our determi-
> nation to resist Japanese aggression, when in reality such determination
> does not exist, that any importance can be attached to the maintenance
> in China of our armed forces insofar as the question of National prestige
> is concerned ... The time may come, however, when it is no longer
> debatable, when we have to withdraw or fight, and when to withdraw
> would be a national disgrace; and we may expect that time to come
> when we are least able to act as we should like.

3. Abandonment of United States businesses. Hart felt that the presence of United States forces was not keeping them from being "squeezed out."

4. Adverse effect on China. Hart considered this factor to be the most important. He wrote:

> It is probable that the withdrawal of our armed forces from the oc-
> cupied territory, particularly from Shanghai, would at least temporarily,
> have an adverse effect on the morale of those Chinese in that city who
> are still loyal to the Chungking regime and whose financial and indus-
> trial activities may be contributing substantially to the economic strength
> of free China ... It is precisely for this reason that he has any hesitation
> in recommending an immediate withdrawal.[26]

The British withdrawal was considered by China as an act of deser-
tion, according to Hart, and he did not want the United States to be
so accused. If it became apparent that the withdrawal would cause a
reaction in China, Japan, or the United States which the diplomats
wanted to avoid, then perhaps a token force might be acceptable. In
that event Hart recommended that the gunboats *Luzon* and *Oahu* be
withdrawn, that the Marines at Tientsin and Chinwangtao be withdrawn and the Fourth Marines in Shanghai be reduced to two companies. Hart would not get approval to carry out his recommendations
until November.

On August 22, Stark finally answered Kimmel's letter of July 26
asking for information on possible courses of action relative to threatened Japanese attacks on the Russian maritime provinces. Stark ad-

mitted that not only had no decision been made at the Argentia meeting, but that he could not find out either in Washington or from London what Britain would do if Japan attacked the Soviet Union. Such an attack would not be unwelcomed, since it would relieve "the pressure now being exerted by Japan to the southward." If Britain declared war on Japan, but the United States did not, Stark supposed that the United States "would follow a course of action similar to the one we are now pursuing in the Atlantic as a neutral."

Again he promised Kimmel that the small high-speed transports needed by the Marines would be returned to the Pacific Fleet at the earliest possible opportunity. Kimmel, in his late July letter, had asked for an additional 20,000 men. Stark said he just did not have them to send and explained why. The Navy needed to recruit 12,000 men per month to meet service requirements projected to June 30, 1942. The current enlistment rate—only 9,300 per month—would leave a shortage by the following June of 32,000 men, well over the number Kimmel had requested. Stark was hopeful, however, that a new appropriation of $1,000,000 to be spent on recruiting advertisements would pay off.[27] Less than a week later, Stark wrote Hart and Kimmel that the advertising campaign was starting to bear fruit. The Navy had 262,000 men in August with an expected 10,000 enlistments anticipated the following month. Concentration in the recruiting drive was in "the South and Middle West farm belt."[28]

August 28 was one of those days when fate pulled the tangled strands of history into a Gordian knot. That day Nomura presented two messages from Konoye to Roosevelt. In the first message Konoye asked for a meeting as soon as possible. Roosevelt called the invitation a "splendid message" and talked enthusiastically of a three-day interview. The second message contained Japan's statement of intentions: that troops would be withdrawn from Indochina as soon as the China Incident was settled or a just peace was established in East Asia; that Japan would take no action against Russia so long as Russia observed the neutrality pact and did "not menace Japan or Manchukuo"; and that Japan had no intentions of using "without provocation" military force against any neighboring country.[29]

If Roosevelt was the eager and willing partner-to-be in the meeting with Konoye, then Hull was his antithesis. He wanted no part of a second Munich and set out to prevent the meeting. He summoned Nomura to his apartment the evening after the ambassador had talked with Roosevelt and informed him "that it was desirable to reach an agreement in principle on major questions prior to the meeting" between the heads of state.[30] Hull was going to call the tunes before the dance started.

On the morning of August 28, Stark had a long talk with Mr. Juiji Kasai, member of the Japanese Parliament. He wrote of that meeting and other events later in the day to both Hart and Kimmel. He told Hart he had been very frank with Kasai, as he had with Nomura in the past. He found that neither had any "stomach for the Tri-partite Agreement," and that Nomura had a sincere desire that the two "countries solve their problems amicably." At this stage Stark still had "some hopes, or to put it in another way, [had] not given up hope that peace in the Pacific may be maintained." He wished that hope was not sustained by such a slender thread.[31] Because he considered that thread so slender, he told his Japanese acquaintances that another move, "such as one into Thailand, would go a long way towards destroying before the American public what good-will still remained."[32]

Earlier in the year Hart had asked that the United States and the Netherlands East Indies make the Sulu Sea a closed area by declaring it to be internal water territory. The Sulu Sea lay between the southwestern Philippine Islands and Borneo; the Japanese fleet would most probably transit it in attacking the Indies. Had Hart's request been carried through, countries would have had to ask for special permission to move their ships through the territorial waters. Stark had opposed the idea, and on August 28 he could justify his decision with a new situation. Oil was being sent from the United States to the Soviet Union through the port of Vladivostok on the western side of the Sea of Japan. Regardless of how tankers approached the maritime provinces and the Sea of Japan, they had to pass close to the Japanese home islands. Had the United States "closed" the Sulu Sea, Japan would have had a precedent to close the waters adjacent to her islands. That the Soviet Union was getting oil while Japan got no oil and that tankers were passing so closely brought a protest to the United States from the Japanese government. Hull pointed out that Japan had a neutrality pact with the Soviet Union and that the oil was to enable the Russians to fight Germany.

In yet another message from Stark on August 28 a new command, the Southeast Pacific Force, was ordered instituted, to be under strategic direction of the Chief of Naval Operations. The force, to consist of two 7,500-ton light cruisers, was given the mission to destroy surface raiders which attacked or threatened United States flag shipping. They were to "interpret an approach of surface raiders within the

Pacific sector of the Panama naval coastal frontier or the Pacific Southeast sub-area as a threat to United States shipping." The western boundary of the area of operations was 100° West longitude. Shoot-on-sight orders, which unofficially were in effect in the Atlantic, had arrived in the Pacific—but under Stark's authority, not Kimmel's.

When Roosevelt met with Nomura on September 3, he was polite and interested but much less enthusiastic than on August 17 or 28 when the meeting with Konoye was first discussed. He told Nomura that before he could meet with Konoye, Japan would have to agree to the Four Principles which Hull had presented to Nomura the previous April and which to date the Japanese government had avoided addressing directly.

Meantime in Tokyo, joint conferences split the Japanese Army and Navy, and the Army and Konoye, even further apart than before. Tojo wanted immediate preparation for war. Nagano and Konoye wanter no war. Nagano equivocated and said that the Japanese Navy would do whatever the premier decided. By compromise between the cabinet and the high military command a new agreement was reached. Preparation for war would commence immediately, while negotiations were to continue with a time restraint. Konoye was given until early October to obtain an agreement with the United States by diplomacy. In October a decision whether or not to make war on the United States, Britain, and the Netherlands East Indies would be made. The pressure was really on Konoye and Nomura to reach a rapprochement before the war machine was set in such furious motion it could not be stopped.

For the next month, while the military leaders of Japan and the United States were busily preparing for war, the diplomats in Tokyo and Washington parried words with little, if any, progress. Basically, the Japanese offers were conditioned to take effect after peace with China, while the concessions she requested of the United States—economic cooperation, cessation of aid to China, suspension of the defensive buildup in the Pacific—were to take place immediately after the United States signed the accord. Konoye had his problems trying to satisfy his own countrymen and the American diplomats. An imperial conference on September 6 had determined the point beyond which negotiations could not go further, and it was apparent that the two countries were heading for a showdown. Konoye wrote in his memoirs:

> By this time we were largely aware of the difficulties confronting the negotiations, as well as the intention of the United States. In other words, when it came to fundamentals, the difficulty was the "Four Prin-

ciples," and when it came to more concrete obstacles, we were faced with the problems of the stationing of troops in China, the establishment of a principle of equal economic opportunity, and the problem of the Tripartite Pact.[33]

Even though Konoye had admitted to Grew that the Four Principles were "splendid as principles," he still had to deal with "certain elements in the Army and the Foreign Ministries," which were powerful and undeniably opposed to agreeing to the principles. Therefore, "since it was evident that to reject the 'Four Principles' would be to doom the American-Japanese negotiations to failure, [he] was hard put to know how to handle this problem."[34]

Hull wanted positive acts, not words, on the part of the Japanese government to show their intent for peace. Japan wanted some concessions from the United States in the form of easing the economic noose. Neither would budge. Both waited for the other to do something first. For Japan the options were becoming fewer and fewer to the point that it was either fight or back down on a number of fronts. Finally, it was Japan which acted—but not until the first week in December.

In the Atlantic in September, the United States Navy extended its area and degree of responsibility further eastward. On August 25, King ordered Atlantic Fleet forces to destroy all surface raiders which attacked shipping along sea lanes between North America and Iceland or which came close enough to threaten such shipping. On September 3, the area of protective defense was extended further eastward to 10° West longitude. Using a German submarine attack on the USS *Greer* as an excuse, Roosevelt, in a speech to the nation on September 11, ordered the U.S. Navy to attack all "German and Italian vessels of war" which entered the defense area of the United States. That area, which Stark called "our ocean" in a letter to Hart, extended to 10° West and 65° North, a point 100 miles due east of Iceland.[35]

The "shoot-on-sight" orders applied only to the Atlantic and the Pacific zone next to South America as far as 100° West longitude. Kimmel, who had heard Roosevelt's speech and who had a copy of King's orders directing him to take such positive action against German and Italian combatants, wrote to Stark inquiring what the shooting policy would be in the Pacific. So far, his orders to ships escorting convoys to the Far East were to protect the convoys from interference and "to avoid the use of force if possible, but to use it if necessary." He asked specifically if he should not change that order to direct attack on German and Italian surface raiders so as to conform to the Atlantic and sub-area in the Pacific. Then followed:

> Along the same lines, but more specifically related to the Japanese situation, is what to do about submarine contacts off Pearl Harbor and the vicinity. As you know, our present orders are to trail all contacts, but not to bomb unless you are in the defensive sea area. Should we now bomb contacts, without waiting to be attacked?

Kimmel could also see that with renewed emphasis on Atlantic operations his forces in the Pacific might be further weakened at a time when he thought they should be strengthened to meet the increased threat of new battleships, cruisers, and carriers being built by Japan. Kimmel asked Stark to let him have the new battleships *North Carolina* and *Washington* after they finished their shakedown cruise, since "that would have a tremendous effect on Japan and would remove any impression that *all* our thoughts are on the Atlantic."[36] (Emphasis Kimmel's.) As with his previous requests, this would also be in vain.

At his Asiatic Fleet headquarters in Manila, on September 17, Hart proposed a change concerning the deployment of his forces in the event of hostilities with Japan. Such eventualities had been dealt with in one *Orange Plan* after another since the late 1920s. Until the outbreak of war in Europe in 1939, war plans called for the Asiatic Fleet to withdraw from the China Station into the Indian Ocean and, while the main battle fleet made its westward advance, to operate against Japanese shipping. In the winter of 1940–1941, as plans evolved to defend the Malay Barrier, the Asiatic Fleet was assigned different wartime missions as spelled out in *War Plan 44*. This plan, originating in the CNO's War Plans Division, earmarked cruisers and destroyers to augment the Asiatic Fleet by a factor of three, so that with British and Dutch forces they might hold the Malay Barrier against a Japanese advance. In the spring of 1941 with emphasis concentrated in the Atlantic, the decision was made in Stark's office that cruisers and destroyers would not be sent out to the Asiatic Fleet. Reinforcement would be made by Britain, but the plan to hold the Malay Barrier still pertained. Hart proposed that "the initial deployment of the cruisers, two-thirds of the destroyers and all the large auxiliaries except submarine tenders be well to the southwest." His proposal was approved on September 25.[37]

On September 23, Stark answered Kimmel's letter of September 12 in which he requested instructions on "shooting orders" to his fleet: his present orders to ships escorting convoys to the Far East were still proper. Stark answered the question concerning attacking Japanese submarines in the vicinity of Pearl Harbor by quoting *Navy Regulations* relative to defending oneself using "sound judgment of responsible officers," and "with all possible care and forebearance."

With such an answer Kimmel should have been able to see that the Navy in the Atlantic operated under different rules than it did in the Pacific. Relative to the request for more support, Stark said the *North Carolina* and *Washington* could not be ready until March, 1942, and he had not made up his mind where they were to go but favored the Atlantic. That seemed logical to Stark, since the British had promised that by the first of the year they would have in East Indian waters: seventeen light and heavy cruisers, one carrier, four battleships, and one or two modern capital ships. These, plus the Dutch units and the U.S. Asiatic Fleet, and Army Air Corps B-17's, "should make Japan think twice before taking action, if she has taken no action by that time."[38]

Stark held up his letter to Kimmel, and the copy to Hart, because Hull had told him that the conversations with Nomura had reached an impasse. As Stark saw it at the time there was no chance at reaching an agreement unless there was an agreement on China and Japan "and just now that seems remote. Whether or not their inability to come to any sort of an understanding just now *is*—or *is not*—a good thing—(he) hesitated to say."[39] (Emphasis Stark's.)

Six days later, on September 29, Stark added a postscript to his letter:

> Admiral Nomura came in to see me this morning. We talked for about an hour. He usually comes in when he begins to feel near the end of his rope; there is not much to spare at the end now. I have helped before but whether I can this time or not I do not know. Conversations without results cannot last forever. If they fall through, and it looks like they might, the situation could only grow more tense. I have again talked to Mr. Hull and I think he will make one more try. He keeps me pretty fully informed and if there is anything of moment I will, of course, hasten to let you know.[40]

Although he wanted to concentrate his forces in the Atlantic, Stark was still as knowledgeable as anyone in Washington on Japanese-American affairs.

Just the day before, Stark had written to Hart: "so far as the Atlantic is concerned, we are all but, if not actually, in it." Relative to the Far East, Stark reported that Hull had not "given up hope of a satisfactory settlement," Nomura was "working hard on his home government" and while it looked to Stark like a deadlock, as long as there were negotiations, there was hope.[41]

CHAPTER 11

Final U.S. Withdrawal from China

In his September 22 letter to Hart, Stark reviewed the question of pulling U.S. Marines out of China. Almost everyone involved with the proposal had agreed with Hart's reasoned weighing of the pros and cons. Stark acknowledged the "soundness" of all of Hart's arguments and admitted that the Commandant, United States Marine Corps, General Thomas Holcomb, agreed with Hart. However, Stark and his staff felt a complete withdrawal of forces would create a bad reaction in China, Japan, and the United States. Stark did agree with the Marine staff that leaving a token force would be inviting trouble and it would be of "little support to the local police." But there was more than police action in the plot. Stark's position was interesting and prophetic.

> So far as China is concerned, we have "our foot in the door"—the door that once was "open", and if I had the say to, it would remain there until I was ready to withdraw it—or until the door opened to such a point that I could gracefully withdraw if and when I saw fit. I agree that proper timing may be extremely difficult. You may be right that they should come out now. I hope I am right in holding on.[1]

Stark sent a copy of a memorandum received from Marshall dated September 12 to both Hart and Kimmel to show them the degree and nature of the Army buildup and plans for the Philippines.

August 26: There sailed from San Francisco part of a regiment of anti-aircraft troops and some reserve supplies.

September 8: There sailed from San Francisco the remainder of the antiaircraft regiment, a tank battalion of 50 tanks, 50 of the latest pursuit planes, and the personnel to man them, which brings the modern pursuit planes in the Philippines up to 80.

September 18: 50 self-propelled mounts for 75 cannon to be shipped from San Francisco, and 50 more tanks.

Today The squadron of nine Flying Fortresses landed in Manila after successfully flying the route Midway, Wake, New Britain, Dutch East Indies.

September 30: Two squadrons (26 planes) of Flying Fortresses will leave San Francisco for Hawaii enroute to the Philippines.

October: A reserve of pursuit planes will have been in process of shipment, about 32 in October, rising to a total of 130 by December.

November: Probably a reserve of six to nine of the super Flying Fortresses, B-24 type planes will be transferred to Manila. These planes will have an operating radius of 1,500 miles, with a load of 14,000 pounds, which means that they can reach Osaka with a full load and Tokyo with a partial load. They have pressure cabins and can operate continuously 35,000 feet for bombing.

December: Another group of Flying Fortresses, some 35 planes, goes to Manila.
A group of dive bombers, some 54 planes, also goes.
A group of pursuit, some 130 planes, along with two additional squadrons to build up the previous pursuit group, will be dispatched.
A 50% reserve is being established for all these planes.[2]

Meanwhile the pressure on Konoye to come up with some progress with the United States was mounting. Through Nomura in Washington and Grew in Tokyo on September 23, 27, and 29, he urged a meeting with Roosevelt. On September 29, Nomura relayed the warning that if nothing came of the proposal for a meeting between the chiefs of the two governments, it was highly probable that Konoye would not be able to retain his position and that he would likely be replaced by a less moderate leader.

On the day of the Nomura warning, Turner in the CNO War Plans Division, offered Stark advice on how to assist in breaking the impasse. Obviously it would take some time for the Japanese Army to withdraw from China, if such agreement was reached, because of distances, numbers of troops, and lack of transportation. Additionally, Turner was concerned over pulling troops out "until a reasonably stable Chinese Government had been established." He suggested that the United States tentatively agree to a schedule of withdrawals, extending over a stated period of time and commencing with the withdrawal of troops from Indochina. Turner could even see why Japan insisted on retaining military control of North China, "at least for the time being." (Japan's excuse was to contain communism.) Before concessions could adequately be discussed between Stark and Hull or be proposed to Konoye, a further hardening of attitudes in Washington and Tokyo precluded any settlement.[3]

On October 2, Hull handed Nomura the United States response to Japan's proposal of September 6. The six-page document reviewed the exchanges between the two countries for the previous six months. Specifically, the Japanese government was told that their September 6 proposals were a "source of disappointment"; that while Japan appeared to accept the Four Principles, it was only with "qualifications and exceptions to the actual application of those principles"; and finally, that since Japan's intentions were still not clear, the United States requested a renewed consideration of her position on freedom of trade, stationing of troops in China, and the Tripartite Pact. The note was the death knell for the Konoye cabinet. Although Nomura was spurred to accomplish more with Hull, and in Tokyo Konoye and Toyoda did all they could through a sympathetic Grew, it was only a matter of time before the deadline drawn at the September 6 meeting would be invoked.

Yet in spite of the inevitability of war because of the impasse in negotiations, the Japanese Navy was still trying to avoid a showdown. In a position paper passed to Konoye on October 12, the Navy stated that it

> ... does not desire a rupture in the negotiations. Thus it wishes as much as possible to avoid war. But as far as the Navy is concerned it can not of itself bring this openly to the surface and say so. At today's conference the Navy Minister is expected to say that the decision for peace or war is entirely up to the Premier, so I beg you to keep this matter in your mind.[4]

In a joint conference later that day Admiral Oikawa, minister of the Navy, stated that either Japan should continue the negotiations to the bitter end or decide war "today." The Navy would "leave the decision entirely up to the Premier," but it favored negotiations. At this juncture the premier added: "If we were to say that we must determine on war or peace here, today, I myself would decide on continuing the negotiations." But Tojo said that Konoye was too hasty and then demanded of Admiral Toyoda if there were any chance of the negotiations succeeding. The answer to that was a qualified "no" as long as the Japanese Army maintained its rigid attitude toward the stationing of troops in China. Tojo had said: "The problem of the stationing of troops, in itself means the life of the Army, and we shall not be able to make any concessions at all." After four hours the conference broke up without having reached a decision. Two days later Tojo requested Konoye to resign, and on October 18 he became premier and home minister, while retaining his post as minister of war.[5]

As Japanese military and diplomatic leaders became more tense and frustrated over not making progress in the negotiations during the first two weeks in October, American naval officers were very much involved in discussions concerning Japan. In Manila, commencing October 5, Hart and MacArthur met with Magruder, Chiang Kai-shek's adviser, and Air Chief Marshall Sir Robert Brooke-Popham, British commander at Singapore. Although Japanese newspapers and the *New York Times* reported that the meeting was taking place, Hart took strong exception to Brooke-Popham's comment to the United Press upon his return to Singapore that he had conferred in Manila with Hart. Hart told Stark that he had discussed only briefly the use of PBY long-range patrol aircraft, that he did not like the "fanfare of publicity which accompanied the above visit ... which the British always seek to give to our talks with them in this area," and that it was "injudicious to provide Nipponese jingoists with ammunition for the aggravation of public opinion." Stark duly requested Hull to "invite attention of the British Embassy to the desirability of keeping such publicity to a minimum." Stark also informed Admiral Sir Charles James Colebrooke Little, Royal Navy, head of the Admiralty delegation in Washington, of Hart's views and that if he concurred, "it would be appreciated if appropriate action might be taken to handle publicity concerning our joint conferences in the Far East in accordance with ..." Hart's views.[6]

While Hart and his fellow commanders conferred on Far Eastern problems, the Cabinet in Washington debated the advisability of the President asking Congress to repeal the Neutrality Act of 1939. Hull, prior to testifying before the House Foreign Affairs Committee in favor of the repeal, asked Stark for his analysis of the "advantages and disadvantages of abolishing the combat zones around the British Isles and elsewhere ... [and] the disadvantages and advantages that would occur should Hitler declare war on the United States."[7]

Stark's memorandum of October 8 to Hull itemized the advantages of sending more shipping to Britain using American ships and crews, the increase in British morale, and the corresponding decrease in German morale. The advantages of a German declaration of war against the United States, as Stark saw it, were that

> ... the United States would be given a free hand in the operation of its armed forces; it would gain important belligerent rights over neutral shipping and commerce; and it would permit the Pacific and Asiatic Fleets to be employed for eradicating German raiders in the Pacific Ocean. ... It would also permit specific offensive plans to be made by the United States Army and Navy. It would tremendously enhance the war effort put forth by this country and we could plan well into the future for the defeat of Germany with some assurance which we cannot now do.[8]

The major disadvantage would be that Japan might come into the war as an active belligerent. The United States would then be fighting on two fronts, which was to be avoided. He added:

> It has long been my opinion that Germany cannot be defeated unless the United States is wholeheartedly in the war and makes a strong military and naval effort wherever strategy dictates. It would be very desirable to enter the war under circumstances in which Germany were the aggressor and in which case Japan might then be able to remain neutral. However, on the whole, it is my opinion that the United States should enter the war against Germany as soon as possible, even if hostilities with Japan must be accepted.[9]

The next day, October 9, Roosevelt asked Congress to repeal Section VI of the Neutrality Act which would then permit the arming of American merchant ships. It was better to ask for a small concession than risk not having the Neutrality Act repealed in toto. Hull testified on October 13, followed by Stimson and Knox who also had Stark's memorandum. The night before the vote in Congress, the destroyer *Kearny*, while assisting in an attack on a German submarine pack 400 miles from Iceland, was torpedoed with the loss of eleven men. The *Kearny* casualities impressed enough congressmen for the repeal of Section VI to be carried by a vote of 251–138—a margin much greater than previously anticipated.

From August 1941, when the decision was made to reinforce the Philippine Islands, until December 7, when the Japanese attacked American Pacific possessions, there was a race between Japan, preparing for offense, and the United States, preparing for defense. Key elements in the American scheme were the B-17 long-range bombers and troops. On October 3, Roosevelt authorized Stimson to deliver aircraft to any territory subject to the jurisdiction of the United States, to any

191

territory within the Western Hemisphere, to the Netherlands East Indies and Australia, and to construct the facilities needed for effecting such delivery. MacArthur's estimate of troop strength requirements for defense of the Philippines was 200,000. To move troops from the United States to augment the existing Army units already in place, planners wanted as many large troop transports as were available for Pacific duty. When the Navy, which had already taken two large Army transports to lift Marines to Iceland, wanted to convert the troop transports *West Point, Mount Vernon,* and *Wakefield* to aircraft carriers to supply Army planes and personnel to overseas bases, Army planners objected vehemently. The controversy came before the Joint Board on October 15 at which time the Army was told to go along with the Navy scheme. (Later events overtook the conversion plans and the three ships were never used as carriers.) The Army in the meantime planned to use eleven small transports to move more than 20,000 troops from San Francisco to the Philippines between November 21 and December 9.

The resignation of Konoye on October 16 was one of the few major Japanese actions of 1941 not known in advance through *Magic*. When the news reached Washington, Roosevelt spent the afternoon conferring with Hull, Stimson, Knox, Stark, Marshall, and Harry Hopkins. Later that night Stark sent a dispatch to the Atlantic, Pacific and Asiatic Fleet commanders, advising them of the Konoye resignation and that if a new cabinet was formed "it will probably be strongly nationalistic and anti-American." Stark also declared that "hostilities between Japan and Russia were a strong possibility" and an attack by Japan on the United States and Britain was "also a possibility."[10]

That same night Stark had his staff warn all U.S. merchant ships in the Pacific of the possibility of hostile action by Japan. Ships in Chinese waters, the China Sea, and the Dutch Indies were to proceed immediately to Manila. Those in the North Pacific westbound, unless bound for Vladivostok, were to proceed to Honolulu or the Philippines, whichever was closest. Ships bound for Honolulu, those in the North Pacific eastbound, those in the South Pacific and coastwise ships on the West Coast were told to continue their voyages, avoiding usual trade routes.[11] Unwittingly such instructions, by clearing U.S. shipping from the North Pacific, contributed to later undetected movements of the Japanese task force which attacked Pearl Harbor.

The next day Commander in Chief, Asiatic Fleet, and the Commandant of the Twelfth Naval District in San Francisco, were advised that effective immediately they were to route all shipping to and from the Far East, India, and East India through Torres Strait between Australia and New Guinea. Ships were to stay well to the southward of the Japanese mandated islands and to take maximum advantage of Dutch and Australian patrolled areas.[12]

On the same day, Stark told Kimmel to take all practicable precautions for the safety of the airfields at Wake and Midway, because of their importance as fueling stops for long-range Army bombers being ferried to the Philippines.[13]

A week later Stark directed that "until further orders all army and navy transpacific troop transports, ammunition ships and such others with sufficiently important cargo" would be escorted both ways between Manila and Honolulu. The Asiatic and Pacific Fleets were to coordinate the escort duty.[14]

Stark wrote Kimmel on October 17, the day after the first surge of message about the Konoye resignation. He modified the gravity of his message.

> Personally I do not believe the Japs are going to sail into us and the message I sent you merely stated the "possibility"; in fact I tempered the message handed to me considerably. Perhaps I am wrong, but I hope not. In any case after long pow-wows in the White House it was felt we should be on guard, at least until something indicated the trend.
>
> If I recall correctly I wrote you or Tommie Hart a forecast of the fall of the Japanese Cabinet a couple weeks ago after my long conference with Nomura.
>
> We shall continue to strive to maintain the status quo in the Pacific. How long it can be kept going I don't know, but the President and Mr. Hull are working on it.[15]

Stark also reported progress on three fronts: recruiting was on the increase, shipping showed a net gain in August for the first time due to "accelerated shipbuilding and better protection to convoys," and air strength was increasing in the Philippines.

With his October 17 letter Stark included a memorandum from Captain Roscoe Ernest Schuirmann, head of the Central Division, which had liaison with the State Department. Stark said Schuirmann summed up his thoughts better than he himself could have. Schuirmann thought there was a tendency to overestimate the change in the Japanese cabinet. Konoye as premier and the Konoye cabinet had been in power for five years. Konoye was premier when the China Incident began and it was he who declared "Japan's policy was to beat China to her knees." The only thing that could be said for the Konoye cabinet was that it may have restrained the extremists among the military. "The new cabinet to be formed will be no better and no worse than the one which has just fallen."[16]

The new cabinet under Tojo was formed on October 18, and on that date and again on October 20 Nomura asked to be allowed to resign. The new foreign minister, Shigenori Togo, urged him to stay on in Washington asserting that the new cabinet was no different than Konoye's in wanting to adjust Japanese-American relations on a fair basis. Nomura knew that the United States would not reconsider and asked again on October 22 permission to resign. Again Togo persuaded him to stay.

While the Japanese cabinet was having its shakedown, Kimmel was taking action in case their decision was war. When he received the Stark warning message of October 16 about the Konoye cabinet falling, he moved smartly to be prepared for the worst. Before he received Stark's subsequent letter of October 17 he sent twelve patrol planes to Midway, two submarines to Wake, additional Marines, ammunition, and stores to Johnston and Wake, and additional Marines to Palmyra; prepared to send six patrol planes from Midway to Wake, replacing the six at Midway from Pearl Harbor; had six submarines prepared to depart for Japanese waters; placed ships on a health cruise to the West Coast on twelve-hour notice; put additional security measures in effect in the operating areas outside Pearl Harbor; and delayed the sailing of the battleship *West Virginia* until November 17 when she was scheduled for overhaul in Puget Sound, Washington. Kimmel also put in his usual plea for more ships of all kinds.[17]

In the opening days of November, decisions were being made simultaneously in Tokyo and Washington which shaped the final nature of Japanese-American relations before war commenced five weeks later. At the end of October increased Japanese troop and air strength in Indochina triggered a frantic plea for additional help from Chiang Kai-shek and Magruder who agreed with him. Chiang appealed to Churchill for air support against a potential Japanese attack on Yunnan Province, which would have cut the Burma Road, source of supplies to China. A parallel message was sent to Roosevelt on October 30 asking for his intercession with Churchill for air support and for the United States to warn Japan against any action against Yunnan or Thailand from bases in Indochina.

On November 1, Hull called a meeting to discuss the Chiang request. Present were State Department representatives and officers from the Army and Navy war plans and intelligence staffs. Hornbeck favored a strong warning to Japan even at the risk of war. Hull, and his other advisers on the Far East, Hamilton and Ballentine, objected to further warnings unless the United States could back them up with force. The military officers questioned the finality of a Japanese victory over China or even Japan's ability to mount the necessary force to launch the attack within two more months. Hornbeck argued that a strong warning could not be equated with military action and, even if that did come to pass, Japan could easily be defeated by the existing power arrayed against her. Led by Schuirmann, the military officers present at the Hull conference of November 1 deferred further discussions until they could present the situation to the Joint Board. Still, at Hornbeck's persistence, the State Department sought military concurrence for positive action against Japan. During another meeting held on Sunday, November 2, it was agreed that Britain be requested to send planes to Thailand and that Japan be warned against moving into Siberia. Schuirmann and his Army colleagues again deferred other proposals until the Joint Board met later in the week.[18]

At Stark's request the regular weekly meeting of the Joint Board was rescheduled from November 5 to November 3, when Schuirmann presented the details of the recent meetings with the State Department. He pointed out that the President, when he returned from meeting with Churchill in August, had issued a warning to Japan and that Hull thought there should be no more warnings unless they could be backed up with credible force. Specifically, Hull wanted to know if the "military authorities would be prepared to support further warnings by the State Department."[19]

In the ensuing discussions, Stark gave his estimate of the current situation in China based upon recent dispatches from Chungking. Next Admiral Ingersoll, deputy chief of naval operations, gave his contribution to the Navy's domination of the discussion. He stressed that the United States had decided months before to concentrate offensive power in the Atlantic in accordance with the *ABC-1 Plan,* and if forced "to fight in the Pacific to engage in a limited offensive effort." Shipping (especially tankers) was too scarce to divert any to the Pacific effort; the Japanese mandated islands lay across the shortest lines of communications; and even if the Pacific Fleet moved to the Far East, there were no facilities, docks, or antiaircraft protection for it. Taking a strong stand against provoking a war with Japan, Ingersoll finished with a statement that some persons in the State Department were "under the impression that Japan would be defeated in military action in a few weeks."[20]

Further discussions brought out that if the United States did provide air support to China, it would leave the Philippines bare of defense, invoke war with Japan, and leave Luzon open "to serious risk of capture." The military leaders acknowledged that a major risk was being taken in even trying to defend the Philippines. The Navy was rushing long-range submarine reinforcements to the area, and the Army was ferrying out new B-17's as fast as they came off the production line. Critically needed fighter aircraft to protect the bombers were enroute by slow transports. The U.S. did not have, in the Far East, a radar warning system or sufficient long-range patrol aircraft to alert the bomber force of impending attack.[21]

In accordance with the decisions made at the Joint Board meeting on November 3, Stark and Marshall two days later sent the President a memorandum on their estimate of the situation in the Far East. After presenting the rationale for their recommendations, they reaffirmed that "Germany was the most dangerous enemy and effort should remain in the Atlantic." Their specific recommendations were:

> That the dispatch of United States armed forces for intervention against Japan in China be disapproved.
>
> That material aid to China be accelerated consonant with the needs of Russia, Great Britain, and our own forces.
>
> That aid to the American Volunteer Group be continued and accelerated to the maximum practicable extent.
>
> That no ultimatum be delivered to Japan.[22]

Two additional recommendations were made. The first was that under certain contingencies military action against Japan should be undertaken. Those contingencies were:

> (1) A direct act of war by Japanese armed forces against the territory or mandated territory of the United States, the British Commonwealth, or the Netherlands East Indies;
>
> (2) The movement of Japanese forces into Thailand to the west of 100° East or south of 10° North; or into Portuguese Timor, New Caledonia, or the Loyalty Islands.[23]

The complementary recommendation to the foregoing was that if the decision was made to go to war against Japan that "complete coordinated action in the diplomatic, economic, and military fields, should be undertaken in common by the United States, the British Commonwealth, and the Netherlands East Indies."[24]

In the meantime Roosevelt had received, from Churchill, Chiang's request for help sent by that route. Churchill suggested that if the

United States sent another warning to Japan, Britain would do likewise; however, he thought that no independent action by Britain would deter Japan. Britain would back the United States in whichever course it elected to take, but Churchill thought at the time that Japan was more likely to "drift into war than to plunge in."[25]

The Stark-Marshall memorandum to the President dated November 5 still did not satisfy all the State Department officials, especially Hornbeck, who thought the United States had a moral obligation to China to prevent her collapse. Another meeting between Hull, Hornbeck, Stark, and Marshall was held. The Army position was that the best aid that could be given China, and which would contribute to the defense of Singapore and the Netherlands East Indies, was an accelerated build-up of Luzon as an air and submarine base. The earliest that air and ground reinforcements could guarantee the safety of Luzon was the middle of December 1941, at which time the Army Air Corps would have become a positive threat to Japanese operations. Not until then should diplomatic or economic pressures be exerted from a military viewpoint, and it would be even more preferable to delay severe diplomatic and economic pressures until February or March 1942 when the Philippine Air Force would be at full strength. Ultimately, Roosevelt went along with the advice of his service chiefs. With the exception of the contingencies under which the United States would go to war against Japan, he passed the Joint Board recommendations of November 5 to Churchill on November 7.

Despite his busy schedule, on November 1 Stark wrote Hart a long letter answering his questions concerning material, ships, radar, and aircraft. Hart had evidently complained about Army cooperation relative to the defense of Manila Bay, because Stark suggested that he consider "the agreement Kimmel and General Short are now using at Pearl Harbor." Hart had also suggested to Stark that Glassford, who still had the Yangtze River Patrol command, be considered for his replacement. Stark was not prepared to give an answer, although he appreciated the fact that Glassford had held that command for two years. The State Department still wanted a flag officer on the Yangtze and the Navy would "have to go along with them." Hart had recommended in a letter of August 19 that whoever was to be his replacement be sent forthwith, since he had passed his normal tour of duty and the retirement age. Stark mixed flattery and compassion in his letter encouraging Hart to stay on. No one else was "so well qualified to serve our country out there in time of stress," so even though he "hated to do it," Stark asked Hart "to continue in the Far East."[26]

While the American decision makers were meeting on what to do about China and Japan in the first part of November, the Japanese Cabinet and top military commanders conferred on the night of November 1–2. Togo, the new foreign minister, wanted to avoid war even if the negotiations with America failed. The military diametrically opposed further delays in attacking the United States. If landing operations against the United States, Britain, and the Netherlands in Southeast Asia were not executed before the end of the year, unfavorable weather would prevent any action for almost another year. The strengthening of forces in the Philippines and Singapore and the constant diminishing of Japanese strategic materials, especially petroleum, entered into the evaluation of courses of action. The diplomats were to be given one last chance: get American agreement on past and present Japanese action prior to November 25. After that date Japan would ask her Tripartite Pact allies, Germany and Italy, to join her against the United States, but she would not fight the Soviet Union at the same time. If Germany would not join in war against the United States under those conditions, Japan would fight alone.

The agreement reached the night of November 1–2 between Togo and the service chiefs called for two plans to be submitted to the United States. Plan A, to be submitted first, addressed the three major stumbling blocks in past discussions: nondiscrimination of trade in China, Japan's membership in the Tripartite Pact, and the stationing of Japanese troops in China. If Plan A failed acceptance, Plan B offered a modus vivendi to buy time wherein Japan was to promise not to expand any further if the United States would relax the economic restrictions. Concomitantly, the military chiefs were to continue their preparations for war so that if the ultimate decision favored that course of action, all would be ready for the attack.

Japan's accelerated preparation for war, which had been going on for months, became quite obvious to Ambassador Grew. He warned Washington officials that the Japanese actions were more than just sword rattling and that armed conflict might become unavoidable and commence with dangerous and dramatic suddenness. Grew's warning was at once timely and prophetic, because on the same day Admiral Nagano, Chief of Naval Operations, accepted the perfected plan of attack on Pearl Harbor, which Admiral Isoroku Yamamoto had been developing since the previous January. Two days later the Emperor formally approved the submission of Plans A and B by Nomura. Nomura was also told that he would finally get the assistance of Saburo Kurusu, which he had requested on August 4.

Parallel to the advance of the Japanese diplomats to their final act before the war, the Japanese military also inched forward to the commencement of the war phase, and on November 5, issued the necessary operational orders with a warning that war with the United States, Britain, and the Netherlands East Indies was inevitable and that general preparation must be complete by early December. On November 7, the date was set for the attack on Pearl Harbor, tentatively December 8, 1941, Tokyo time.

In Washington the President's cabinet met on November 7 to discuss the seriousness of the Far Eastern situation. Hull warned that an attack might come "anywhere at any time."[27] In the same meeting Roosevelt was told unanimously by his cabinet that the American people would support him if the United States went to war against Japan even under the contingencies recommended by the Joint Board two days earlier. To prepare the country for the increased possibility of war with Japan, the cabinet agreed that Armistice Day speeches on this theme should be the order of the day. Before Knox and Welles, who did give speeches on November 11, could emphasize the developing crisis, Churchill upstaged them on November 9 in a speech at the Lord Mayor's Banquet in London. Acknowledging that the United States was doing all it could to preserve peace in the Pacific, he stated that should such efforts fail and war begin, "the British declaration would follow within the hour."[28] Churchill's assertion of help was serious because at the time the *Prince of Wales, Repulse,* and carrier *Indomitable* were rushing to Singapore just for such eventualities.

In the evening of November 7, Nomura presented part of Plan A to Hull, asked for a prompt decision, and requested a meeting with Roosevelt. On the same day Stark wrote to Kimmel approving the disposition of forces which Kimmel had made in October when the Japanese Cabinet changed hands. He devoted the next three pages of his letter to reasons why he could not grant any requests for additional support with the exception of long-range submarines, which would be sent as soon as they were built. Boiled down to hard facts, the Stark excuses meant that the Atlantic theater had priority. He closed his letter with his usual appraisal of the Pacific situation: events were "moving steadily towards a crisis . . ." It did not look good, and a "month may see, literally, most anything."[29]

On the diplomatic front the nation's leaders were going through their motions without any hopes of changing the future. Only the timing of the break was unknown. Nomura presented the details of Plan A to Roosevelt and Hull on November 10. They already knew from intercepted messages that Japan intended to renew the Tripartite Pact on November 25 and that Nomura had been given that date as a deadline by which he was to have reached an agreement with the United States. Assurances given in Plan A, playing down Japan's role in the Tripartite Pact, seemed all the more deceitful. The explanations on trade in China and the stationing of troops were really nothing new. It was no surprise to Nomura that Roosevelt and Hull were not even lukewarm toward the proposals. When he reported the discouraging results of his meeting to Togo, the foreign minister was frantic. He replied promptly that Nomura must impress the United States that the situation in Japan was critical. Nomura was reminded again, as if he needed it, that his deadline was November 25. Nomura's morale was dealt a further blow when Hull rejected Plan A on November 15. The blow was assuaged somewhat when Ambassador Saburo Kurusu arrived the same day to assist him in presenting Plan B, the final act short of war.

On November 8, Stark confirmed by letter to Hart the news that had already been sent by radio—the Marines were to be withdrawn from China. Hart was also told that the Japanese situation looked like an impasse and that anything could happen in the "next month or two." Stark reported that he had "been pressing Marshall to press the British for more air force in the Singapore area," and that he thought the United States was justified in insisting that the Malay Barrier be strengthened since the British position in Europe had improved. He conceded that the British Navy was sending marked increases to the Eastern theater, but he regretted their not having been sent sooner since they might have "acted as a very great deterrent."[30] The *Prince of Wales* and *Repulse* were still enroute to Singapore, but the *Indomitable* had gone aground near Jamaica.

One of the last exchanges of letters between Stark and Kimmel was initiated by the latter on November 15. His tone was particularly hard as he wrote:

> In repeated correspondence I have set forth to you the needs of the Pacific Fleet. These needs are real and immediate. I have seen the material and personnel diverted to the Atlantic. No doubt they are needed there. But I must insist that more consideration be given to the needs of the Pacific Fleet.[31]

Kimmel obviously perturbed, complained further that the strength of the fleet limited his freedom of action and the lack of modern equipment in the ships limited their effectiveness. He required approximately 9,000 men to fill complements and he could use another 10,000. Kimmel's closing paragraph was the climax to his numerous letters pleading for additional support.

> If this fleet is to reach and maintain a satisfactory degree of readiness for offensive action, the foregoing requirements must be met; and it must not be considered a training fleet for support of the Atlantic and the shore establishment.[32]

Stark replied immediately on November 25. He said that it was just impossible to "take inadequate forces and divide them into two or three parts and get adequate forces anywhere." The inadequate forces factor had governed the terms of the *ABC-1* and *Rainbow 5* plans "which were accepted by all as about the best compromise we could get out of the situation actually confronting us." Stark addressed Kimmel's complaints rather obliquely. King had convinced Secretary Knox that destroyers in West Coast ports could be better used on Atlantic duty. Stark had staved off that proposal for the time being, even though he agreed that King was desperate for escort ships. Kimmel would not get more ships—he would be lucky to hold what he already had. On the personnel situation, Stark was no more optimistic. Recruiting was down 15 percent after the sinking of the destroyer *Reuben James* and Stark had just received presidential approval to use draftees in his previously all-volunteer navy. Probably with tongue in cheek and as if he could forget, the referee between the two fleet commanders closed with:

> One thing I forgot to mention was your "the Pacific Fleet must not be considered a training fleet for support of the Atlantic Fleet and the Shore Establishment." I'll hand that one to King. Once in a while something happens which gives real interest. I think I'll have a gallery ready to see King when he reads that, particularly after a recent statement of his that he noted he was getting fewer men and had less percentage of complement than did the Pacific Fleet, etc. etc[33].

On November 17, Kurusu had nothing substantive to offer in his first meeting with Roosevelt. In subsequent conferences with Hull over the next few days it was obvious that there was no real basis for an immediate agreement. Contrary to their instructions from Togo, Kurusu and Nomura on their own initiative proposed a modus vivendi: Japan to withdraw her troops from southern Indochina for a lifting of the freezing orders. Hull was not enthusiastic about the idea, because, as he told the Japanese proponents, he was afraid the troops would be used elsewhere for some "equally objectionable movement."[34]

However, Hull did agree to discuss the proposal with the British and Dutch government.

In their message to Tokyo, Nomura and Kurusu advised that Plan B not be submitted. Togo again was most unhappy with his Washington team. They were told they were not following explicit instructions, they had taken unwarranted initiatives and made unacceptable proposals. Only if the United States accepted Plan B in its entirety could Japan withdraw troops from southern Indochina. Nomura pleaded for some give-and-take, and not to embark on yet another war after fighting four years in China without a final decision. His pleas were to no avail. Back came the order to submit Plan B. On November 20, Thanksgiving Day, Plan B was presented to Hull. In substance Plan B was an agreement wherein the United States would lift the freezing orders, provide oil to Japan, help Japan get commodities from the Netherlands East Indies, and discontinue aid to China. For its part Japan would make no further advances in Southeast Asia or Southwest Asia and would withdraw troops from southern Indochina after peace with China. Hull's immediate reaction was reported to Togo, whose return advice to Nomura was that if the United States would use its good offices to bring Japan and China to peace terms there would be no need for aid to China. Confident that the United States was so desirous of a truce that she would agree to some version of Plan B, Togo succeeded in convincing Tojo to extend the deadline from November 25 to November 29. The intercepted message which contained this news also included the ominous warning that after November 29, if there were no agreement, "things are automatically going to happen."[35]

Meanwhile, the State Department's Far Eastern Division had been working on a temporary agreement to be proposed to Japan, based on Hull's often repeated principles, which would allow for a continuation of the negotiations while providing the basis for a comprehensive settlement of Pacific problems. The proposal was submitted to Hull on November 11. From yet another source, Dr. Harry Dexter White, director of monetary research and an economist in the Treasury Department, came an all en-compassing proposal not only to tide over the discussions, but to bring lasting peace to the Pacific area. The basis of his thesis was a drastic change in economic policy between the United States and Japan. On November 18, Secretary Morganthau sent Hull and Roosevelt copies of the proposal, entitled *Outline of Proposed Basis for Agreement between* the United States and Japan.

It was accepted and revised by the far eastern division on the same day and sent immediately to Stark and Marshall for comments.

On November 20, Hull met with the British minister, Sir Ronald Campbell, to discuss Nomura's modus vivendi. The next day he had similar talks with the ministers of Australia and the Netherlands, Richard G. Casey and Alexander Laudon, respectively, and two meetings with Schuirmann, the liaison officer from the Navy Department. On the morning of November 21, the day after he had received Plan B from Nomura and Kurusu, Hull met with Admiral Stark and General Gerow, acting in Marshall's absence, to discuss the *Outline* and also the newest development—Plan B. Hull requested comments from both officers on the *Outline* from a "military and naval standpoint."[36]

In his memorandum to Hull on the same day Stark took strong exceptions to those provisions in the *Outline* which would limit the size of American naval forces in the Pacific; which specified that the United States would use its influence to get Britain to sell Hong Kong to China (with the United States providing a loan for the purpose); and which required Japan to sell to the United States a specified tonnage of merchant shipping. He, with Gerow, thought that a provision that Japan should withdraw troops from Manchuria should be deleted, because he thought that neither Japan nor Russia would agree to mutual withdrawals. Stark ended his analysis of the paper with the idea that since the *Outline* was assumed to "abrogate the tripartite treaty on the part of Japan," it would be better to state that fact specifically.[37]

The next day, Saturday, November 22, the State Department's Far Eastern Division completed the draft counterproposal to Plan B, the Nomura and Kurusu offer of November 20. The draft counterproposal had two sections which brought together the joint efforts of the various individuals and offices which were attempting to keep the talks with Japan going. The first section contained a proposed modus vivendi to last three months as an alternative to Plan B. The second section was in two parts: the first was a statement of principles and agreements on economic relationships and was basically the November 11 paper from the Far Eastern Division; the second part was Dr. White's much-revised proposal incorporating the ideas of Stark and Gerow.

Also on November 22, Hull held a meeting attended by the ambassadors of Britain and China and the ministers of Australia and the Netherlands. He briefed them on the Japanese Plan B proposal and

the draft of the American counterproposal, which had just been finished that day. Later in the day he met with Nomura and Kurusu to
tell them that he had discussed their proposal with other governments
and that he expected to have an answer for them on Monday, November 24.

Over the weekend the Far Eastern Division completely revised the
draft counterproposal. In the early afternoon of November 24, Hull
conferred with Schuirmann and by telephone with Knox and Stimson.
Later in a conference with Stark and Marshall, Hull discussed the
revisions. Still later, after having talked with his military contacts,
Hull met again with the Allied diplomats to bring them up to date
on the revisions and to learn what they had heard from their respective governments on the Japanese proposals and the American response to them. Hull was most disappointed to learn that only the
Dutch minister had heard from his government, which was favorable
to the approach the United States was making. The Chinese ambassador, Dr. Hu Shih, objected violently to the provision of the modus
vivendi proposed by the United States which would allow Japan to
keep approximately 25,000 troops in northern Indochina during the
three months and to another provision which would permit a limited
amount of oil to Japan. Besides the Chinese objections there was the
lack of response from the English-speaking allies. No small wonder
that the Secretary of State was pessimistic.

Roosevelt, too, was pessimistic on November 24 as he sent
Churchill a review of the Japanese Plan B and the United States
counterproposal; he thought the counterproposal was fair, but that
"its acceptance or rejection is really a matter of internal Japanese
politics," and that he was "not very hopeful and we must all be prepared for real trouble, possibly soon."[38]

Stark was also concerned. On the same day he sent a top secret
message to all Pacific fleet commanders and district commandants on
the West Coast, stating that chances of a favorable outcome of the
negotiations with Japan were very doubtful. Stark thought that the
status of the negotiations, plus the provocative statements of Tojo and
the movements of Japanese military and naval forces pointed to "a
surprise aggressive movement in any direction including [an] attack on
[the] Philippines or Guam" as possibilities. Marshall had seen Stark's
message, concurred in it, and requested that the naval commanders
inform their Army counterparts.[39]

On Tuesday morning, November 25, Hull met with Knox and
Stimson to discuss the final version of the modus vivendi. Stimson

thought there was little chance of Japan accepting the truce. After meeting for an hour and a half the trio adjourned to meet again at one o'clock in the White House with Roosevelt, Stark, and Marshall. In the discussion the President brought up the fact that it was likely that the United States would be "attacked perhaps [as soon as] next Monday, for the Japanese are notorious for making an attack without warning..."[40] Stark, in a postscript to his November 25 letter to Kimmel, described briefly his meeting with Roosevelt and Hull and that in the recent past he had been "in constant touch with Mr. Hull." Neither one "would be surprised over a Japanese attack."[41]

Later in the day Hull received the British and Chinese responses —both negative—to his draft counterproposals. The British diplomats thought the offer of economic help too high and the demands made on Japan too low. They would have preferred that all Japanese troops be evacuated from all of Indochina and that petroleum not be offered in any amount. The Chinese were even more adamant. Between November 22, when they were told about the American modus vivendi, and November 25, almost every avenue of communicating with the decision makers in Washington was used to register protests against easing economic restrictions on Japan, "selling out China," destroying Chinese morale, etc. Even before Dr. Hu Shih, the Chinese ambassador, called on Hull the evening of November 25, Chiang Kai-shek had had his political adviser, Owen Lattimore, cable Lauchlin Currie, personal secretary to Roosevelt; had appealed to Churchill to intercede with the United States; and had cabled his brother-in-law, Mr. T. V. Soong, who happened to be in Washington, to protest directly to Knox and Stimson about the modus vivendi. In addition, the Chinese diplomats deliberately leaked stories to the American press that China was being betrayed. In the face of all the actions against the modus vivendi Hull attempted to defend it on the basis that the United States sought just peace in China and a lasting settlement of Pacific problems. Hu Shih was not convinced.

Other bits of intelligence entered into the purview of Stark, and consequently Hull, which affected the decisions on Japanese relations. By *Magic* the Navy had learned that Togo had instructed Nomura on November 24 that Plan B in its entirety was the *minimum* condition which could be accepted by Japan for even a temporary agreement. The American modus vivendi, when measured alongside Plan B, would fall way short of Japanese acceptance. Also, naval intelligence and the Army's G-2 had learned that a large Japanese expeditionary force was embarking on some thirty to fifty ships at Shanghai. It was

Stimson who passed this information to Hull and the White House immediately after he returned to his War Department office from the noon meeting with the War Council on November 25.

At the same time Stark and Ghormley in London had been exchanging information on a reported concentration of Japanese forces in the Pelew Islands—forces supposedly being prepared for an attack on Portuguese Timor or the Netherlands East Indies. If this proved true, it would fit one of the contingencies in the joint November 5 memorandum to the President which recommended automatic United States military action against Japan. Stark checked the report out with the Asiatic and Pacific Fleet staffs and determined that there was not yet a threat to the Dutch possession. Ghormley was told to inform Vice Admiral Furstner, Minister of Marine in the Dutch government in England, and also the British Chief of Naval Staff, that the Japanese Fourth Fleet was at Saipan as normal; that air, submarine, and patrol activity in the mandated islands was on the increase, but "fairly well distributed." Stark was more concerned about the "apparent preparations in China, Formosa and Indo-China for an early aggressive movement of some character."[42]

Stark's analysis on November 24 was a reinforcement of a British intelligence estimate passed to him on November 22 that Thailand was the most probable objective and that Japanese occupation of the Kra Isthmus would be sound strategy in preparation for further attacks on Malaya and the Netherlands East Indies.[43]

Given such indication of Japanese aggression in the offing and the cryptographic intelligence of minimum Japanese conditions for agreement, Hull was certainly conditioned not to expect any further progress with Nomura. The final increment of nonsupport to his modus vivendi was received during the night of November 25–26. Churchill, to whom Chiang had appealed directly for intercession with the United States, told Roosevelt that of course it was up to the United States "to handle the situation," and "that we certainly do not want an additional war," *but*

> ...What about Chiang Kai-shek? Is he not having a thin diet? Our anxiety is about China. If they collapse, our joint dangers would enormously increase. We are sure that the regard of the United States for the Chinese will govern your action. We feel that the Japanese are most unsure of themselves.[44]

In the morning of November 26 Stimson received a call from Mr. Soong who, acting on instructions from Chiang, wanted to discuss the American modus vivendi. Stimson called Hull about it and was told then by Hull that he had decided "to kick the whole thing over"—to tell the Japanese that he had "no other proposition at all." Stimson then called Roosevelt to ascertain whether he had received the intelligence on the Japanese move to the south from Shanghai. Stimson recorded that the President "fairly blew up." He said he had not seen it and that this information changed "the whole situation because it was evidence of bad faith on the part of the Japanese that while they were negotiating for an entire truce—an entire withdrawal—they should be sending this expedition down there to Indo-China."[45]

Whether the decision not to submit the modus vivendi preceded or followed Stimson's call to Roosevelt has been examined and discussed ad infinitum. Hull in congressional investigation testimony and in his *Memoirs* has said that "early" in the morning of November 26 he wrote a memorandum for Roosevelt, which he gave orally and to which the President agreed, recommending that the modus vivendi not be submitted to Japan. Instead, only the long settlement, the *Outline,* was to be presented. Hull gave as his reasons for this abrupt change of procedure the lack of response or half-hearted support of the Allies and "the wide publicity of the opposition." The foreign diplomats were not consulted nor told until after the fact. More important, Knox, Stimson, Stark, and Marshall were not consulted before the decision was made to change the procedure. It was purely a Hull and Roosevelt decision and most evidence points to the fact that it was the latter's decision alone.

At 10:30 A.M. Schuirmann passed the information to the Navy Department that the attempt to get a truce would not be made. Hull himself called Stark at 11:05, probably with the same information. The Army and Navy wanted desperately to buy time, just any amount, until the troops and aircraft enroute or ordered could reach the Philippines in December. Now for certain the talks and relations would be broken and "things would happen automatically." Japanese forces were obviously in motion towards some objective south of Shanghai. War was inevitable and the United States with its meager force in the Far East was not ready.

The Joint Board met almost immediately after learning the shocking diplomatic news. From 11:30 A.M. to 1:00 P.M. the military leaders discussed their next moves and what those of Japan might be. Attention concentrated on Southeast Asia and the Japanese forces moving in strength into the area. There was no suspicion that the Japanese carrier striking force which was to attack Pearl Harbor in less than two weeks was already enroute.

Early in the afternoon of November 26 Stark and Hull exchanged telephone calls, Hull to Stark at 1:20 and vice versa at 2:35. Records of the conversations are not available. Since Hull was to see Roosevelt later in the afternoon and still later to submit the ten-point *Outline* settlement to Nomura, it can be assumed that these meetings might have prompted the calls. At 2:15 Roosevelt met the Chinese, Hu Shih and Soong, and gave them the assurances they wanted to hear—there would be no modus vivendi offered to Japan and no "selling China down the river." Hull's meeting with Roosevelt followed that with the Chinese, after which he returned to his office for a 5:00 P.M. meeting with Nomura and Kurusu.

The Japanese diplomats had already indicated to their foreign office by telephone that they expected the United States to reject Plan B. They also expected a counterproposal as a modus vivendi, not a comprehensive settlement agreement. They hardly were prepared for what was presented to them. After they had had time to scan the paper Hull gave them, they were shocked at the terms. They thought they could not even forward it to their government without further informal discussion. Kurusu observed that there were a number of impossibilities and in particular he could not see how his government could consider paragraphs 3 and 4, which read:

3. The Government of Japan will withdraw all military, naval, air, and police forces from China and Indo-China.
4. The Government of the United States and the Government of Japan will not support—militarily, politically, economically—any government or regime in China other than the National Government of the Republic of China with capital temporarily at Chung-king.[46]

Although the United States proposal was plainly labeled "Tentative and Without Commitment," was not an ultimatum per se, had no deadlines in time, and gave no threats of counteraction for non-acceptance, it nevertheless was a bitter dose for Japan. She was being asked to give up all she had gained in four years of costly fighting and to keep out of the European war in exchange for a new commercial treaty with the United States *or* to face continued economic restrictions and eventual strangulation. Since Hull would not budge from his position of offering only a full settlement, the ambassadors asked for a meeting with Roosevelt the next day, November 27. Hull agreed.

On that day, as a result of the Joint Board meeting the previous noon, Stark sent the following despatch to the Commanders in Chief of the Asiatic and Pacific Fleets (information to the Commander in Chief Atlantic Fleet and the special naval observer in London):

This despatch is to be considered a war warning. Negotiations with Japan looking toward stabilization of conditions in the Pacific have ceased and an aggressive move by Japan is expected within the next few days. The number and equipment of Japanese troops and the organization of naval task forces indicates an amphibious expedition against either the Philippines, Thai or Kra peninsula or possibly Borneo. Execute an appropriate defensive deployment preparatory to carrying out the tasks assigned in WPL 46. . . .[47]

In addition, on November 27 as a result of the Joint Board meeting of the day before, Stark and Marshall presented Roosevelt another memorandum on the situation in the Far East. The memorandum basically agreed with the earlier one of November 5, which listed certain contingencies under which joint action would be taken automatically by the United States, Britain, and the Dutch in the Far East. Joint military counteraction against Japan would be taken "only in case Japan attacks or directly threatens the territory or mandated territory of" the *ADB* powers, or "should the Japanese move forces into Thailand west of 100° East or south of 10° North, Portuguese Timor, New Caledonia, or the Loyalty Islands." Again, Thailand was considered the most likely objective, and direct attacks on Malaya and the East Indies were thought improbable "until the threat exercised by the United States forces in Luzon is removed." The most essential requirement was to gain time; the greatest immediate concern was the safety of the *"Pensacola* convoy," carrying troops and equipment, which was then near Guam, and another convoy just leaving Shanghai with the U.S. Marines—both convoys headed for Manila. Some 21,000 troops were scheduled to sail from the United States by December 8. If only the reinforcements arrived there before hostilities commenced, the Joint Board thought Japan would "be hindered and perhaps seriously blocked." In view of the race with time, the Joint Board recommended that:

> . . . prior to the completion of the Philippine reinforcement, military counteraction be considered only if Japan attacks or directly threatens United States, British, or Dutch territory as above outlined; in case of a Japanese advance into Thailand, Japan be warned by the United States, the British, and the Dutch governments that advance beyond the lines indicated may lead to war; prior to such warning no joint military opposition be undertaken; steps be taken at once to consummate agreements with the British and Dutch for the issuance of such warning.[48]

The Joint Board memorandum was not the only one of significance submitted on November 27. A very optimistic Hornbeck argued

209

against any further attempts to gain time. Rather caustically he pointed out that diplomacy had already bought six months and that now the President should tell the Army and Navy what to do instead of asking them what they could do. He thought war *less* likely than a week before and he made his point by giving odds on the unlikelihood of war with Japan. He thought that there was only a one-to-five chance of war by December 15, a three-to-one chance before January 15, and an even chance by March 1, 1942.[49] Ten days later Hornbeck's betting instincts and analysis proved to be tragically erroneous.

During the same day, November 27, Hull told the British, Dutch, and Australian diplomats of the decision to withhold the modus vivendi and of the completed action of presenting to Japan the United States terms for a settlement. In the afternoon Roosevelt had a cordial but uncompromising conference with Nomura and Kurusu, and he backed Hull's position that there was nothing else to offer at that time. Meanwhile in Tokyo, the Japanese military chiefs met with the senior cabinet members in a liaison conference to discuss the proposed settlement agreement. Despite the tirades of Tojo and his condemnation of the American offer as an ultimatum, the moderates gained one more day of grace by convincing the others to wait for the results of Nomura meeting with Roosevelt. The next day American officials in Washington knew by *Magic*, almost as quickly as Nomura and Kurusu did, that the liaison conference had decided as expected that the Imperial government could by no means use the United States offer as a basis for negotiations. However, the Japanese ambassadors were not to give the impression that negotiations were de facto ruptured, but to say that it would be two or three days before they would have an answer from Tokyo.

The Japanese message to the ambassadors in all probability was not available in time for the War Council meeting at noon on November 28. Roosevelt, Hull, Knox, Stimson, Marshall, and Stark discussed possible Japanese objectives, while Hull reaffirmed one more time that there was "practically no possibility of an agreement with Japan," and that the "safeguarding of our national security was in the hands of the Army and the Navy." Hull also reiterated that a surprise attack would probably be part of Japan's strategy.[50]

In the course of the same discussion Roosevelt thought the Japanese force moving from Shanghai might well be headed for the Kra Isthmus to attack Thailand, seize Rangoon in Burma, and cut off China's supply route, the Burma Road, at its beginning. If Japan did take Kra, Britain would fight and if Britain fought, the United States would have to join in. Among the problems were the fact that the United States could not attack the Japanese forces without warning and that it could not allow the Japanese force to steam right by the Philippines and wait for it to hit targets undisturbed. Roosevelt considered a personal message to Emperor Hirohito, since a similar tactic had been fairly effective at the time of the *Panay* incident. His advisers pointed out to him that taking issue with a completed attack and warning about forces crossing a line or passing a point, the substance of the proposed message, were not the same at all. Stimson suggested that such a communication would not inform the American people of the dangers involved. The tentative decision was a message to be given to Congress—therefore to the people—and a secret message to the emperor. Hull, Knox, and Stimson were given the task of drafting both messages, while Roosevelt took a short rest in Warm Springs, Georgia.

By this time it was known that the Japanese forces in southern Indochina had been increased to 70,000 troops and 150 aircraft and that the force moving south from Shanghai had another 25,000 troops embarked. On November 28, the War Plans Division took stock of the U.S. Army strength in the Philippines and reinforcements scheduled to arrive in the immediate future. As of that date, there were 29,000 troops, 2,700 enroute, and another 19,000 due to leave the United States the first week of December. Counting 80,000 Philippine troops due to be mobilized by December 15, MacArthur would have only 130,700 men by mid-December, appreciably less than the 200,000 he had expected by October 1. As for air strength, there were 81 P-40E fighters on hand, with 64 due to arrive before December 7; 52 A-24 dive bombers en route, and 35 B-17 bombers on hand. Ground force material reinforcement consisted of antiaircraft artillery for one regiment, 109 tanks and 50 75mm self-propelled mounts. There were 40 105mm howitzers; 178 75mm guns were scheduled but not due to arrive until later in December or January.[51]

The decision to withdraw the U.S. Marines from China had been made the first week in November. The Shanghai contingent of 900 was en route to Manila when Stark issued his war warning. On November 18, the Navy decided to withdraw the Commander, Yangtze Patrol, and the gunboats *Luzon* and *Oahu* from China, and to close the Navy Purchasing Office in Shanghai. Most of the other units of the Asiatic Fleet already were in the Philippines.

The buildup of forces in the Philippines and the increasing force differential favoring MacArthur caused service rivalry over command

and control. Shortly after taking over from General Grunert, Mac-Arthur had requested, on October 31, that he be given over-all command of Navy elements in the Far East. General Marshall had held that request to himself. Admiral Hart, in his maneuverings for partial control, proposed that the Navy have tactical command of Army air elements when aircraft were to attack shipping in waters where the U.S. Navy was operating—a request which MacArthur found "entirely objectionable." MacArthur had no hesitation, when Marshall did not give him a satisfactory answer, in taking his case directly to Stark by letter on October 18. Stark handed the problem back to Marshall. The Army War Plans Division in Washington sided with MacArthur's solution of leaving elements in their own command structure and effecting operational cooperation through *coordination of assignment missions*. The Navy Department was informed of this decision on November 18. The "war warning" message of November 27 did have some influence on bringing the two feuding commanders in chief together, since Mac-Arthur informed Marshall on November 28 that "intimate liaison and cooperation and cordial relation exist between Army and Navy" in the Philippines.[52]

On November 28, as Roosevelt journeyed to Warm Springs the State, Army and Navy staffs plunged into the task of drafting a congressional speech. By noon the next day material from the Army and Navy had been received by Hull and incorporated by Hornbeck into a twenty-page draft. The speech was to have covered United States foreign policy in the Far East since 1833 and relations with Japan since 1908, with particular emphasis on Japanese aggression in the last four years. Knox, who acknowledged the assistance of Stark and Turner sent a copy of his draft directly to Roosevelt.

While the Washington team figured out how best to tell the American people of Japan's impending attack, information was received on November 29 which strengthened the belief that Thailand was Japan's next target. Intercepted messages disclosed that Japan was arranging with pro-Japanese factions in Thailand to put Britain in the position of being the first invader of Thai territory, thereby invoking a declaration of war against her. If Japan moved into British territory just opposite the Thai border, British forces probably would defend the route to Singapore by going into Thailand to block the advance.

The most alarming news, which complemented the intelligence on the situation in Thailand, came from Tokyo. Tojo in a highly provocative and venomous speech received in Washington on November 29, Saturday, made no pretense of Japan's future actions against Britain and the United States:

> The fact that Chiang Kai-shek is dancing to the tune of Britain, America, and communism at the expense of able-bodied and promising young men in his futile resistance against Japan is only due to the desire of Britain and the United States to fish in the troubled waters of East Asia by pitting the East Asiatic peoples against each other and to grasp the hegemony of East Asia. This is a stock in trade of Britain and the United States.
>
> For the honor and pride of mankind we must purge this sort of practice from East Asia with a vengeance.[53]

Saturday was also the known deadline when Nomura was to have reached an agreement with the United States or "things were to happen automatically." That fact was not lost on Hull. Late that evening he telephoned Roosevelt and after a long conversation in which he reviewed the situation, Roosevelt decided to return to Washington on Monday.

The next morning, Sunday, Hull talked twice with Stark, at 10:30 and 12:08, before calling Roosevelt again to bring him up to date. During the day a message from Tokyo to Nomura was translated, which directed the ambassador to keep the negotiations going. Later Kurusu telephoned Tokyo that he and Nomura had an appointment with Hull for the next day, that Roosevelt was returning early from a trip because of Tojo's speech, and that such speeches put him and Nomura "in a very difficult position."

Also on Sunday at 1:28 P.M. the State Department received from Ambassador John Gilbert Winant in London a message from Churchill to Roosevelt. Churchill thought a statement should be made to Japan that any further act of aggression would "lead immediately to the gravest consequence." He realized that Roosevelt had "constitutional difficulties," and he was willing to make a similar or joint declaration with Roosevelt. He ended with an apology to his "dear friend, for presuming to press such a course upon [him], but [he was] convinced that it might make all the difference and prevent a melancholy extension of the war."[54]

On the same Sunday afternoon Lord Halifax called on Hull to pass him a *most secret* British memorandum. The British were convinced that Japan intended to land troops on the Kra Isthmus and they had plans to move quickly to beat them to strategic points so as to hold a line across the isthmus near Singora. In order to determine

Japanese moves, the Royal Air Force was reconnoitering "in an arc of 180 miles from Tedta Bharu for three days commencing November 29th." The British Commander in Chief, Far East, had requested the U.S. Commander in Chief, Asiatic Fleet, to conduct similar air reconnaissance on a line from Manila to Cam Ranh Bay, Indochina. The British commander in the Far East had asked permission to go into Thailand at the Kra Isthmus if his air reconnaissance established "the fact that escorted Japanese ships" were approaching the coast of Thailand. He wanted an immediate answer. Now Halifax wanted to know what the United States would do if the British did invade Thailand. Hull could not give an answer, but he promised that he would lay the whole matter before Roosevelt when he returned the next day from Warm Springs.[55]

The *most secret* information which Halifax had given Hull about a possible Japanese landing on Kra Isthmus had been received by Stark two days earlier. The Commandant, Fourteenth Naval District, had relayed to Stark intelligence information received through the British consul in Honolulu that Japan would attack the Kra Isthmus on December 1 without warning or ultimatum and that the attackers would proceed directly from Hainan and Formosa. Although Hull took no subsequent positive action other than informing Roosevelt the next day, Stark had already reacted. He had sent a message to Hart late in the night of November 29, before Halifax had even met with Hull on the subject, and ordered Hart to "cover by air the line Manila-Camrahn Bay on three days commencing upon receipt" of the despatch. The Asiatic Fleet planes were to observe only, not to appear to be attacking, but "to defend themselves if attacked." MacArthur was to be informed if the Japanese did approach Thailand.[56]

In Tokyo over the same weekend the last attempts to prevail against Tojo's determination to go to war failed. Nomura and Kurusu had suggested, when they sent the United States settlement terms, that the Navy minister be informed in hopes that he might help them avert war. That attempt failed because Admiral Oikawa could not overcome Tojo's powerful clique. In the liaison conference two former premiers, Konoye and Admiral Yonai, urged that peace be maintained, but again Tojo had his way. On November 30, Tojo was summoned by the Emperor to explain a rumor passed by Prince Takamatsu that the Imperial Navy wanted to avoid war. Tojo defended his militant side of government. The Emperor had only to ask the Navy minister and the Chief of Naval Staff, Admiral Nagano, to be told that the Navy would fight and win. Tojo's last opposition had finally capitulated. On December 1, the formal decision for war was made in an Imperial conference.

On Monday morning, December 1, Hull met with Nomura and Kurusu, who told him that the Japanese answer to the proposed agreement of November 28 would be presented in a few days. At 11:45 that morning Hull and Stark conferred with Roosevelt immediately after his return to Washington. No record of the meeting exists, but it is safe to assume that the proposed congressional speech, the message to the Emperor, Tojo's latest speech, Churchill's note, and Halifax's memorandum on Britain's intentions concerning the Kra Isthmus were covered. Since later facts so indicate, sometime soon after his return Roosevelt decided against making the speech to Congress or the people, and against issuing a joint statement with Churchill but to send a direct appeal to the emperor.

That same day, and possibly before the meeting of Roosevelt, Hull, and Stark, messages intercepted between Togo and the Japanese ambassador, Oshima, in Berlin were received in Washington. Germany had been increasing its pressure on Japan to attack Britain and the United States and so Oshima was directed to reply that "war may suddenly break out between the Anglo Saxon nations and Japan . . . quicker than anyone dreams."[57] Another interception that day disclosed that the Japanese Foreign Office had ordered its embassies in London, Hong Kong, Singapore, and Manila to dispose of their code machines and that the machine in Batavia had been returned to Japan.

During the same day Schuirmann inquired of Hamilton whether the State Department would object to Hart's suggestion that the gunboat *Mindanao* be withdrawn to the Philippines. After clearing the idea with Hornbeck, Hamilton informed Schuirmann there was no objection. And so another increment of United States presence in China came "off the station."[58]

Late on December 1, Roosevelt had a brief conference with Sumner Welles, who was directed to confer with Lord Halifax. (Hull had taken to his bed due to exhaustion.) After Welles met with Halifax he returned to the White House for another meeting with Roosevelt which lasted for an hour and a half. Ever since these three meetings were first disclosed to the public in the congressional investigations of the Pearl Harbor attack, there has been speculation as to what was discussed. Welles testified that he did not remember what transpired. There is every reason now to believe that it was a Roosevelt tactic to answer Halifax and Britain, through an indirect contact, as to whether or not the United States would fight Japan if Britain fought Japan

215

and whether or not the United States would support a British move into Thailand to counter a Japanese invasion there.

Very late on December 1, Stark on Roosevelt's orders directed Hart to charter three "small vessels to form a 'defensive information patrol' " as soon as possible and "within two days if possible." The minimum requirements to establish the chartered vessels as United States men-of-war were a United States naval officer in command and the mounting of a small gun and one machine gun. Filipino crews with a minimum number of ratings were authorized to accomplish the mission, which was to observe and report by radio "Japanese movements in west China Sea and the Gulf of Siam." One of the vessels was to be stationed between Hainan and Hue, Indochina, one off the Indochina coast between Cam Ranh Bay and Cape St. Jacques, and the other off Pointe de Camau in southern Indochina. Hart was to report immediately the "measures taken to carry out the President's views." He was also asked "what reconnaissance measures [were] being regularly performed at sea by both Army and Navy," whether by air, surface vessels, or submarines and what he thought of the effectiveness of the submarine reconnaissance.[59] None of the vessels arrived on station until after December 8 (Manila time).

Navy patrol aircraft and submarines were already employed in reconnaissance operations when Stark's dispatch to complement the British searches was received in Manila on December 1. Reports were immediately initiated to Washington with significant information sent also to the British Commander in Chief, Far East. On November 30, only a light cruiser and an auxiliary were sighted; on December 1, there were negative reports "even including the close vicinity [of] Camrahn Bay." On December 2, the Navy patrols reported twenty-one large transports anchored in Cam Ranh Bay with six planes patrolling overhead. On the same day nine Japanese I-61 type submarines were sighted in a line abreast with five-mile spacing at latitude 13° 10' North, longitude 110° 00' East heading south at ten knots. Because the United States planes had "been sighted on the Indo-China coast for three successive days," search in that locality was "discontinued for the present." On December 3 and 4 there were negative results from the reconnaissance.[60]

On December 2, in Washington, Roosevelt asked the Japanese ambassadors through Welles what the Japanese intentions were regarding the increased strength in Indochina. Kurusu claimed he did not know but would get an answer from Tokyo. In the same meeting assurances were given that in a few days there would be an answer to the United States proposal of November 26. At noon on December 2, Knox, Stimson, and Welles met with Roosevelt to discuss the next steps. At that time Roosevelt was still considering sending a message to the emperor and addressing Congress and the country.

Late on December 2, Togo sent Nomura the answer to Roosevelt's question concerning the increased Japanese forces in Indochina. Nomura was very perturbed with the answer which he was ordered to give: that the troops were a precautionary measure against Chinese troops across the border. Nomura knew it would not be accepted by the United States and immediately returned a dispatch pleading with Togo to come up with something better or the United States would "take a bold step." On December 4, Togo answered Nomura that what he had said was "of course, true," but it "would be very delicate matter to give any more explanations." Nomura was told again to "reply in accordance with [Togo's] aforementioned message."[61]

The last of Kimmel's letters to Stark before the attack, which has been made public, was dated December 2. Kimmel gave a long detailed review of the personnel and material situation at Wake, Midway, and Johnston Islands. He and Short had each received directives from Washington concerning the use of Army troops and equipment in relief of U.S. Marine garrisons in the islands. Kimmel understood the Navy Department version that the Army would reinforce the Navy and Marine forces in case of necessity, not as Short's War Department message indicated. The latter's message stated that the Army "would take over the defense of some outlying bases from the Navy in accordance with an agreement to be reached by the Commanding General and [Kimmel]."[62]

Kimmel presented a good case against turning complete control over to the Army until special battalions had been formed, equipped, and trained for the tasks. According to the Commanding General, Hawaiian Air Detachment, Army aircraft could not operate more than fifteen miles from land and could not fly from aircraft carriers to get to the islands, so the Navy and Marine Corps would have to continue air support. In fact, Kimmel reported on December 3 that Admiral William Halsey in the *Enterprise* would launch twelve Marine fighters for the defense of Wake Island. The *Enterprise,* escorted by three heavy cruisers, a squadron of destroyers, and two squadrons of patrol aircraft, was to return to Pearl Harbor immediately after the Wake reinforcement.

Kimmel hit again and again at the folly of sending Army units into the outlying islands. He had checked with Short and his staff and confirmed that the only guns—either surface or antiaircraft—which the Army could send to those islands were .30-caliber machine guns and rifles. He reminded Stark of his often cited report of "inadequacy of the Army anti-aircraft guns." "So far, very little had been done to improve [that] situation." If the Marines had to give up their anti-aircraft batteries to Army replacements and return to Hawaii, they too would be in Oahu without any equipment other than rifles. Finally, Kimmel wanted the Navy to have command and control of the development of base defense in the other islands. He was sure that Stark would "subscribe to the principle that all these outlaying bases must be under Navy command and the forces must be subject to the orders of the Commander in Chief [Pacific Fleet] without any qualifications whatsoever."[63]

In a final postscript Kimmel objected to the poor utilization of his cruiser force in convoy work. The Navy Department had ordered that a single cruiser be used in convoys of not more than eight ships to the Far East, which meant there would have been seven cruisers continuously on convoy duty. Kimmel wanted no more than four so employed. His closing words were at once pessimistic and optimistic in the light of events in the immediate offing:

> . . . the demands for trans-Pacific escorts may decrease if it becomes impossible to route ships to Manila but it will still be necessary to supply the Asiatic Fleet and our allies in the Far East.[64]

In the first days of December there were additional indications that war was near. Two messages intercepted and translated on December 2 instructed Japanese embassies on what to do "on the outbreak of war with England and the United States," or in the event of a "full fledged war." On Thursday December 4, a message to the Japanese embassy in Washington gave instructions on burning telegraphic codes and destroying code machines. Ambassador Nomura was directed to keep in his custody a certain code key "until the last moment."[65] On December 3, Stark informed Hart and Kimmel that the various Japanese embassies had been instructed to destroy codes and machines. On December 4, as Japanese clerks burned classified material in Washington, Stark was ordering the bulk of American classified materials to be destroyed in Tokyo, Bangkok, Peiping, Shanghai, Tientsin, and Guam.[66]

Also during the first week of December Stark again became involved with naval strategic problems concerning the Netherlands East Indies which were being discussed in London. Even though earlier reports of Japanese concentrations in the Pelews were evaluated as unlikely, the Dutch naval command in London was still nervous about a possible attack by Japan either from the north or east. The Admiralty and Admiral Ghormley suggested to the Dutch naval staff that the matter was one of a political as well as a military nature and warranted discussions at the foreign minister level. When the Dutch foreign minister met with Britain's Anthony Eden, the latter suggested a unilateral declaration by the Netherlands similar to the one Britain made relative to a defense area off the Malayan coast at Jahore. The substance of the declaration would be that all ships entering the area must first inform the Netherlands naval authorities of their intentions and call at specific ports for routing instructions. This suggestion appealed to Admiral Furstner, the senior Dutch admiral in London, who then sought concurrence in declaring such a defense area south and west of a line from Davao in Mindanao to Waigeo in New Guinea and then east along the equator.[67]

Stark took strong exception to the idea of declaring such a large area dangerous to shipping and directed Ghormley to communicate his views to the Admiralty and the Dutch naval staff. He reasoned that the small area off Malaya declared dangerous by Britain was a different matter altogether, as to size. Of much greater concern to Stark were the delays for United States shipping transiting the area and the possible actions Japan might take in retaliation. In the first instance, Stark doubted that the "Dutch could set up promptly a naval control system" so as not to delay United States reinforcements sailing to the Philippines via Torres Strait. On the other hand, if such a large area were closed, Japan would have a precedent to close the Okhotsk Sea, the Sea of Japan, and all the western portion of the South China Sea and the Gulf of Siam. Since the United States shipping to Russia crossed the Okhotsk Sea and the Sea of Japan, and the United States, Britain, and the Netherlands East Indies were executing reconnaissance measures in all directions, the Japanese closures would be most prejudicial to the interests of the three allied powers. He then recommended that if "Dutch authorities consider [that] some warning should be given Japan," it should take the form of a declaration that "in view of the current situation Japanese naval vessels or expeditionary forces crossing the Davao-Waigeo line would be considered hostile and would be attacked."[68] Before Ghormley's suggestion from Stark to Furstner could be discussed and put into operation, war had begun.

In addition to the Dutch request for support, Thailand on December 4 also appealed once again to possible Anglo-American allies for their assurances that a Japanese invasion of their country would be met automatically with armed assistance. Since the previous August, immediately after Japan annexed southern Indochina to her control, Thailand had sought with very little success to obtain arms and financial help from Britain and the United States. To be sure, Stark and Marshall had suggested to Roosevelt in their memorandum of November 5, reaffirmed by another on November 27, that in the event of Japanese moves in Thailand south of 10° N or west of 100° E the United States would automatically respond. Additionally, the two service chiefs had recommended seeking cooperation with Britain and the Netherlands and that warnings to Japan be made by the same lineup of possible allies, but Roosevelt vacillated. It was one thing to aid Britain in the Atlantic; it was more questionable, given the strong current of isolationism running in Congress and in the country, to aid Britain and the Netherlands if their Far East colonies were attacked. It was even more unlikely that the necessary support would be forthcoming in Congress for a declaration of war if Japan invaded another Asian country. The Thai diplomats in Washington received no American assurances, although a general consensus prevailed that Thailand was one of Japan's next targets.

On December 5, more bits of the international mosiac were exposed. By *Magic* or reconnaissance the United States had reasonably good knowledge of Japanese military and diplomatic moves with one glaring exception. Attention was so fixed on the obvious moves in the Far East that no one was even remotely aware of the Japanese carrier force steaming undetected towards Pearl Harbor.

Hull knew in advance of the December 5 visit by Nomura and Kurusu what Tokyo had ordered them to answer to Roosevelt's earlier question concerning increased Japanese troop strength in Indochina. The fabrication, given as directed, was that the troops were "precautionary measures," because of Chinese troop movements near the Indochina border. Hull recorded in his *Memoirs* that he informed the Japanese ambassadors that "it was the first time that he knew the Japanese were on the defensive in Indo-China."[69] Hull refused further discussion of the Japanese proposals of November 20, because he knew, again by *Magic,* that Japan had decided to compromise no more.

When Roosevelt had returned from Warm Springs on December 1, he had rejected a proposal by Churchill that a joint warning be given to Japan about further moves in Southeast Asia. One December 5, Halifax tried again with Hull. He told Hull that "the time has now come for immediate cooperation with the Dutch East Indies by mutual understanding. This relates to the matter of defense against Japan."[70] Almost simultaneously with the Hull-Halifax conference, British RAF reconnaissance aircraft out of Malaya sighted three Japanese convoys rounding Cape Cambodia and entering the Gulf of Siam. The composite force constituted a formidable threat, since it consisted of a battleship, seven cruisers, forty-six transports, and a number of escorting destroyers. Before the final course could be determined—west to Malaya or northwest to Thailand—contact was lost for thirty hours due to heavy monsoon rains. When contact was regained, the convoys were just hours away from the Malayan coast.

Information on the impending Japanese invasion reached Washington by several routes. Stark had the first news at 7:55 A.M. Saturday, December 6, from Hart in Manila. Schuirmann passed the information on the convoys to Hull, and Stark conferred with Hull by telephone at 1:09 P.M. and 5:15 P.M. In mid-morning, Hull also received from Ambassador Winant in London a *triple priority and most urgent* message giving information on the initial sighting. This was followed by another message from Winant with similar urgency at 3:05 P.M. which stated, among other things:

> British feel pressed for time in relation to guaranteeing support Thailand fearing Japan might force them to invite invasion on pretext protection before British have opportunity to guarantee support but wanting to carry out President's wishes in message transmitted by Welles to Halifax.[71]

The Welles-Halifax meeting on December 1 had taken place on Roosevelt's orders, immediately after his return from Warm Springs. Persistent questioning of Welles during later congressional investigations of the Pearl Harbor attack shed no further light on what Roosevelt's wishes were at the time, nor have subsequent searches ever disclosed a copy of the message mentioned by Winant as having been passed by Welles to Halifax.[72]

Meanwhile, on the opposite side of the world and much closer to the inevitable clash of arms, interesting events were filling the frantic and confusing final days of Anglo-American pre-war relations in the Far East. Vice Admiral Tom Phillips, who arrived in Singapore in the *Prince of Wales* on December 2, conferred with Hart and MacArthur in Manila December 4–6. Under the pressure of time, after months of non-productive *ADB* conferences, a detailed plan for the employment of naval and air forces was agreed to and sent to Washington for approval. It arrived in the Navy Department at 11:00 P.M. December 6. Phillips, meanwhile, had learned of the Japanese convoys nearing the Malayan coast and hurried to Singapore to lead the *Prince of Wales* and *Repulse* to their tragic fate—sinking by Japanese aircraft.

On the afternoon of December 6 as Hart and Phillips wound up their agreement, Captain John M. Creighton, United States naval attache at Singapore, sent the following message to Hart:

> Brooke-Popham received Saturday [Friday, December 5, Washington time] from War Department London:
>> American armed support has now been assured us [the British] in following cases:
> (a) We have to execute our plans to prevent landing Isthmus of Kra by Japs or counteract Jap invasion elsewhere in Siam.
> (b) Attack is made on Dutch Indies and we proceed to their defense.
> (c) Japs attack US the British. Accordingly, put plan into action without reference to London if you have good information that Jap expedition is advancing apparently with intention of landing in Kra, or if any part of Thailand is violated by the Japs.
>> Should NEI be attacked, put plans agreed upon between Dutch and British into operation.[73]

No such agreement was known to Hart, who immediately fired off a dispatch to Stark: "Learn from Singapore we have assured Britain armed support under three or four eventualities. Have received no corresponding instructions from you." Nor would he receive any response to this last dispatch. Hart did receive approval to the deployment plans of his Asiatic Fleet forces, which had been worked out with Phillips. That approval was drafted during the morning of December 7 and reached Hart after war had started.

On Saturday afternoon, December 6, there were still decisions being made and courses of action being weighed. Halifax had asked Hull on November 30 what the United States would do if Britain invaded Thailand in order to resist a Japanese landing on the Kra Isthmus, and Hull had discussed this inquiry with Roosevelt on December 1. After a week of diplomatic probing and maneuvering by Halifax and Australian Minister Richard G. Casey, Roosevelt still had not given the assurances of assistance which they sought. In fact, the United States decision makers would not agree with Churchill's earlier request for a joint strong warning to Japan. Now on December 6, in the face of a major Japanese assault and British pressures for clarification on America's stand, Roosevelt reconsidered the options worked out among the State, Navy, and War Departments just the weekend before: a unilateral warning, a joint warning, a message to Congress, a message to the country, or a message to Emperior Hirohito. Roosevelt selected first the choice least recommended by his diplomatic and military advisers—a personal message to Hirohito, urging the Emperor for the sake of humanity to withdraw his forces from Indochina. Should he fail to get a response from the emperor, Roosevelt planned to address Congress and the country.

The original draft of the message to the Emperor was made more positive as to the dire consequences which would follow if the two countries did not continue their peaceful relations. It was sent to Grew from Washington at 9:00 P.M. December 6 and was received in the Tokyo post office an hour later (12 noon December 7, Tokyo time). Delivery was not made until 10:30 P.M., so that by the time Grew could arrange a meeting with Foreign Minster Togo it was after midnight, December 8. At that meeting Grew read Roosevelt's message to Togo and requested an audience with the emperor as soon as possible. Not until a second request was made for a meeting with the emperor did Togo condescend. Just hours later at 7:00 A.M. Grew was summoned by Togo to be told that negotiations had been broken off. Not until later did he learn that Pearl Harbor had been attacked several hours earlier.

Late in the afternoon of December 6, Australian Minister Casey conferred with Roosevelt about a strongly worded warning which was to be sent jointly by Britain, Australia, New Zealand, Canada, and the Union of South Africa to Japan. Casey wanted Roosevelt's concurrence in the warning before Australia would go along with sending it. Casey received that concurrence, but it was conditional as to timing. At 9:30 P.M. December 6 he sent an urgent message to the Australian minister for external affairs in Canberra, who promptly relayed the information to the British secretary of state for dominion affairs of the United Kingdom in London. The message from Canberra to London is paraphrased as follows:

> Subject to conditions that President gives prior approval to text of warning as drafted and also gives signal for actual delivery of warning, we concur in draft as a joint communication from all His Majesty's Governments. I point out that message from Australian Minister at Washington just received notes that,
> 1. President has decided to send message to Emperor.
> 2. President's subsequent procedure is that if no answer is received by him from the Emperor by Monday evening,
> (a) he will issue his warning on Tuesday afternoon or evening,

223

(b) warning or equivalent by British or others will not follow until Wednesday morning, i.e., after his own warning has been delivered repeatedly to Tokyo and Washington.[74]

Even though Roosevelt's announced timetable put the British warning off until at least Tuesday or Wednesday of the next week, there were strong indications that he had given assurances to Britain of United States assistance and cooperation should Britain go into Thailand to counterattack Japanese invading forces there. The message from Creighton to Hart was not based on rumor. It was almost verbatim what Brooke-Popham had received from London. As critical as American cooperation was to British plans and the urgency with which it was sought, a message that it finally had been given would not have been fabricated. In addition, the substance of the Creighton message meshed exactly with that which Stark and Marshall had twice in the previous month recommended to Roosevelt.

During Saturday afternoon, December 6, significant messages to Nomura were intercepted and translated. The first was a "pilot message," which announced that a fourteen-part answer to the United States proposal of November 26 was on its way. The State Department was told of the pilot message and the general nature of the first parts by 7:30 P.M. By early evening the first thirteen parts had been translated; they were delivered to Knox by 9:00 P.M. and to the President by 9:30 P.M. One of Roosevelt's first reactions was to call Stark, but when he was told that the CNO was at the National Theater, he elected not to have him paged or called out of his box for fear that the ever-alert public might misinterpret Stark's sudden departure. Stark was told of the first thirteen parts when he arrived home later that evening. Actually, the American readers found no surprises in the first parts because already a November 28 interception had indicated an inevitable break.

By a telephone call at 8:00 P.M. an aide of Stimson requested the Navy Department duty officer to compile certain information regarding the location and numbers of the naval ships of the United States, Britain, the Netherlands, Japan, and Russia in the Pacific before 9:00 the next morning. Knox, when consulted about the request, asked that it be delivered to him before 10:00 the next morning. Also that evening Knox, Hull, and Stimson exchanged telephone calls between 8:00 and 9:00, most probably to discuss their scheduled meeting in Hull's office at 10:30 Sunday morning. High on the agenda was a draft of the President's speech to Congress in which he was to warn Japan again about aggressive moves in Southeast Asia.

On Sunday morning the fourteenth part of the Japanese answer was intercepted and translated. It was delivered to the White House and then taken to the President in his bedroom by his naval aide, Captain John R. Beardall. Hull, Knox, and Stimson were also given copies. The last sentence of this last part read:

> The Japanese Government regrets to have to notify hereby the American Government that in view of the attitude of the American Government it cannot but consider that it is impossible to reach agreement through further negotiations.[75]

There was no war threat there, just what was already known, that the negotiating was over. There was little reaction among the three secretaries, nor did Roosevelt attempt to call Hull about the message after all the parts were known.

At 10:45 A.M. another message to Nomura had been translated and delivered to Roosevelt and to the Hull conference. It directed Nomura to present the fourteen-part message to Hull at 1:00 P.M. At about noon the Japanese embassy called Hull's office to request a 1:00 P.M. meeting, but shortly thereafter asked for a postponement until 1:45. Japanese clerks were having more difficulty translating the last part than the U.S. Navy's cryptographic team had had.

The secretaries' meeting lasted until approximately 11:30 A.M. at which time Stimson went home to lunch and Knox returned to his office in the Navy Department. In the White House, Roosevelt and Chinese Ambassador Hu Shih had a short meeting in the course of which Roosevelt spoke of the scheduled Hull-Nomura appointment. He thought that it was a prelude to "foul play" and that within the next forty-eight hours something "nasty" might happen in Thailand, Malaya, the Dutch Indies, and "possibly" the Philippines. Hu Shih left at 1:10 P.M.

Fifteen minutes later, at 7:55 A.M. Hawaiian time, more than a hundred Japanese aircraft commenced their attack on Pearl Harbor. With surprise as an additional key factor, the attack was most effective in a loss-inflicted to loss-sustained ratio. Japan lost forty-eight aircraft and three 45-ton midget submarines. The United States lost eighty Navy and ninety-seven Army aircraft. Personnel casualties were: Navy, 2,117 officers and men killed, 960 missing, and 876 wounded; Army, 226 officers and men killed, 396 wounded. The battleship *Arizona* was a total loss; the battleships *Oklahoma, Nevada, West Virginia* and *California,* three destroyers, a mine layer and a target ship were severely damaged but eventually repaired; the battleships *Tennessee,*

Pennsylvania, and *Maryland,* the cruisers *Helena, Honolulu,* and *Raleigh,* a seaplane tender, a repair ship, and a dry dock were damaged but soon repaired.

In Washington, twenty-five minutes after the attack began, Knox —who was talking to Stark and Turner in the Navy Department—received Kimmel's terse message:

> Air raid on Pearl Harbor. This is not drill.[76]

First word of the attack went to Roosevelt by telephone, and he in turn phoned it to Hull and Stimson. The attack was as big a surprise in Washington as it had been in Hawaii. Navy Department duty officers, in compiling the Stimson and Knox request for information on the Pacific navies, had listed all Japanese ships involved in the attack as being either at Sasebo or Kure in the Japanese home islands. Knox at first thought the message was a mistake and told Stark, "This must mean the Philippines." It was no mistake. The Philippines would be hit later that day with MacArthur's B-17 bombers receiving special attention.

Hull, who had been informed of the attack just minutes before Nomura and Kurusu arrived for their final meeting at 2:05 P.M., kept them waiting for fifteen minutes. He gave the appearance of reading their answer to the American note of November 26 and then told the uncomfortable diplomats:

> ... In all my fifty years of public service I have never seen a document that was more crowded with infamous falsehoods and distortions— infamous falsehoods and distortions on a scale so huge that I never imagined until today that any Government on this planet was capable of uttering them.[77]

On the opposite side of the world a massive Japanese air and sea assault against Thailand commenced simultaneously with the Pearl Harbor attack. At 3:00 P.M. Washington time Japanese air forces hit Singapore for the first time and an hour later Khota Baru in British Malaya was under air attack.

In Washington at 3:00 P.M. Roosevelt met with Stark, Marshall, Hull, Knox, Stimson, and Harry Hopkins to discuss the attack and what was to be said to Congress the next day. The President asserted his prerogative of keeping the speech short rather than accepting a much longer version which reviewed all the negotiations and which Hull recommended. During these deliberations the Imperial Japanese Government declared war on the United States and Britain at

4:00 P.M. Washington time. At 8:30 Roosevelt met with Cabinet officials, read a draft of his proposed speech to Congress and still later with majority and minority congressional leaders in attendance discussed the events of the previous week and the then known facts of the attacks.

Churchill, during the evening of December 7, inquired whether he should declare war on Japan or wait until the President had addressed Congress. An immediate answer was sent favoring the latter course of action. Shortly after noon on December 8, Roosevelt addressed a joint session of Congress and within an hour all but one representative had approved a resolution declaring war—a resolution which the President signed at 4:10 P.M. Britain and the British Commonwealth countries followed with similar declarations immediately.

Japan, which had been actively seeking German agreement for a joint war since December 3, had her wishes formalized when Germany and Italy declared war on the United States on December 11. On the same day the United States reciprocated with declarations of war on the two. Finally, the political and military problems of Roosevelt and his advisers of how to convince Congress and the people to aid Britain in defeat of Germany and to deter Japan were partially solved. The United States and Britain were directly involved in a world war against common enemies recognized by an emotionally aroused American people. With the Pacific Fleet emasculated, there was little choice as to strategy. The United States would have to fight according to *Plan Dog*.

CHAPTER 12

Deterrence
as a Strategic Concept

The events of World War II, as with all history, grow dim with time. Recollections fade, new alliances and alarms are the order of the day, and new generations grow up oblivious of the past. In the perspective of time, events in the Pacific in the five years before Pearl Harbor were merely ephemeral. The shock of December 7, 1941, set off national and international reaction that completely overshadowed the diplomatic and strategic preliminaries to what became a great world war. Yet lessons learned about concepts and strategy in the past are worth reviewing in the light of the present.

In the present age of intercontinental ballistic missiles with nuclear warheads poised in readiness to mete out awesome destruction on any target in the world, deterrents of the 1930s pale into puny insignificance. The concepts of a strategy using deterrents, military or economic, despite the technological improvements in the tools of war and the complex interrelationships of modern world commerce, remain valid with time.

In a democracy there is always a problem of citizen approval of allocating sufficient resources—manpower, money, and productive capacity—to maintain an effective national defense even though, ironically enough, national defense is equated with national survival. Just as differences in viewpoint over what constitutes sufficient defense in peacetime have caused heated debates, there has been even more divisiveness over maintaining, much less using, a credible deterrent. In the 1930s, there existed, as there still does, lack of agreement within the United States over whether the government should become involved in European and Asian affairs with force. Indicative of the isolationist times was a popular pacifist saying: "Big ships make big wars; little ships make little wars and no ships make no wars." A sizable number of American citizens and a majority in Congress would have overthrown the experience of centuries of traditional international relations which called for having enough strength, solely or with allies, to protect national interests.

Another truism which bridges time is that diplomats who represent their government in negotiations without actual or potential force behind them negotiate from weak positions. If their opponents have decidedly superior actual and potential force, those opponents may with impunity ignore or reject any proposals or agreements. The democratic nation, not choosing to field large military forces unnecessarily, usually seeks by a combination of existing military forces, diplomacy, economic pressures, and cooperation with other like-minded powers to deter any aggression or acts by other powers in violation of principles or national interests. Such was the strategy of the United States which evolved prior to the Pearl Harbor attack and, to be sure, the fleet and naval leadership were deeply involved.

As Japanese, German, and Italian military might increased rapidly in the mid-1930s, American diplomats found themselves in progressively weaker positions. The potential power of the United States was still greater than any of the militants, but that power was not being channeled into war machinery. The Army, which had shrunk to less than 120,000 men, was still at low ebb and the Navy was not even up to the limits of naval treaty strength. The actual and relative military power of the Axis powers gave them terrifying advantage. There should be no wonder that Cordell Hull "should be 'plugging' for a bigger Navy" in 1936.[1]

Against Japanese naval strength, strong military force, and the propensity to use force to gain objectives in the Orient, the Navy and State Department representatives had the weak Asiatic Fleet, the presence of the United States Fleet at Hawaii, and economic pressures. Though the areas, times, and degrees of use varied, the two main forces used to deter Japan from using her localized advantage against United States interests and assumed responsibilities were naval and economic. The problem facing the American strategists was how to deter the Japanese from expanding southward into Indochina and especially the Netherlands East Indies, using the relatively weak forces available. The problem intensified after the decision to first concentrate American effort in the Atlantic to defeat Germany.

The U.S. Asiatic Fleet had, as its mission, to protect American nationals and their property and, after 1937 by its presence in China, to temper Japanese action which adversely affected American interests. The effectiveness of the Asiatic Fleet as a deterrent was derived not from the strength of the fleet itself but from what it represented, namely, a country capable of dramatic economic reprisals and additional naval action. (A near-parallel analogy exists in 1970 in the presence of the U.S. Seventh Army in the Federal Republic of Germany vis-à-vis much stronger Soviet forces arrayed against it.) If the decisions were made by the Japanese to risk the American use of either or both the underlying sources of potential power, the naval forces on station in the Orient would be sadly inadequate in every respect. This fact had been recognized clearly since Mahan expressed his views on sea power.

In 1938 the Hepburn Board, reviewing the future needs of the Navy, specially recommended "adequate air and submarine protection securely based on Guam" to make that island "secure against anything short of a major effort on the part of any probable enemy."[2] If the use of the fleet at Pearl Harbor "on the flank of any Japanese move to the south" served Stimson[3] as a deterrent against Japan in 1932, would not a secure base at Guam to which units of the United States Fleet might deploy to operate thousands of miles closer to Japan and "which would provide for the security of the Asiatic Fleet in time of sudden emergency" be even more deterring? The Japanese definitely thought so earlier. The removal of the threat of fortified Guam was *sine qua non* to their acceptance of the Washington Naval Treaty in 1922. For many reasons Congress did not approve the Apra Harbor improvement bill which was the first step in building up the base at Guam in 1939. In retrospect, Guam, with adequate defenses, would have strengthened considerably the *Orange* and *Rainbow 5* war plans, most probably would have served as a stronger deterrent than the fleet in Hawaii, and quite possibly would have received the same destructive treatment as the fleet at Pearl Harbor.

Coincidentally, days before the Hepburn Board Report was published, the Asiatic Fleet commander, Yarnell, in a personal letter informed Leahy, the Chief of Naval Operations, of his views of problems in the Pacific. Leahy by memorandum passed extracts of Yarnell's letter to Roosevelt. Yarnell's recommenadtions were:

3.   (a)   An announcement to Japan that the United States, Great Britain, France and the Netherlands East Indies, that [violations of the Nine Power] Treaty will not be recognized.
      (b)   No money to be loaned to Japan by any of the signatory powers.

    (c)   Prohibition of shipment of war material to Japan.

    (d)   Strengthening of Pacific and Guam specifically.

        1.   Decided increase of Army and Navy aviation in the Pacific.

        2.   Increase of submarine force.

        3.   Increase of base facilities.

        4.   Increase of AA defense.

        5.   Base an increased number of heavy cruisers on Hawaii.

    (e)   The other nations to increase their forces accordingly and to take similar measures.

    (f)   For every note written, there should be some increase of our strength in the Far East.

4.   It is only by such means that respect will be gained for our diplomatic efforts. Japan at present is in a dangerous position with respect to her . . . military men in China who must be supplied from overseas. Any threat against this line of communications by a competent and ample force . . . will have a profound effect on her attitude of mind regarding the settle of the present controversy.[4]

Most of Admiral Yarnell's suggestions were adopted, but generally too late in 1941 to deter the Japanese.

On September 1, 1939, the Navy War Plans Division was concerned over Japanese moves "in the event that England and France enter war with Germany" and recommended to the Chief of Naval Operations "that the United States take such immediate steps as may be practicable to provide a deterrent effect against such aggressive measures by Japan."[5] Later, in December, the War Plans Division was more specific in its recommendations. The Netherlands East Indies were particularly vulnerable to Japanese demands, since Britain and France were fully occupied in Europe and the Netherlands were so exposed to German pressures. Because of the war in Europe and the increased opportunity for Japan to take further actions, the war plans staff recommended strengthening the United States military position in the Far East before spring in order to "serve as some additional deterrent to further Japanese expansion plans, and possibly to make more forceful the efforts of the State Department in that direction." Specifically, they recommended increasing without delay the Army Air Force in the Philippines and possibly its garrison, with an increase of at least one squadron of Navy patrol planes to make more effective such an Army augmentation. The Navy recommendations for increasing the creditability of deterrents was discussed in a Joint Board meeting on December 9; however, no action was taken since the Army could not at the time comply.[6]

Since the Army was incapable of reinforcing its Far East forces,

the Navy studied actions which it could take alone. On learning that
the Japanese Navy intended to move into the Netherlands East Indies
in May 1940, Captain Crenshaw of the War Plans Division suggested
discussing with the State Department and the President the interesting
possibility of sending a division of *Omaha*-class cruisers to the Indies
to make similar moves. Captain Schuirmann, liaison officer with the
State Department, discussed with Dr. Hornbeck and Mr. Hamilton the
proposal that, if Japan sent a small occupation force for the protection
of the Netherlands East Indies, the United States send a similar force.
A variation of the same idea was also suggested to the State Department representatives—that the United States suggest to Japan a joint
occupancy of the Netherlands East Indies. Hornbeck and Hamilton
thought that unless the United States were prepared to go to war in
the event such joint occupancy were opposed by Japan, that such a
move should not be made. In addition, they thought the proposals
unfeasible since the Japanese had already stated that they wanted
the status quo preserved. Having received the diplomatic reaction to
their ideas, the Navy staff let them drop.

The "grasping at straws" to deny the Netherlands East Indies to
Japan gave way to more practicable United States considerations of
joint actions with the Netherlands and Britain. To this end Hart, at
Stark's suggestion, initiated talks in October 1940 with Dutch and
British force commanders at Singapore and Batavia. Hart's letter expressing disappointment at lack of cooperation in the Far East between Dutch and British commanders was analyzed by Hornbeck for
State Department use. Hornbeck's evaluation is quoted in part to
show the American thinking on deterrents at the time.

5. The only thing which will deter the Japanese from an attempt to
   seize the Netherlands East Indies will be their fear of opposing
   forces. By refusing to confer with the British for defense of the
   Indies, the Dutch are only doing themselves harm.
6. The certainty of British aid to the Dutch would probably not be
   sufficient of itself permanently to deter the Japanese.
7. The fullest use of our joint resources calls for Staff discussions that
   would go immeasurably beyond the "exchange of information" basis
   on which we are now working. It should be possible for the United
   States, without making any political commitment, to proceed on
   certain assumptions, if there is a possibility that we will be acting
   jointly with the British or Dutch.
8. A Japanese attack on British or Dutch possessions, or both, is a most
   likely development unless the Japs are fairly certain that we will
   intervene. The occasion approaches which will be our last chance

to maintain our right and interests in the Far East except entirely
on our own and starting from scratch.[7]

Cooperation among the powers in the Far East had been urged by
Yarnell; and Richardson, when he was Assistant CNO, had insisted
on allies who would not leave the United States "in the lurch." Now
Hart and Stark proposed agreements with a view to possible joint action, yet history shows that the united front came only in extremis and
certainly too late *to deter* or to oppose Japan effectively.

On January 16, 1941, the President in a White House conference
announced his decision to make no further reinforcement of the
Asiatic Fleet. The background behind the decision is most significant
because two schools of thoughts were involved—one advanced by
Yarnell, the former Commander in Chief, Asiatic Fleet, relative to
Japan and a much more moderate one advanced by Stark. Though in
this instance Stark again was able to persuade Roosevelt to accept his
reasoning, most of Yarnell's recommendations ultimately were tried.

Stark must be given credit for his consistency in the application
of his concept to naval and economic pressures against Japan. As indicated in his *Plan Dog* Stark did not want to do anything which
would bring Japan into the war until Germany was defeated. Just
three days prior to Roosevelt's decision not to reinforce the Asiatic
Fleet, Stark had written Kimmel that he did not want to become involved in the Pacific, if it were possible to avoid it. A month later
Stark had written that there was a chance that further moves against
Japan would "precipitate hostilities rather than prevent them." He
wanted to give Japan no excuse for coming into the war in case the
United States was forced into hostilities with Germany. The degree to
which he was willing to go was indicated in his full support of Welles
in the State Department *not* to embargo oil to Japan and his unrelenting attempts to counter the more daring proposals of Yarnell to stand
up to Japan. On the reinforcement question, Stark had the complete
support of Admiral Joseph Mason Reeves, who had been Commander
in Chief, United States Fleet, in 1935.

The record does not show definitely who initiated the proposal
which triggered the discussion on the reinforcement of the Asiatic
Fleet; it could conceivably have been Yarnell. The proposal was to
send immediately to the Asiatic Fleet the aircraft and ships which in
the Navy Basic War Plan *Rainbow 3* were termed the "Asiatic Fleet
Reenforcement." In the war plan the detachment to the Asiatic Fleet
was to be sent from Pearl Harbor "as soon after the outbreak of war
as it could be prepared for the trip." The detachment was not de-

233

signed for operations in the Philippines, but for operations initially from bases in the Malay Barrier "in cooperation with the British and Dutch naval, land and air forces there."[8] "The reenforcement ... if it had ever arrived, would have about trebled the surface power of [the] Asiatic Fleet."

In early January 1941, Stark analyzed for Secretary Knox the effects of reinforcing the Asiatic Fleet. If it were for the purpose of deterring Japan from advancing against Malaya and the Netherlands East Indies, Stark was not so sure that the United States would go to war against Japan. If war did result, "the demands of that war [would] be such that" the United States could "do little to aid the British Isles or to assist the British Navy in the Alantic Ocean." It was Stark's opinion that the British Isles could not hold out against Germany unless the United States continued her supply of materials "to those Isles and, probably, actively enter the war with [its] major naval forces deployed in the Atlantic." Should the United States make war with its major naval forces against Japan, Stark believed that Britain would be defeated by Germany, that the United States would then be left with decidedly inferior naval forces in the Atlantic to protect its national interests, and that then the United States would be unable to withdraw from the war with Japan without heavy losses of ships and prestige. Should the reinforcement of the Asiatic Fleet not deter Japan, but actually encourage her to strike, the United States might be creating a situation that would result in national disaster. Stark's advice then and later was that the United States avoid war with Japan, and his analysis was consisent with his *Plan Dog* and often repeated views on defeating Germany first. He was not willing to risk actions which might lead to war with Japan or to risk the loss of his naval forces needed in the Atlantic.

Admiral Yarnell may be said to have had the opposite viewpoint. He was willing to send naval forces to the Far East to deter Japan and to use force if the Japanese moved into southern Indochina. His suggestions to the Secretary of the Navy may be summarized as follows: strengthen the Philippines with forces from Panama and Hawaii; send a division of heavy cruisers on a visit to New Zealand, Australia, and Singapore; maintain a striking force of cruisers and carriers at Pearl Harbor; discuss plans of coordinate action with the British and Dutch; the British should maintain as large a naval and air force in Singapore as possible consistent with the situation in Europe and take positive action if Japan moves south from Hanoi to Cam Ranh Bay and Saigon.[10]

234

Admiral Stark commented on the Yarnell suggestions item by item in a letter to the Secretary of the Navy on January 17. Relative to strengthening the Philippines, Stark stated: "Anything we can send would probably be inadequate for a successful bluff or deterrent to Japan. It would certainly be inadequate to defend the Philippines, and it is doubtful if it could be withdrawn in time to preserve Singapore, Malay, or the Dutch East Indies. It is inadequate for effective action of any serious nature from the Philippines." On the heavy cruiser visits to New Zealand, Australia, and Singapore, he commented: "From a military standpoint I think a division of heavy cruisers in such an area on the outbreak of war would be unfortunate." And finally, the taking of positive action against Japan if she moved south from Hanoi was interpreted by Stark as meaning war with Japan, and he did not "recommend war against Japan if she seize[d] all of Indo-China."[11] In retrospect, the Philippines were strengthened, cruisers were sent on visits to New Zealand and Australia, and "positive action" was taken by freezing assets and invoking a complete oil embargo after the Japanese forces moved south in Indochina. Yarnell's suggestions were tried with Stark fighting them every step of the way.

The final phase of the deterrent concept took on new meaning with the fast-moving events in the fall of 1941. The previous attitude —that it was impossible to defend the Philippines—gave way to optimism over General MacArthur's new army and the arrival of B-17 bombers, submarines, and additional troops. On November 5, Stark and Marshall gave Roosevelt an *Estimate concerning Far Eastern Situation.* Although the programmed buildup of forces in the Philippines was indicated, there was also an unwarranted overevaluation of strength "on hand" as indicated in the following extract of the estimate:

> The present combined naval, air and ground forces will make attack on the islands a hazardous undertaking. By about the middle of December, 1941, United States air and submarine strength in the Philippines will have become a positive threat to any Japanese operations south of Formosa. The U.S. Army air forces in the Philippines will have reached its projected strength by February or March, 1942. The potency of this threat will have then increased to a point where it might well be a deciding factor in deterring Japan in operations in the areas south and west of the Philippines. By this time, additional British naval and air reinforcements to Singapore will have arrived. The general defensive strength of the entire southern area against possible Japanese operations will then have reached impressive proportions.[12]

The last attempt to deter Japan failed by months. In an intriguing game of historical supposition, it is most interesting to speculate whether Japan would have been deterred if the final Philippine buildup had been attained.

Only in the last few months before war commenced in the Pacific was there an attempt to build up a force in the Philippines which could be considered a deterrent. The main deterrent, in concept and strength, was the United States Fleet, later renamed the Pacific Fleet, in Hawaii. When Hart asked for additional cruisers in September 1939, Stark reviewed the *Orange* War Plan, conferred with the State Department and Roosevelt, and with their concurrence, sent the requested detachment to Hawaii instead of the Far East. Hart received a tender, a squadron of patrol aircraft, and six new submarines in lieu of cruisers. Stark, in explaining his rationale to Richardson, thought the decision to send the detachment to Hawaii under the "present world conditions" was sound, but that it would be difficult to assess how much effect the cruisers in Hawaii might have on Japan's foreign policy. At any rate the president and the State Department "okayed [the decision] one hundred percent."[13] The cruisers were to have plenty of company before too long.

At the end of the annual naval maneuvers in the spring of 1940 the United States Fleet was in Hawaiian waters. On May 7, Stark wrote to Richardson that he had "just hung up the telephone after talking with the President and by the time this reaches you you will have received word to remain in Hawaiian Waters for a couple of weeks." Two weeks later Richardson—still in Hawaii and uninformed about the plans for his fleet and facing problems of scheduling and training —wrote Stark to find out why the fleet was there and how long would it stay. Stark's reply was: "You are there because of the deterrent effect which it is thought your presence may have on the Japs going into the East Indies." Stark added that if Japan were to go into the Netherlands East Indies, he did not know nor did anyone else "in Gods' green earth" just what the United States would actually do. Richardson was told to remember that the Japanese did not know either what the United States was going to do and as long as they did not know "they may hesitate, or to be deterred."[14] With the fleet to be used as a deterrent, it would appear that a cycle had been completed. When Roosevelt came into office in 1933, the fleet was then at Pearl Harbor as a deterrent against Japan.

Richardson did not accept the validity of the concept that the fleet at Pearl Harbor was a deterrent to Japan. He visited Washington to persuade the President to return the fleet to the West Coast where it could be better supported and trained. In a memorandum covering talks with Roosevelt, Richardson recorded that he could be convinced "of the desirability of retaining the battleships on the West Coast if [he could] be given a good statement which will convince the American people, and the Japanese Government, that in bringing the battleships to the West Coast we are not stepping backward."[15] Roosevelt told Stark, relative to moving the fleet: "When I don't know how to move I stay put."[16] So the fleet "stayed put" despite Richardson's pleas.

Stark reiterated the problem once more to Richardson in November 1940: "As you know, the matter of withdrawing the Fleet from Hawaii is delicate, and could hardly be accomplished without a certain amount of preparation in Washington. It does not appear that we can withdraw it without some good pretext."[17] There would be no "good statement" or "pretext;" the fleet was held at Pearl Harbor by the deterrent idea which first put it there "for a couple of weeks." Its withdrawal might be considered by Japan as the withdrawal of a deterrent, thereby giving encouragement to any moves which were held in abeyance because of the deterrent. Kimmel relieved Richardson on February 1, 1941, and continued the recital of complaints about deficiencies in the fleet. The deterring fleet, lacking the support ships necessary to move it westward from Hawaii and having its effectiveness constantly diminished as the expansion to a two-ocean navy accelerated to full speed, remained in place. Despite its deteriorating battle efficiency, to the Japanese it still posed a threat and therefore a deterrent. Finally, it was not recalled to the West Coast of the United States, and a major part of the battle line was either sunk or incapacitated by the Japanese attack on Pearl Harbor.

The question of the oil export restrictions was a thorny one. Japan received the bulk of her oil from the United States. As the possibility of war increased, the export of oil to Japan was tantamount to furnishing a probable enemy with important logistic support. On the surface such actions would appear strategically unsound, but several considerations colored the whole picture. By 1939 Japan had accumulated huge oil reserves, and in the period of accumulation the American people were little concerned over future national security. There was no attempt to curtail the profitable oil trade *while* the reserves were being built. When operations in China cut into the reserves and huge orders were placed to compensate for the increased use, the international situation had changed. Oil in 1940 had become a strategic commodity due to the war in Europe, and Japan was tied to the Axis powers fighting in that area.

Secretaries Morgenthau, Stimson, Knox, and Ickes and many

naval officers thought that curtailing shipments of oil to Japan would deter further aggression, reasoning that for want of oil she could not fight elsewhere. It would appear that this faction had a low estimate of the accumulated reserve, or else chose to ignore the fact that a total embargo did not run the tap dry immediately. Conservative estimates gave Japan nine to twelve months reserve at "normal" war usage. The group led by Stark and Welles, who wanted limited shipments continued (which amounted to near the former total flow through circumvention) reasoned that though the price of peace in the Pacific came high, it was worth it until the defeat of Germany was assured. Again it is interesting to speculate whether continuing the oil shipments would have kept Japan out of the war long enough for the deterrent force in the Philippines and in the British Far Eastern Fleet to become completely effective, or whether Japan would have reacted regardless of the oil policy. Fears of Japanese seizure of the oil in the Dutch East Indies started even before the war in Europe and certainly contributed to the ultimate decision to build up the British and American forces in the Far East in late 1941. Those deterrents in the Philippines and the augmented British Fleet and the United States Fleet "on her eastern flank" were effective against Japan until the decision to strike Pearl Harbor was made. Then that which Stark feared happened. With prospects of diminishing oil reserves and ever-growing deterrents facing her, Japan decided she had to strike while she could. Those forces which posed the greatest threat to her were the first to be attacked and quickly eliminated.

The attack on Pearl Harbor and the Philippines marked the end of a most significant phase in Japanese-American foreign relations. The years of planning for war with Japan were at an end. In the preceding five years the old unrealistic *Orange* War Plan reached its last stage of development. Fortunately for the United States it was not given the ultimate test, for although the objectives and estimated requirements were pared down from the original, the last *Orange* Plan was still overly ambitious. The chronic shortage of troops, the lack of a train to support a fleet movement, the weakness of the Philippine defenses, and the unknown capabilities of the Japanese in the mandated islands were factors which could not be ignored. Attempts to visit the strategically located islands, so inconveniently straddling American lines of communications to the Orient, failed, lending more weight to suspicions of illegal fortifications. To have allowed the islands to pass from Spanish possession through German hands to the Japanese was a strategic mistake due to lack of foresightedness. Not to enure that the islands were kept in accordance with the mandate was an accepted strategic risk, since Guam and the Philippines were undefended by the Washington Treaty of 1922.

As German successes continued in 1940, American naval leaders appreciated still more the necessity of cooperation with allies in the Atlantic and Pacific. The strategic thinking found expression in Admiral Stark's *Plan Dog*. Subsequent conferences with the British in early 1941 produced an agreement on strategy in the Atlantic, but meetings with the British and Dutch at Singapore and Batavia were much less productive. In the present era of numerous bilateral and multilateral defense alliances between the United States and most of the non-Communist world, it is difficult to appreciate the problems in 1941 of reaching joint agreements with obvious allies faced with a common threat. Certainly the *ABC* accord stands out as an exception. The frustrations of arriving at an acceptable *ADB* plan against Japan and the equally serious disagreements over American participation in the defense of Singapore have been described. On reflection there could be serious arguments that even with the culmination of an *ADB* plan, without the forces to make it effective, there would have been little change in the deterrent effects on Japan. Even agreed-upon operations plans would prove little against one major strength factor of Japan—air superiority. MacArthur's B-17 bombers, which sat parked in neat rows on Clark Air Base in the Philippines and were completely destroyed in one raid, and the *Prince of Wales* and *Repulse* were all victims of that superiority in the opening hours of the war.

The weakness of United States power in the Far East in 1941 stands in stark contrast to power after the war. It is interesting to observe that the active military efforts of the United States since World War II have been in the Far East: in Korea with many allies and in Vietnam with few allies. In both cases the burden of effort was carried by the United States and therein spells the difference in the situation existing in 1941. The United States has extended its sphere of influence into Asia with powerful air and naval superiority to back up its national policies, unilaterally if necessary.

As power has changed in the Far East since 1941, so has it changed in the same period in bureaucratic Washington. All Presidents since Roosevelt have taken those military actions they deemed necessary in the international arena without the fears of congressional disapproval which permeated the thinking of Roosevelt and his advisers and which were appreciated by and shared with Churchill in 1941. As presidential power has increased, that of the military leadership has been bridled. Gone are the days when a chief of naval op erations helped shape United States foreign policy *directly* with a president and secretary of state. The pre-World War II *ad hoc* ar rangements which evolved out of the demands of practicality and ex pediency have been formalized by act of Congress in the Joint Chiefs of Staff and the National Security Council. A new echelon—the Secre tary of Defense with his ever-expanding staff organization—has been interposed between the President and the service chiefs and service secretaries. The CNO may still approach the President directly, but he would have a very difficult time, even with a definitely naval-oriented President such as Roosevelt, exerting the influence which Stark did.

According to his correspondence, official documents, and the per sonal memoirs of others, Stark did exert his influence on foreign policy. His *Plan Dog* was the blueprint for the initial participation of the United States in the war. He had the support of Welles, and most often Roosevelt and Hull, in the discussions on deterrent strategy. Cer tainly Stark did enjoy a favorable relationship with Roosevelt, yet his near-opposite in strategic thinking, Yarnell, also had influence. He too had most of his "get tough" ideas tried. The Roosevelt technique of orchestrating the divergent views of his subordinates applied to naval strategy as well as in the political fields.

The United States Navy in the period discussed was certainly the dominant American force in the Pacific and naval strategy and naval influence were deeply involved in almost all relations with Japan. Though the naval influence was pronounced and the U.S. Navy must take its share of the mistakes made, the final decisions, as always, were made by the Commander in Chief, the President of the United States.

APPENDIX A

"Plan Dog"

Op-12-CTB   November 12, 1940

MEMORANDUM FOR THE SECRETARY

Referring to my very brief touch in a recent conference as to the desirability of obtaining at once some light upon the major decisions which the President may make for guiding our future naval effort in the event of war, and in further immediate preparation for war, you may recall my remarks the evening we discussed War Plans for the Navy. I stated then that if Britain wins decisively against Germany we could win everywhere: but that if she loses the problem confronting us would be very great; and, while we might not *lose everywhere*, we might possibly, not *win anywhere*.

As I stated last winter on the Hill, in these circumstances we would be set back upon our haunches. Our war effort, instead of being widespread, would then have to be confined to the Western Hemisphere.

I now wish to expand my remarks, and to present to you my views concerning steps we might take to meet the situation that will exist should the United States enter war either alone or with allies. In this presentation, I have endeavored to keep in view the political realities in our own country.

The first thing to consider is how and where we might become involved.

(a) War with Japan in which we have no allies. This might be precipitated by Japanese armed opposition should we strongly reinforce our Asiatic Fleet or the Philippines Garrison, should we start fortifying Guam, or should we impose additional important economic sanctions; or it might be precipitated by ourselves in case of overt

241

Japanese action against us, or by further extention of Japanese hegemony.

(b) War with Japan in which we have the British Empire, or the British Empire and Netherlands East Indies, as allies. This might be precipitated by one of the causes mentioned in (a), by our movement of a naval reinforcement to Singapore, or by Japanese attack on British or Netherlands territory.

(c) War with Japan in which she is aided by Germany and Italy, and in which we are or are not aided by allies. To the causes of such a war, previously listed, might be added augmented American material assistance to Great Britain, our active military intervention in Britain's favor, or our active resistance to German extention of military activities to the Western Hemisphere.

(d) War with Germany and Italy in which Japan would not be initially involved and in which we would be allied with the British. Such a war would be initiated by American decision to intervene for the purpose of preventing the disruption of the British Empire, or German capture of the British Isles.

(e) We should also consider the alternative of now remaining out of war, and devoting ourselves exclusively to building up our defense of the Western Hemisphere, plus the preservation by peaceful means of our Far Eastern interests, and plus also continued material assistance to Great Britain.

As I see it, our major national objectives in the immediate future might be stated as preservation of the territorial, economic, and ideological integrity of the United States, plus that of the remainder of the Western Hemisphere; the prevention of the disruption of the British Empire, with all that such a consummation implies; and the diminution of the offensive military power of Japan, with a view to the retention of our economic and political interests in the Far East. It is doubtful, however, that it would be in our interest to reduce Japan to the status of an inferior military and economic power. A balance of power in the Far East is to our interest as much as is a balance of power in Europe.

The questions that confront us are concerned with the preparation and distribution of the naval forces of the United States, in cooperation with its military forces, for use in war in the accomplishment of all or part of these national objectives.

I can only surmise as to the military, political, and economic situation that would exist in the Atlantic should the British Empire collapse. Since Latin-America has rich natural resources, and is the only important area of the world not now under the practical control of strong military powers, we can not dismiss the possibility that, sooner or later, victorious Axis nations might move firmly in that direction. For some years they might remain too weak to attack directly across the sea; their effort more likely would first be devoted to developing Latin American economic dependence, combined with strongly reinforced internal political upheavals for the purpose of establishing friendly regimes in effective military control. The immediacy of danger to us may depend upon the security of the Axis military position in Eastern Europe and the Mediterranean, the degree of our own military preoccupation in the Pacific, and the disturbing influence of unsatisfied economic needs of Latin-America.

The present situation of the British Empire is not encouraging. I believe it easily possible, lacking active American military assistance, for that empire to lose this war and eventually be disrupted.

It is my opinion that the British are over-optimistic as to their chances for ultimate success. It is not at all sure that the British Isles can hold out, and it may be that they do not realize the danger that will exist should they lose in other regions.

Should Britain lose the war, the military consequences to the United States would be serious.

If we are to prevent the disruption of the British Empire, we must support its vital needs.

Obviously, the British Isles, the "Heart of the Empire," must remain intact.

But even if the British Isles are held, this does not mean that Britain can win the war. To win, she must finally be able to effect the complete, or, at least, the partial collapse of the Germain Reich.

This result might, conceivably, be accomplished by bombing and by economic starvation through the agency of the blockade. It surely can be accomplished only by military successes on shore, facilitated possibly by over-extension and by internal antagonisms developed by the Axis conquests.

Alone, the British Empire lacks the man power and the material means to master Germany. Assistance by powerful allies is necessary both with respect to men and with respect to munitions and supplies. If such assistance is to function effectively, Britain must not only continue to maintain the blockade, but she must also retain intact geographical positions from which successful land action can later be launched.

Provided England continues to sustain its present successful resistance at home, the area of next concern to the British Empire ought to be the Egyptian Theater.

Should Egypt be lost, the Eastern Mediterranean would be opened to Germany, and Italy, the effectiveness of the sea blockade would be largely nullified; Turkey's military position would be fully compromised; and all hope of favorable Russian action would vanish.

Any anti-German offensive in the Near East would then become impossible.

The spot next in importance to Egypt, in my opinion, is Gibraltar, combined with West and Northwest Africa. From this area an ultimate offensive through Portugal, Spain and France, with the help of populations inimical to Germany, might give results equal to those which many years ago were produced by Wellington. The western gate to the Mediterranean would still be kept closed, provided Britain holds this region.

This brief discussion naturally brings into question the value to Britain of the Mediterranean relative to that of Hong Kong, Singapore and India. Were the Mediterranean lost, Britain's strength in the Far East could be augmented without weakening home territory.

Japan probably wants the British out of Hong Kong and Singapore; and wants economic control, and ultimately military control, of Malaysia.

It is very questionable if Japan has territorial ambitions in Australia and New Zealand.

But does she now wish the British out of India, thus exposing that region and Western China to early Russian penetration or influence? I doubt it.

It would seem more probable that Japan, devoted to the Axis alliance only so far as her own immediate interests are involved, would prefer not to move military forces against Britain, and possibly not against the Netherlands East Indies, because, if she can obtain a high degree of economic control over Malaysia, she will then be in a position to improve her financial structure by increased trade with Britain and America. Her economic offensive power will be increased. Her military dominance will follow rapidly or slowly, as seems best at the time.

The Netherlands East Indies has 60,000,000 people, under the rule of 80,000 Dutchmen, including women and children. This political situation can not be viewed as in permanent equilibrium. The rulers are unsupported by a home country or by an alliance. Native rebellions have occurred in the past, and may recur in the future.

244

These Dutchmen will act in what they believe is their own selfish best interests.

Will they alone resist aggression, or will they accept an accommodation with the Japanese?

Will they resist, if supported only by the British Empire?

Will they firmly resist, if supported by the British Empire and the U. States?

Will the British resist Japanese aggression directed only against the Netherlands East Indies?

Should both firmly resist, what local military assistance will they require from the United States to ensure success?

No light on these questions has been thrown by the report of the proceedings of the recent Singapore Conference.

The basic character of a war against Japan by the British and Dutch would be the fixed defense of the Malay Peninsula, Sumatra and Java. The allied army, naval, and air forces now in position are considerable, and some future reenforcement may be expected from Australia and New Zealand. Borneo and the islands to the East are vulnerable. There is little chance for an allied offensive. Without Dutch assistance, the external effectiveness of the British bases at Hong Kong and Singapore would soon disappear.

The Japanese deployment in Manchukuo and China requires much of their Army, large supplies and merchant tonnage, and some naval force. It is doubtful if Japan will feel secure in withdrawing much strength from in front of Russia, regardless of non-aggression agreements. The winter lull in China will probably permit the withdrawal of the forces they need for a campaign against Malaysia. The availability of ample supplies for such a campaign is problematical.

Provided the British and Dutch cooperate in a vigorous and efficient defense of Malaysia, Japan will need to make a major effort with all categories of military force to capture the entire area. The campaign might even last several months. Whether Japan would concurrently be able successfully to attack Hong Kong and the Philippines, and also strongly to support the fixed positions in the Mid-Pacific, seems doubtful.

During such a campaign, due to her wide dispersion of effort, Japan would, unquestionably be more vulnerable to attack by the United States (or by Russia) than she would be once Malaysia is in her possession.

This brings us to a consideration of the strategy of an American war against Japan, that is, either the so-called "Orange Plan," or a modification. It must be understood that the Orange Plan was drawn up to govern our operations when the United States and Japan are at war, and no other nations are involved.

You have heard enough of the Orange Plan to know that, in a nutshell, it envisages our Fleet's proceeding westward through the Marshalls and the Carolines, consolidating as it goes, and then on to the recapture of the Philippines. Once there, the Orange Plan contemplates the eventual economic starvation of Japan, and, finally, the complete destruction of her external military power. Its accomplishment would require several years, and the absorption of the full military, naval, and economic energy of the American people.

In proceeding through these Mid-Pacific islands, we have several subsidiary objectives in mind. First, we hope that our attack will induce the Japanese to expose their fleet in action against our fleet, and lead to their naval defeat. Second, we wish to destroy the ability of the Japanese to use these positions as air and submarine bases from which to project attacks on our lines of communication to the mainland and Hawaii. Third, we would use the captured positions for supporting our further advance westward.

Most of the island positions are atolls. These atolls, devoid of natural sources of water other than rainfall, and devoid of all supplies, are merely narrow coral and sand fringes around large shallow areas where vessels may anchor. Alone, they are undefendable against serious attack, either by one side or the other. They do, however, afford weak positions for basing submarines and seaplanes. Our Fleet should have no difficulty in capturing atolls, provided we have enough troops, but we could not hold them indefinitely unless the Fleet were nearby.

We know little about the Japanese defenses in the Mid-Pacific. We believe the real islands of Truk and Ponape in the Carolines are defended with guns and troops, and we believe that some of the atolls of the Marshalls may be equipped as submarine and air bases, and be garrisoned with relatively small detachments of troops.

The Marshalls contain no sites suitable for bases in the absence of the Fleet, though there are numerous good anchorages. With the Fleet at hand, they can be developed for use as seaplane and submarine bases for the support of an attack on real islands such as Ponape and Truk. With the Fleet permanently absent, they will succumb to any serious thrust.

Our first real Marshall-Caroline objective is Truk, a magnificent harbor, relatively easily defended against raids, and capable of conversion into an admirable advanced base. When we get this far in the accomplishment of the "Orange Plan," we have the site for a base where we can begin to assemble our ships, stores, and troops, for further advance toward the Philippines. It would also become the center of the defense system for the lines of communications against flank attack from Japan.

Getting to Truk involves a strong effort. We would incur losses from aircraft, mines and submarines, particularly as the latter could be spared the operations in Malaysia. We would lose many troops in assaulting the islands.

Going beyond Truk initiates the most difficult part of the Orange Plan, would take a long time, and would require the maximum effort which the United States could sustain.

Truk is not looked upon as a satisfactory final geographical objective. It is too far away to support useful operations in the China Sea. It can not be held in the absence of fairly continuous Fleet support. No matter what gains are made in the Mid-Pacific, they would undoubtedly be lost were the Fleet to be withdrawn to the Atlantic. We would have then to choose between a lengthy evacuation process, and a major loss of men, material and prestige.

In advancing to the capture of Ponape and Truk, the Orange Plan contemplates proceeding promptly, delaying in the Marshalls only long enough to destroy Japanese shore bases, to capture the atolls necessary to support the advance and to deny future bases to Japan.

We have little knowledge as to the present defensive strength of the Marshall and Caroline groups, considered as a whole. If they are well defended, to capture them we estimate initial needs at 25,000 thoroughly trained troops, with another 50,000 in immediate reserve. If they are not well defended, an early advance with fewer troops might be very profitable. Several months must elapse from the present date before 75,000 troops could be made ready, considering the defense requirements of Alaska, Hawaii, and Samoa, and our commitments with respect to the internal political stability of the Latin-American countries.

We should consider carefully the chances of failure as well as of success. An immediate success would be most important morally, while a failure would be costly from the moral viewpoint. Before invading Norway, Germany trained for three months the veterans of the Polish campaign. Remembering Norway, we have the example of two methods of overseas adventure. One is the British method; the other is the German method.

The question of jumping directly from Hawaii to the Philippines has often been debated, but, so far as I know, this plan has always been ruled out by responsible authorities as unsound from a military viewpoint. Truk is 1900 miles from Yokohama, 5300 miles from San Francisco, 3200 from Honolulu, and 2000 miles from Manila. I mention this to compare the logistic problem with that of the Norway incident. An enormous amount of shipping would be required. Its availability under present world conditions would be doubtful.

Of course the foregoing, (the Orange Plan), is a major commitment in the Pacific, and does not envisage the cooperation of allies. Once started the abandonment of the offensive required by the plan, to meet a threat in the Atlantic, would involve abandoning the objectives of the war, and also great loss of prestige.

A totally different situation would exist were the Philippines and Guam rendered secure against attack by adequate troops, aircraft, and fortifications. The movement of the Fleet across the Pacific for the purpose of applying direct pressure upon Japan, and its support when in position, would be less difficult than in the existing situation.

Should we adopt the present Orange Plan today, or any modification of that plan which involves the movement of very strong naval and army contingents to the Far East, we would have to accept considerable danger in the Atlantic, and would probably be unable to augment our material assistance to Great Britain.

We should, therefore, examine other plans which involve a war having a more limited objective than the complete defeat of Japan, and in which we would undertake hostilities only in cooperation with the British and Dutch, and in which these undertake to provide an effective and continued resistance in Malaysia.

Our involvement in war in the Pacific might well make us also an ally of Britain in the Atlantic. The naval forces remaining in the Atlantic, for helping our ally and for defending ourselves, would, by just so much, reduce the power which the United States Fleet could put forth in the Pacific.

The objective in a limited war against Japan would be the reduction of Japanese offensive power chiefly through economic blockade. Under one concept, allied strategy would comprise holding the Malay Barrier, denying access to other sources of supply in Malaysia, severing her lines of communication with the Western Hemisphere, and raiding communications to the Mid-Pacific, the Philippines, China, and Indo-China. United States defensive strategy would also require army reenforcement of Alaska and the Hawaiian Islands, the establishment of naval bases in the Fiji, Samoan and Gilbert Islands areas, and denial to Japan of the use of the Marshalls as light force bases. We might be able to re-enforce the Philippine garrison, particularly with aircraft. I do not believe that the British and Dutch alone could hold Malay Barrier without direct military assistance by the United States. In addition to help from our Asiatic Fleet, I am convinced that they would need further reenforcement by ships and aircraft drawn from our Fleet in Hawaii, and possibly even by troops.

Besides military aid for the allied defense forces, our intervention would bring them a tremendous moral stimulus.

An alternative concept of the suggested limited war would provide additional support from the main body of the Fleet either by capturing the Marshalls, or by capturing both the Marshalls and Carolines. This, or a similar fleet activity, would be for the purpose of diverting away from Malaysia important Japanese forces to oppose it, and thus reducing the strength of their assault against the Dutch and British.

But we should consider the prospect that the losses which we would incur in such operations might not be fruitful of compensating results. Furthermore, withdrawal of the Fleet from captured positions for transfer to the Atlantic would be more difficult.

It is out of the question to consider sending our entire Fleet at once to Singapore. Base facilities are far too limited, the supply problem would be very great, and Hawaii, Alaska, and our coasts would be greatly exposed to raids.

One point to remember, in connection with a decision to adopt a limited offensive role, as in both of the alternative plans just mentioned, is that, in case of reverses, public opinion may require a stronger effort. For example, should Japanese success in the Far East seem imminent, there would be great pressure brought to bear to support our force there, instead of leaving it hanging in the air. Thus, what we might originally plan as a limited war with Japan might well become an unlimited war; our entire strength would then be required in the Far East, and little force would remain for eventualities in the Atlantic and for the support of the British Isles.

Let us now look eastward, and examine our possible action in the Atlantic.

In the first place, if we avoid serious commitment in the Pacific, the purely American Atlantic problem, envisaging defense of our coasts, the Caribbean, Canada, and South America, plus giving strong naval assistance to Britain, is not difficult so long as the British are able to maintain their present naval activity. Should the British Isles

249

then fall we would find ourselves acting alone, and at war with the world. To repeat, we would be thrown back on our haunches.

Should we enter the war as an ally of Great Britain, and not then be at war with Japan, we envisage the British asking us for widespread naval assistance. Roughly, they would want us, in the Western Atlantic Ocean from Cape Sable to Cape Horn, to protect shipping against raiders and submarine activities. They would also need strong reenforcements for their escort and minesweeping forces in their home waters; and strong flying boat reconnaissance from Scotland, the Atlantic Islands, and Capetown. They might ask us to capture the Azores and the Cape Verde Islands.

To their home waters they would have us send submarines and small craft, and to the Mediterranean assistance of any character which we may be able to provide. They would expect us to take charge of allied interests in the Pacific, and to send a naval detachment to Singapore.

This purely naval assistance, would not, in my opinion, *assure* final victory for Great Britain. Victory would probably depend upon her ability ultimately to make a land offensive against the Axis powers. For making a successful land offensive, British man power is insufficient. Offensive troops from other nations will be required. I believe that the United States, in addition to sending naval assistance, would also need to send large air and land forces to Europe or Africa, or both, and to participate strongly in this land offensive. The naval task of transporting an army abroad would be large.

To carry out such tasks we would have to exert a major naval and military effort in the Atlantic. We would then be able to do little more in the Pacific than remain on a strict defensive.

Were we to enter the war against Germany and Italy as an ally of Great Britain, I do not necessarily anticipate immediate hostile action by Japan, whatever may be her Axis obligation. She may fear eventual consequences and do nothing. We might be faced with demands for concessions as the price of her neutrality. She might agree to defer her aggressions in the Netherlands East Indies for the time being by a guarantee of ample economic access to the Western Hemisphere and to British and Dutch possessions. But she might even demand complete cessation of British and American assistance to China.

The strong wish of the American government and people at present seems to be to remain at peace. In spite of this, we must face the possibility that we may at any moment become involved in war. With war in prospect, I believe our every effort should be directed toward the *prosecution of a national* policy with *mutually supporting diplo-*

matic and military aspects, and having as its guiding feature a determination that any intervention we may undertake shall be such as will ultimately best *promote our own national interests.* We should see the best answer to the question: "Where should we fight the war, and for what objective?" With the answer to this question to guide me, I can make a more logical plan, can more appropriately distribute the naval forces, can better coordinate the future material preparation of the Navy, and can more usefully advise as to whether or not proposed diplomatic measures can adequately be supported by available naval strength.

That is to say, until the question concerning our final military objective is authoritatively answered, I can not determine the scale and the nature of the effort which the Navy may be called upon to exert in the Far East, the Pacific, and the Atlantic.

It is a fundamental requirement of our military position that our homeland remain secure against successful attack. Directly concerned in this security is the safety of other parts of the Western Hemisphere. A very strong pillar of the defense structure of the Americas has, for many years, been the balance of power existing in Europe. The collapse of Great Britain or the destruction or surrender of the British Fleet will destroy this balance and will free European military power for possible encroachment in this hemisphere.

I believe that we should recognize as the foundation of adequate armed strength the possession of a profitable foreign trade, both in raw materials and in finished goods. Without such a trade, our economy can scarcely support heavy armaments. The restoration of foreign trade, particularly with Europe, may depend upon the continued integrity of the British Empire.

It may be possible for us to prevent a British collapse by military intervention.

Our interests in the Far East are very important. The economic effect of a complete Japanese hegemony in that region is conjectural. But regardless of economic considerations, we have heretofore strongly opposed the further expansion of Japan.

We might temporarily check Japanese expansion by defeating her in a war in the Far East, but to check her permanently would require that we retain possession of, and militarily develop, an extensive and strategically located Asiatic base area having reasonably secure lines of communication with the United States. Retaining, and adequately developing, an Asiatic base area would mean the reversal of long-standing American policy.

Whether we could ensure the continued existence of a strong

British Empire by soundly defeating Japan in the Far East is questionable, though continuing to hold on there for the present is a definite contribution to British strength.

Lacking possession of an Asiatic base area of our own, continued British strength in the Far East would doubtless prove advantageous to us in checking Japan permanently.

The military matters discussed in this memorandum may properly receive consideration in arriving at a decision on the course that we should adopt in the diplomatic field. An early decision in this field will facilitate a naval preparation which will best promote the adopted course. As I see affairs today, answers to the following broad questions will be most useful to the Navy:

(A) Shall our principal military effort be directed toward hemisphere defense, and include chiefly those activities within the Western Hemisphere which contribute directly to security against attack in either or both oceans? An affirmative answer would indicate that the the United States, as seems now to be the hope of this country, would remain out of war unless pushed into it. If and when forced into war, the greater portion of our Fleet could remain for the time being in its threatening position in the Pacific, but no major effort would be exerted overseas either to the east or the west; the most that would be done for allies, besides providing material help, would be to send detachments to assist in their defense. It should be noted here that, were minor help to be given in one direction, public opinion might soon push us into giving it major support, as was the case in the World War.

Under this plan, our influence upon the outcome of the European War would be small.

(B) Shall we prepare for a full offensive against Japan, premised on assistance from the British and Dutch forces in the Far East, and remain on the strict defensive in the Atlantic? If this course is selected, we would be placing full trust in the British to hold their own indefinitely in the Atlantic, or, at least, until after we should have defeated Japan decisively, and thus had fully curbed her offensive power for the time being. Plans for augmenting the scale of our present material assistance to Great Britain would be adversely affected until Japan had been decisively defeated. The length of time required to defeat Japan would be very considerable.

If we enter the war against Japan and then if Great Britain loses, we probably would in any case have to reorient towards the Atlantic. There is no dissenting view on this point.

(C) Shall we plan for sending the strongest possible military assistance both to the British in Europe, and to the British, Dutch and Chinese in the Far East? The naval and air detachments we would send to the British Isles would possibly ensure their continued resistance, but would not increase British power to conduct a land offensive. The strength we could send to the Far East might be enough to check the southward spread of Japanese rule for the duration of the war. The strength of naval forces remaining in Hawaii for the defense of the Eastern Pacific, and the strength of the forces in the Western Atlantic for the defense of that area, would be reduced to that barely sufficient for executing their tasks. Should Great Britain finally lose, or should Malaysia fall to Japan, our naval strength might then be found to have been seriously reduced, relative to that of the Axis powers. It should be understood that, under this plan, we would be operating under the handicap of fighting major wars on two fronts.

Should we adopt Plan (C), we must face the consequences that would ensue were we to start a war with one plan, and then, after becoming heavily engaged, be forced greatly to modify it or discard it altogether, as, for example, in case of a British fold up. On neither of these distant fronts would it be possible to execute a really major offensive. Strategically, the situation might become disastrous should our effort on either front fail.

(D) Shall we direct our efforts toward an eventual strong offensive in the Atlantic as an ally of the British, and a defensive in the Pacific? Any strength that we might send to the Far East would, by just so much, reduce the force of our blows against Germany and Italy. About the least that we would do for our ally would be to send strong naval light forces and aircraft to Great Britain and the Mediterranean. Probably we could not stop with a purely naval effort. The plan might ultimately require capture of the Portuguese and Spanish Islands and military and naval bases in Africa and possibly Europe; and thereafter even involve undertaking a full scale land offensive. In consideration of a course that would require landing large numbers of troops abroad, account must be taken of the possible unwillingness of the people of the United States to support land operations of this character, and to incur the risk of heavy loss should Great Britain collapse. Under Plan (D) we would be unable to exert strong pressure against Japan, and would necessarily gradually reorient our policy in the Far East. The full national offensive strength would be exerted in a single direction, rather than be extended in areas far distant from each other. At the conclusion of the war, even if Britain should finally collapse, we might still find ourselves possessed of bases in Africa suitable for assisting in the defense of South America.

Under any of these plans, we must recognize the possibility of the involvement of France as an ally of Germany.

I believe that the continued existence of the British Empire, combined with building up a strong protection in our home areas, will do most to ensure the status quo in the Western Hemisphere, and to promote our principal national interests. As I have previously stated, I also believe that Great Britain requires from us very great help in the Atlantic, and possibly even on the continents of Europe or Africa, if she is to be enabled to survive. In my opinion Alternatives (A), (B), and (C) will most probably not provide the necessary degree of assistance, and, therefore, if we undertake war, that Alternative (D) is likely to be the most fruitful for the United States, particularly if we enter the war at an early date. Initially, the offensive measures adopted would, necessarily, be purely naval. Even should we intervene, final victory in Europe is not certain. I believe that the chances for success are in our favor, particularly if we insist upon full equality in the political and military direction of the war.

The odds seem against our being able under Plan (D) to check Japanese expansion unless we win the war in Europe. We might not long retain possession of the Philippines. Our political and military influence in the Far East might largely disappear, so long as we were fully engaged in the Atlantic. A preliminary to a war in this category would be a positive effort to avoid war with Japan, and to endeavor to prevent war between Japan and the British Empire and the Netherlands East Indies. The possible cost of avoiding a war with Japan has been referred to previously.

I would add that Plan (D) does not mean the immediate movement of the Fleet into the Atlantic. I would make no further moves until war should become imminent, and then I would recommend redistribution of our naval forces as the situation then demanded. I fully recognize the value of retaining strong forces in the Pacific as long as they can profitably be kept there.

Until such time as the United States should decide to engage its full forces in war, I recommend that we pursue a course that will most rapidly increase the military strength of both the Army and the Navy, that is to say, adopt alternative (A) without hostilities.

Under any decision that the President may tentatively make, we should at once prepare a complete Joint Plan for guiding Army and Navy activities. We should also prepare at least the skeletons of alternative plans to fit possible alternative situations which may eventuate. I make the specific recommendation that, should we be forced into a war with Japan, we should, because of the prospect of war in the Atlantic also, definitely plan to avoid operations in the Far East or the Mid-Pacific that will prevent the Navy from promptly moving to the Atlantic forces fully adequate to safeguard our interests and policies in the event of a British collapse. We ought not now willingly engage in any war against Japan unless we are certain of aid from Great Britain and the Netherlands East Indies.

No important allied military decision should be reached without clear understanding between the nations involved as to the strength and extent of the participation which may be expected in any particular theater, and as to a proposed skeleton plan of operations.

Accordingly, I make the recommendation that, as a preliminary to possible entry of the United States into the conflict, the United States Army and Navy at once undertake secret staff talks on technical matters with the British military and naval authorities in London, with Canadian military authorities in Washington, and with British and Dutch authorities in Singapore and Batavia. The purpose would be to reach agreements and lay down plans for promoting unity of allied effort should the United States find it necessary to enter the war under any of the alternative eventualities considered in this memorandum.

H. R. Stark

APPENDIX B

The outline of a proposed basis for agreement which Secretary Hull handed to the Japanese Ambassadors follows, in full:

Strictly Confidential, Tentative and Without Commitment.

WASHINGTON, *November 26, 1941*

OUTLINE OF PROPOSED BASIS FOR AGREEMENT
BETWEEN THE UNITED STATES AND JAPAN

SECTION I

Draft Mutual Declaration of Policy

The Government of the United States and the Government of Japan both being solicitous for the peace of the Pacific affirm that their national policies are directed toward lasting and extensive peace throughout the Pacific area, that they have no territorial designs in that area, that they have no intention of threatening other countries or of using military force aggressively against any neighboring nation, and that, accordingly, in their national policies they will actively support and give practical application to the following fundamental principles upon which their relations with each other and with all other governments are based:

(1) The principle of inviolability of territorial integrity and sovereignty of each and all nations.

(2) The principle of noninterference in the internal affairs of other countries.

(3) The principle of equality, including equality of commercial opportunity and treatment.

(4) The principal of reliance upon international cooperation and conciliation for the prevention and pacific settlement of controversies and for improvement of international conditions by peaceful methods and processes.

256

The Government of Japan and the Government of the United States have agreed that toward eliminating chronic political instability, preventing recurrent economic collapse, and providing a basis for peace, they will actively support and practically apply the following principles in their economic relations with each other and with other nations and peoples:

(1) The principle of nondiscrimination in international commercial relations.

(2) The principle of international economic cooperation and abolition of extreme nationalism as expressed in excessive trade restrictions.

(3) The principle of nondiscriminatory access by all nations to raw material supplies.

(4) The principle of full protection of the interests of consuming countries and populations as regards the operation of international commodity agreements.

(5) The principle of establishment of such institutions and arrangements of international finance as may lend aid to the essential enterprises and the continuous development of all countries and may permit payments through processes of trade consonant with the welfare of all countries.

SECTION II

Steps to be Taken by the Government of the United States and by the Government of Japan

The Government of the United States and the Government of Japan propose to take steps as follows:

1. The Government of the United States and the Government of Japan will endeavor to conclude a multilateral nonaggression pact among the British Empire, China, Japan, the Netherlands, the Soviet Union, Thailand, and The United States.

2. Both Governments will endeavor to conclude among the American, British, Chinese, Japanese, the Netherland, and Thai Governments an agreement whereunder each of the Governments would pledge itself to respect the territorial integrity of French Indochina and, in the event that there should develop a threat to the territorial integrity of Indochina, to enter into immediate consultation with a view to taking such measures as may be deemed necessary and advisable to meet the threat in question. Such agreement would provide also that each of the Governments party to the agreement would not seek or accept preferential treatment in its trade or economic relations

257

with Indochina and would use its influence to obtain for each of the signatories equality of treatment in trade and commerce with French Indochina.

3. The Government of Japan will withdraw all military, naval, air, and police forces from China and from Indochina.

4. The Government of the United States and the Government of Japan will not support—militarily, politically, economically—any government or regime in China other than the National Government of the Republic of China with capital temporarily at Chungking.

5. Both Governments will give up all extraterritorial rights in China, including rights and interests in and with regard to international settlements and concessions, and rights under the Boxer Protocol of 1901.

Both Governments will endeavor to obtain the agreement of the British and other governments to give up extraterritorial rights in international settlements and in concessions and under the Boxer Protocol of 1901.

6. The Government of the United States and the Government of Japan will enter into negotiations for the conclusion between the United States and Japan of a trade agreement, based upon reciprocal most-favored-nation treatment and reduction of trade barriers by both countries, including an undertaking by the United States to bind raw silk on the free list.

7. The Government of the United States and the Government of Japan will, respectively, remove the freezing restrictions on Japanese funds in the United States and on American funds in Japan.

8. Both Governments will agree upon a plan for the stabilization of the dollar-yen rate, with the allocation of funds adequate for this purpose, half to be supplied by Japan and half by the United States.

9. Both Governments will agree that no agreement which either has concluded with any third power or powers shall be interpreted by it in such a way as to conflict with the fundamental purpose of this agreement, the establishment and preservation of peace throughout the Pacific area.

10. Both Governments will use their influence to cause other governments to adhere to and to give practical application to the basic political and economic principles set forth in this agreement.

MODUS VIVENDI

1. The Government of the United States and the Government of Japan, both being solicitous for the peace of the Pacific, affirm that

their national policies are directed toward lasting and extensive peace throughout the Pacific area and that they have no territorial designs therein. They undertake reciprocally not to make by force or threat of force, unless they are attacked, any advancement, from points at which they have military establishments, across any international border in the Pacific area.

2. The Japanese Government undertakes forthwith to withdraw its armed forces now stationed in southern French Indochina, not to engage in any further military activities there, including the construction of military facilities, and to limit Japanese military forces in northern French Indochina to the number there on July 26, 1941, which number in any case would not exceed 25,000 and which number would not be subject to replacement.

3. The Government of the United States undertakes forthwith to remove the freezing restrictions which were placed on Japanese assets in the United States on July 26 and the Japanese Government agrees simultaneously to remove the freezing measures which it imposed in regard to American assets in Japan. Exports from each country would thereafter remain subject to the respective export control measures which each country may have in effect for reasons of national defense.

4. The Government of the United States undertakes forthwith to approach the British and the Dutch Governments with a view to those Governments' taking, on a basis of reciprocity with Japan, measures similar to those provided for in paragraph three above.

5. The Government of the United States would not look with disfavor upon the inauguration of conversations between the Government of China and the Government of Japan directed toward a peaceful settlement of their differences nor would the Government of the United States look with disfavor upon an armistice during the period of any such discussions. The fundamental interest of the Government of the United States in reference to any such discussions is simply that they be based upon and exemplify the fundamental principles of peace which constitute the central spirit of the current conversations between the Government of Japan and the Government of the United States.

In case any such discussions are entered into between the Government of Japan and the Government of China, the Government of the United States is agreeable to such discussions taking place in the Philippine Islands, if so desired by both China and Japan.

6. It is understood that this modus vivendi is of a temporary nature and shall not remain in effect for a period longer than three months unless renewed by common agreement.

Notes

NOTES TO CHAPTER 1

1. Memo: Captain Bastedo to Chief of Naval Operations, 8 December 1936, Naval History Division Files, Washington, D.C. (hereafter cited as NHD), A 16-3/Warfare, Misc.

2. Memo: Chief of Naval operations to Captain Bastedo, 12 January 1937, Ibid.

3. Telegram: American Embassy, Peiping, to Secretary of State, 27 July 1936, National Archives, Washington, D.C. (hereafter cited as NA), 811.30/253.

4. Letter: Secretary of the Navy to Secretary of State, 5 June 1936, NA 811.3394/231.

5. Telegram: Ambassador Grew to Secretary of State, 13 July 1936, NA 811.3362i/15.

6. Memo: Mr. Hamilton *after* talking with Hill, Canaga, Puleston and Standley, 14 July 1936, Ibid.

7. Memo: Mr. Hamilton, 15 July 1936, Ibid.

8. Memo: Mr. Hamilton, 16 July 1936, Ibid.

9. Memo: President Roosevelt to Chief of Naval Operations, 10 August 1936, NHD A8/Intelligence.

10. Memo: conversation between President Roosevelt, Acting Secretary of State Moore, and Assistant Secretary of State Sayre, 16 November 1936, NA 711B.00111/6.

11. Ibid.

12. Letter: Commander in Chief, Asiatic Fleet, to Chief of Naval Operations, 17 November 1936, NA Navy File FF 6.

NOTES TO CHAPTER 2

1. Rear Admiral Julius Augustus Furer, *Administration of the Navy Department in World War II* (Washington: Department of the Navy, 1959), p. 6.

2. Maurice Matloff and Edwin M. Snell, *Strategic Planning for Coalition Warfare, 1941–1942,* United States Army in World War II series (Washington: Department of the Army, 1953), p. 3.

3. Personal letter: General Marshall to Representative Ross A. Collins, 21 June 1940, quoted by Mark Skinner Watson in *Chief of Staff: Prewar Plans and Preparations,* United States Army in World War II series (1950), p. 25.

4. Letter: American Embassy, Tokyo, to Secretary of State, 4 August 1937, NA 811.3394/270.

5. Telegram: Secretary of State to American Embassy, Tokyo, 11 May 1937, NA 811.3394/255.

6. Telegram: American Embassy, Tokyo, to Secretary of State, 19 May 1937, NA 811.3394/257.

7. Letter: Secretary of the Navy to Secretary of State, 15 May 1937, NA 894.3311/401.

8. Memo: Dr. Stanley K. Hornbeck, 16 August 1937, NA 793.94/9652.

9. Ibid.

10. Telegram: Commander in Chief, Asiatic Fleet, to Secretary of State, 19 August 1937, NA 793.94/9492.

11. Telegram: Consul General, Shanghai, to Secretary of State, 26 August 1937, NA 793.94/9696.

12. Telegram: Secretary of State to Ambassador Johnson, 10 August 1937, NA 893.0146/550a.

13. Ibid.

14. Telegram: Secretary of State to Consul General, Shanghai, 19 August 1937, NA 793.94/9519.

15. Telegram: Commander in Chief, Asiatic Fleet, to Chief of Naval Operations, 1 September 1937, NA 793.94/9829.

16. Telegram: Secretary of State to Consul General, Shanghai, 5 September 1937, NA 793.94112/12.

17. Memo: President Roosevelt to Secretary of State, 2 October 1937, NA 711.93/380½.

18. Memo: Secretary of State to President Roosevelt, 4 October 1937, Ibid.

19. Telegram: Commander in Chief, Asiatic Fleet, to Chief of Naval Operations, 22 September 1937, NA 393.1115/1057.

20. Letter: Chief of Naval Operations to Secretary of State, 14 September 1937, NA 894.3311/435.
21. Telegram: Commander in Chief, Asiatic Fleet, to Commander, Yangtze Patrol, 21 September 1937, NA 793.94/10169.
22. Telegram: Commander in Chief, Asiatic Fleet, to Secretary of State, 26 October 1937, NA 793.94/10840.
23. Telegram: Commander in Chief, Asiatic Fleet, to Chief of Naval Operations, 26 October 1937, NA 793.94/10849.
24. Memo: conversation between Mr. Hamilton and Admiral Richardson, 28 October 1937, NA 793.94/10975.
25. Memo: Mr. Hamilton, Ibid.
26. Memo: Mr. Hamilton, 10 December 1937, NA 893.0146/598.
27. Letter: Commander in Chief, Japanese Fleet in China, to Commander in Chief, Asiatic Fleet, 21 December 1937, quoted in telegram from Commander in Chief, Asiatic Fleet, to Chief of Naval Operations, 24 December 1937, NA 793.94/11791.
28. Letter: joint reply to Commander in Chief, Japanese Fleet in China, 23 December 1937, Ibid.

NOTES TO CHAPTER 3

1. Anthony Eden, *Memoirs: Facing the Dictators* (Boston: Houghton Mifflin Co., 1962), pp. 619–20.
2. Memo: Captain Ingersoll to Chief of Naval Operations, January 1938, NHD: Correspondence British-U.S. Conversations in London 1938–39.
3. *Hearings Before the Joint Committee on the Investigation of the Pearl Harbor Attack* (hereafter cited as *Pearl Harbor Attack*), 79th Congress, 39 vols. (Washington, D.C.: United States Government Printing Office, 1946), part 9, p. 4273.
4. Telegram: Commander in Chief, Asiatic Fleet, to Chief of Naval Operations, 5 January 1938, NA 793.94112/150.
5. Watson, *Chief of Staff*, p. 415.
6. Ibid., p. 92.
7. Letter: Chief of Naval Operations to Commander in Chief, United States Fleet, and Commander in Chief, Asiatic Fleet, 2 February 1938, NHD: Correspondence British-U.S. Conversations in London 1938–1939. Also CNO File.
8. Ibid.
9. Memo: Mr. Hamilton to Secretary of State, 10 March 1938, NA 811.30 Asiatic Fleet (hereafter cited as AF) /444.

10. Telegram: Ambassador Grew to Secretary of State, 22 April 1938, NA 394.115 Panay/443.
11. Telegram: Ambassador Johnson to Secretary of State, 12 June 1938, NA 793.94/13197.
12. Telegram: Secretary of State to American Embassy, Hankow, 13 June 1938, Ibid.
13. Telegram: Ambassador Johnson to Secretary of State, 15 June 1938, NA 793.94/13227.
14. Telegram: Secretary of State to Ambassador Johnson, 5 July 1938, NA 793.94/13235.
15. Telegram: Ambassador Johnson to Secretary of State, 7 July 1938, NA 393.1115/3354.
16. Telegram: Secretary of State to Consul General, Shanghai, 9 July 1938, NA 393.1115/3360.
17. Telegram: Ambassador Johnson to Secretary of State, 12 July 1938, NA 393.1115/3383.
18. Telegram: Ambassador Grew to Secretary of State, 17 July 1938, NA 811.30 AF/460.
19. Telegram: Consul General Lockhart to Secretary of State, 9 July 1938, NA 793.94/13412.
20. Telegram: Consul, Tsingtao, to Secretary of State, 9 July 1938, NA 394/1123 Massie, T. H., Mrs./17.
21. Ibid.
22. Telegram: Secretary of State to Ambassador Johnson, 24 July 1938, NA 811.30 AF/460.
23. Telegram: Consul, Chefoo, to Secretary of State, 25 July 1938, NA 811.30 AF/466.
24. Telegram: First Secretary of the Embassy, China, to Secretary of State, 27 July 1938, NA 811.30 AF/468.
25. Telegram: *Oahu* to Commander in Chief, Asiatic Fleet, 27 July 1938, NA 811.30 AF/468.
26. Telegram: *Oahu* to Commander in Chief, Asiatic Fleet, 1 August 1938, NA 811.30 AF/477.
27. Telegram: Commander in Chief, Asiatic Fleet, to Chief of Naval Operations, 3 August 1938, NA 811.30 AF/1481.
28. Telegram: *Oahu* to Commander in Chief, Asiatic Fleet, 4 August 1938, NA 811.30 AF/483.
29. Telegram: *Oahu* to Commander in Chief, Asiatic Fleet, 5 August 1938, NA 811.30 AF/485.
30. Telegram: *Oahu* to Commander in Chief, Asiatic Fleet, 6 August 1938, NA 811.30 AF/486.

31. Telegram: Commander in Chief, Asiatic Fleet, to Chief of Naval Operations, 15 August 1938, NA 811.30 AF/502.

32. Telegram: Secretary of State to Ambassador Grew, 15 August 1938, Ibid.

33. Telegram: Ambassador Grew to Secretary of State, 19 August 1938, NA 811.30 AF/517.

34. Telegram: *Oahu* to Commander in Chief, Asiatic Fleet, 19 August 1938, NA 811.30 AF/519.

35. Telegram: Commander in Chief, Asiatic Fleet, to Chief of Naval Operations, 20 August 1938, NA 811.30 AF/520.

36. Telegram: Chief of Naval Operations to Commander in Chief, Asiatic Fleet, 20 August 1938, NA 811.30 AF/527.

37. Telegram: Commander in Chief, Asiatic Fleet, to Chief of Naval Operations, 29 August 1938, NA 811.30 AF/563.

38. Telegram: Chief of Naval Operations to Commander in Chief, Asiatic Fleet, 30 August 1938, Ibid.

39. Telegram: *Oahu* to Commander in Chief, Asiatic Fleet, 2 September 1938, NA 811.30 AF/564.

40. Ibid.

41. Memo: M.M.H. (initials of Max Hamilton) to Secretary of State, 3 September 1938, NA 811.30 AF/564.

42. Telegram: Navy Purchasing Officer, Shanghai, to *Monocacy,* 8 September 1938, NA 811.30 AF/566.

43. Telegram: Navy Purchasing Officer, Shanghai, to *Monocacy,* 12 September 1938, NA 811.30 AF/516.

44. Telegram: Commander, Yangtze Patrol, to *Oahu,* 14 September 1938, NA 811.30 AF/579.

45. Telegram: Consul General, Shanghai, to Secretary of State, 26 September 1938, NA 811.30 AF/609.

46. Telegram: *Monocacy* to Commander, Yangtze Patrol, 27 September 1938, NA 811.30 AF/613.

47. Letter: Secretary of the Navy to Secretary of State, 28 July 1938, NHD: CNO July 1938.

48. Watson, *Chief of Staff,* pp. 97–98.

NOTES TO CHAPTER 4

1. Telegram: Ambassador Grew to Secretary of State, 10 February 1939, NA 793.94/14683.

2. Telegram: Consul General, Shanghai, to Secretary of State, 24 February 1939, NA 893.102S/1743.

3. Telegram: Consul General, Shanghai, to Secretary of State, 10 March 1939, NA 893.102S/1769.

4. Telegram: Consul at Hankow to Secretary of State, 23 April 1939, NA 393.1115/4210.

5. Telegram: Consul General, Shanghai, to Secretary of State, 11 May 1939, NA 893.102S/1796.

6. Telegram: Commander in Chief, Asiatic Fleet, to Chief of Naval Operations, 12 May 1939, NA 893.102S/1810.

7. Telegram: Ambassador Grew to Secretary of State, 13 May 1939, NA 893.102S/1800.

8. Telegram: Secretary of State to Consul at Amoy, 17 May 1939, NA 893.102 Kulangsu/130.

9. Telegram: Secretary of State to Consul at Swatow, 23 June 1939, NA 811.30 AF/763a.

10. Memo: Rear Admiral Ghormley on informal conversations, 12 June 1939, NHD: Correspondence British-U.S. Conversations in London, 1938–39.

11. Telegram: Ambassador Kennedy to Secretary of State, 27 June 1939, NA 893.102 Tientsin/317.

12. Same as note 10 above.

13. Letter: Chief of Naval Operations to Commander in Chief, United States Fleet, and Commander in Chief, Asiatic Fleet, 23 June 1939, NHD: same as note 10 above.

14. Matloff and Snell, *Coalition Warfare,* p. 5.

15. Ibid., p. 7.

16. Watson, *Chief of Staff,* pp. 103–4.

17. Memo: Chief of Naval Operations to Under Secretary of State, 11 August 1939, NHD A16-3/Warfare, Misc.

18. Captain Tracy B. Kittredge, USNR, unpublished monograph on "The United States Navy in World War II," NHD sect. III, vol. 1, note 83, p. 240.

19. Matloff and Snell, *Coalition Warfare,* p. 9.

20. Letter: Admiral Yarnell to Secretary of the Navy, 20 July 1939, NA 793.94/15339.

21. Memo: Director, War Plans Division, to Chief of Naval Operations, 1 September 1939, NHD A16/Mobilization.

22. Letter: Admiral Yarnell to Chief of Naval Operations, 2 September 1939, NHD A16-3/Warfare, Misc.

23. Francis Clifford Jones, *Japan's New Order in East Asia; Its Rise and Fall, 1937–45* (London: Oxford University Press, 1954), p. 153.

24. Cordell Hull, *The Memoirs of Cordell Hull,* 2 vols. (New York: Macmillan Company, 1948), p. 720.

25. Telegram: Consul General, Shanghai, to Secretary of State, 14 September 1939, NA 893.102S/1885.

NOTES TO CHAPTER 5

1. Pearl Harbor Attack, part 14, p. 923.

2. Ibid., pp. 924–27.

3. Ibid., p. 932.

4. Samuel E. Morison, *The Rising Sun in the Pacific, 1931–April 1942,* vol. III in History of United States Naval Operations in World War II (Boston: Little, Brown and Co., 1951), p. 43.

5. Kittredge, "U.S. Navy in World War II," sect. III, vol. 1, note 83, p. 240

6. Matloff and Snell, *Coalition Warfare,* pp. 9–10.

7. Memo: Mr. Frank Duvall to Dr. Stanley K. Hornbeck, 9 May 1940, NA 711.94/2116.

8. *Pearl Harbor Attack,* part 14, pp. 933–34.

9. Ibid., p. 935.

10. Winston Churchill, *Their Finest Hour* (Boston: Houghton Mifflin Co., 1949), pp. 24–25.

11. Memo: Captain Crenshaw to Chief of Naval Operations, 15 May 1940, NHD EA-EZ, case 805.

12. Memo: Captain Schuirmann on State Department conference, 15 May 1940, Ibid.

13. Kittredge, "U.S. Navy in World War II," sect. III, vol. 1, part C, ch. 12, p. 267.

14. Ibid., quoted from ALUSNA London dispatch 101200, May 1940.

15. Ibid., p. 269, quoted from ALUSNA London dispatch 171815, May 1940.

16. Telegram: First Secretary Smyth to Secretary of State, 14 May 1940, NA 740.0011 European War 1939/2922.

17. Letter: Admiral Hart to Admiral Stark, 7 June 1940, NHD EA-EZ, case 805.

18. Telegram: Secretary of State to Ambassador Grew, 16 May 1940, NA 893.0146/768.

19. *Pearl Harbor Attack,* part 14, pp. 938–39.

20. Ibid., pp. 940–42.

21. Matloff and Snell, *Coalition Warfare,* p. 13.

22. Ibid.

23. *Pearl Harbor Attack,* part 14, p. 943.

24. Ibid., p. 944.

25. William L. Langer and S. Everett Gleason, *The Challenge to Isolation, 1937–1940* (New York: Harper & Brothers, 1952), p. 611 ff.

26. Memo: Admiral Stark to President, 2 June 1940, NA 811.3310/ 1606½.

27. Memo: F.D.R. to Under Secretary of State, 3 June 1940, Ibid.

28. Letter: Admiral Hart to Admiral Stark, 7 June 1940, NHD EA-EZ, case 805.

29. Telegram: American Consul, Canton, to Secretary of State, 7 June 1940, NA 811.30 AF/853; letter: American Consul General, Canton, to Consul General for Japan, Canton, 18 September 1940, NA 811.30 AF/911.

30. Memo: Director of Naval Intelligence to Chief of Naval Operations, 8 June 1940, NA 893.0146/846.

31. Telegram: Consul, Tientsin, to Secretary of State, 11 June 1940, NA 893.0146/788.

32. Telegram: First Secretary of the Embassy, Peiping, to Secretary of State, 12 June 1940, NA 893.0146/791.

33. Telegram: First Secretary of the Embassy, Peiping, to Secretary of State, 28 August 1940, NA 893.0146/844.

34. Memo: By Dr. Hornbeck of visit by Commander McCracken, 25 June 1940, NA 893.102S/2091½.

35. Matloff and Snell, *Coalition Warfare,* p. 14.

36. Ibid., pp. 14–15.

37. Langer and Gleason, *Challenge to Isolation,* p. 549.

38. Ibid., p. 548.

39. *Pearl Harbor Attack,* part 14, pp. 1014–15.

40. Langer and Gleason, *Challenge to Isolation,* p. 550.

41. Hull, *Memoirs,* 1:793.

42. Langer and Gleason, *Challenge to Isolation,* p. 551.

43. Ibid.

44. Ibid., pp. 595–96.

45. *Pearl Harbor Attack,* part 15, pp. 1914–26.

46. Ibid., p. 1932.

47. Ibid., pp. 1929–30.

48. Ibid., p. 1594.

49. Ibid., part 5, p. 2453.

50. Ibid., part 3, p. 1409.

51. Langer and Gleason, *Challenge to Isolation,* p. 597.

52. Ibid.

53. Ibid., pp. 510–11.

54. *Pearl Harbor Attack,* part 14, p. 946.

55. Ibid., p. 947.
56. Ibid., part 3, p. 1055.
57. Ibid.
58. Ibid., part 14, p. 948.
59. Watson, *Chief of Staff*, p. 113.
60. Hull, *Memoirs*, 1:897–99.
61. Memo by Under Secretary of State Welles of conversation with Ambassador St. Quentin, 27 June 1940, NA 893.24/828.
62. Memo by Dr. Hornbeck, 25 June 1940, NA 893.102S/2091½.
63. Telegram: Acting Secretary of State to Ambassador Grew, 17 August 1940, NA 893.102S/2194a.
64. Telegram: Ambassador Grew to Secretary of State, 18 August 1940, NA 893.102S/2193.
65. *Pearl Harbor Attack,* part 14, pp. 963–64.
66. Ibid., pp. 956–57.
67. Ibid., p. 957.
68. Ibid., p. 958.
69. Ibid., pp. 958–59.
70. Ibid., pp. 952–53.
71. Memo: Joint Planning Committee to Admiral Stark and General Marshall, 27 September 1940; NHD: CNO File A16-1, September to December 1940.
72. Letter: Admiral Hart to Admiral Stark, 3 October 1940, NHD EA-EZ, case 805.
73. Watson, *Chief of Staff*, p. 117.
74. Pearl Harbor Attack, part 14, p. 962.
75. William L. Langer and S. Everett Gleason, *The Undeclared War, 1940–1941* (New York: Harper & Brothers, 1953), p. 43.
76. Memo: Secretary of the Navy to President, 9 October 1940, NHD A16-1, September to December 1940.
77. Memo: F.D.R. to Secretary of the Navy, 10 October 1940, Ibid.
78. *Pearl Harbor Attack,* part 14, pp. 1006–12.
79. Langer and Gleason, *Undeclared War,* p. 43.
80. *Pearl Harbor Attack,* part 14, p. 963.
81. Ibid., p. 969.
82. Ibid., p. 971.
83. Ibid., p. 972.
84. Memo of conversation between Secretary of State and British Ambassador, 25 November 1940, NA 740.0011 Pacific War/40.
85. *Pearl Harbor Attack,* part 14, p. 973.

86. Ibid., p. 980.
87. Ibid., p. 983.

NOTES TO CHAPTER 6

1. *Oil in Japan's War,* Report of the Oil and Chemical Division, United States Strategic Bombing Survey, Washington, D.C., 1946, p. 1.
2. Ibid., p. 11; Herbert Feis, *Road to Pearl Harbor* (Princeton: Princeton University Press, 1950), p. 268.
3. Feis, *Road to Pearl Harbor,* p. 89.
4. Ibid., p. 41.
5. Ibid., p. 90.
6. Ibid., pp. 90–91.
7. Ibid., pp. 92–93.
8. Memo: Commander McCollum to Director of Naval Intelligence, 2 November 1940, NHD: CNO L11-4/EF37.
9. Director of Naval Intelligence to Chief of Naval Operations, 26 August 1940, NHD: CNO JJ 7 1941.
10. Memo: Director of Naval Intelligence to Secretary of the Navy, 30 August 1940, NHD: CNO JJ7 1941.
11. Ibid.
12. *Pearl Harbor Attack,* part 14, p. 961.
13. Feis, *Road to Pearl Harbor,* p. 123.
14. Langer and Gleason, *Undeclared War,* p. 35; cf. Watson, *Chief of Staff,* p. 115 ff.
15. Memo: Commander McCollum to Director of Naval Intelligence, 2 November 1940, NHD: CNO L11-4/EF37.
16. Ibid.
17. Feis, *Road to Pearl Harbor,* p. 136.
18. Memo: *Japanese Oil Situation,* dated 20 November 1940, incl. (A) to HR: Rear Admiral Ghormley to Chief of Naval Operations, 11 February 1941, NHD: CNO JJ7/EF37-JJ7-3/EF37.
19. Feis, *Road to Pearl Harbor,* p. 136.
20. Letter: Rear Admiral Ghormley to Chief of Naval Operations, NHD: same as note 18 above.
21. Letter: Secretary of the Navy to Secretary of State, 3 April 1941, NHD: CNO A4-5(2)EF37.
22. Letter: Secretary of the Navy to Secretary of State, 15 April 1941, NHD: CNO A4-5(3)EF37.
23. Letter: Secretary of the Navy to Secretary of State, 23 May 1941, Ibid.

24. Feis, *Road to Pearl Harbor,* p. 227.
25. Letter: Chief of Naval Operations to Mr. Welles, 22 July 1941, NA 894.24/1498½.
26. Letter: Director, War Plans Division, to Chief of Naval Operations, 19 July 1941, NHD A11-A15.
27. *Pearl Harbor Attack,* part 5, pp. 2382–84.
28. Feis, *Road to Pearl Harbor,* p. 241.

NOTES TO CHAPTER 7

1. Kittredge, "U.S. Navy in World War II," sect. III, vol. 1, part B, ch. 11, p. 253.
2. Ibid., part A, ch. 10, p. 213.
3. Ibid., part B, ch. 10, pp. 254–55.
4. Watson, *Chief of Staff,* n. 79, p. 118.
5. *Pearl Harbor Attack,* part 14, p. 971.
6. Memo: Chief of Naval Operations to Secretary of the Navy, Op-12-CTB, 12 November 1940, (the original *Plan Dog* is in the Roosevelt Library, Hyde Park, New York; a copy is in Appendix A).
7. Ibid., p. 248.
8. Ibid., p. 250.
9. Ibid., p. 250, 251.
10. Churchill, *Their Finest Hour,* pp. 690–91.
11. Watson, *Chief of Staff,* p. 122.
12. Matloff and Snell, *Coalition Warfare,* p. 28.
13. Watson, *Chief of Staff,* p. 123.
14. Ibid., p. 124.
15. Letter: Joint Planning Committee to Joint Board, 21 January 1941, NHD: Dir., WPD Special File.
16. Memo: F.D.R. to Secretary of the Navy, 26 January 1941, NHD Misc. File #1.
17. Appendix II to letter cited in note 15 above.
18. *Pearl Harbor Attack,* part 15, p. 1487.
19. Matloff and Snell, *Coalition Warfare,* p. 33.
20. Ibid.
21. Churchill, *Their Finest Hour,* pp. 497–98.
22. Kittredge, "U.S. Navy in World War II," sect. IV, vol. 1, part A, ch. 14, p. 348.
23. Lord Lothian became seriously ill shortly after he returned from London in November. He died December 12, 1940.
24. Quotes from *The Far East* paper, NHD: U.S.-U.K. Conversations 1941 file.

25. Ibid.
26. Kittredge, "U.S. Navy in World War II," sect. IV, vol. 1, part A, ch. 14, p. 350.
27. Minutes of the joint meeting of the Army and Navy Sections, 13 February 1941; NHD: U.S.-U.K. Conversations 1941 file.
28. Ibid.
29. Kittredge, "U.S. Navy in World War II," sect. IV, vol. 1, part A, ch. 14, p. 352.
30. Ibid., p. 355.
31. The official title was: U.S. Serial 011512-12(R), B.U.S. (J)(41)30; cf. *Pearl Harbor Attack,* part 15, pp. 1485–1541.
32. *Pearl Harbor Attack,* part 15, p. 1490.
33. Ibid., pp. 1491–92.
34. Ibid., pp. 1511–12. The Pacific Area was North of 30° North and West of 140° East, North of the equator and East of 140° East, South of the equator and East of 180° to South American coast and 74° West.
35. Ibid., p. 1516.

NOTES TO CHAPTER 8

1. Letter: Commander in Chief, Asiatic Fleet, to Chief of Naval Operations, 17 November 1936, NA Navy File FF6.
2. Memo: Admiral Yarnell to Chief of Naval Operations, 2 September 1939, NHD: CNO File A16-3/Warfare, Misc.
3. *Pearl Harbor Attack,* part 16, p. 2446.
4. Memo: Joint Planning Committee to Chief of Naval Operations and Chief of Staff, 27 September 1940, NHD A16-1, September to December 1940.
5. *Pearl Harbor Attack,* part 16, pp. 2448–49.
6. Ibid., p. 2449.
7. Ibid.
8. Letter: Chief of Naval Operations to Commander in Chief, Asiatic Fleet, 12 December 1940, NHD A16-3/A7-3.
9. Watson, *Chief of Staff,* p. 392.
10. Report by Captain Purnell, Batavia talks, 10–14 January 1941, Encl. "C" to letter: Commander in Chief, Asiatic Fleet, to Chief of Naval Operations, 18 January 1941, NHD ABDA-ANZAC Correspondence 1941–1942.
11. Dispatch: Chief of Naval Operations to Commander in Chief, Asiatic Fleet, 15 February 1941, NHD ABDA-ANZAC.

12. Letter: Commander in Chief, Asiatic Fleet, to Chief of Naval Operations, 4 March 1941, NA 811.30 AF/926½.

13. Memo: Chief of Naval Operations to President, 26 March 1941, Ibid.

14. Kittredge, "U.S. Navy in World War II," sect. IV, vol. 1, part A, ch. 14, p. 372.

15. Watson, *Chief of Staff*, p. 394.

16. Dispatch: Chief of Naval Operations to Commander in Chief, Asiatic Fleet, 5 April 1941, NHD ABDA-ANZAC.

17. *Pearl Harbor Attack*, part 15, p. 1516.

18. Matloff and Snell, *Coalition Warfare*, n. 9, p. 66; Watson, *Chief of Staff*, pp. 395–96.

19. Letter: Commander L. R. McDowell, Secretary for Collaboration, to Captain A. W. Clarke, RN, Secretary of the British Military Mission, 7 June 1941, NHD ABDA-ANZAC.

20. *Pearl Harbor Attack*, part 15, p. 1490.

21. Ibid., pp. 1677–79.

22. Letter: Rear Admiral Turner to Rear Admiral Dankwerts, RN, 3 October 1941, NHD ABDA-ANZAC.

23. Dispatch: Special Naval and Military Observers, London, to Chief of Naval Operations, 25 October 1941, NHD ABDA-ANZAC.

24. Watson, *Chief of Staff*, p. 399.

25. Dispatch: Chief of Naval Operations to Special Naval and Military Observers, London, 6 November 1941, NHD ABDA-ANZAC.

26. Ibid.

NOTES TO CHAPTER 9

1. *Pearl Harbor Attack*, part 14, pp. 985–92.

2. Ibid., p. 991.

3. Ibid., part 1, p. 322.

4. Ibid., p. 324.

5. Hull, *Memoirs*, 2:982.

6. Memo: General Marshall, 17 January 1941, quoted by Watson in *Chief of Staff*, pp. 124–25.

7. *Pearl Harbor Attack*, part 14, p. 994.

8. Ibid., p. 998.

9. Ibid., p. 999.

10. Ibid., part 16, p. 2144.

11. Ibid.

12. Telegrams: Consul General, Canton, to Secretary of State, 15 & 18 January 1941, NA 811.30 AF/919 & 921.

13. Langer and Gleason, *Undeclared War*, p. 316.

14. *Pearl Harbor Attack,* part 16, p. 2147.
15. Memo: Captain Schuirmann to State Department, 4 February 1941, NA 740.0011 PW/117.
16. *Pearl Harbor Attack,* part 16, p. 2152.
17. Ibid.
18. Ibid., pp. 2150–51.
19. Ibid., pp. 2144–48.
20. Feis, *Road to Pearl Harbor,* p. 157.
21. *Pearl Harbor Attack,* part 33, p. 1283.
22. Ibid., part 16, p. 2227.
23. Ibid.
24. Ibid., p. 2229.
25. Ibid.
26. Ibid., p. 2149.
27. Ibid.
28. Ibid., p. 2153.
29. Ibid., pp. 2153–54.
30. Ibid., p. 2159.
31. Ibid., p. 2160.
32. Ibid., p. 2163.
33. Hull, *Memoirs,* 2:942–43.
34. Feis, *Road to Pearl Harbor,* p. 178.
35. Cf. Ch. VIII for discussion of *ADB* Plan.
36. *Pearl Harbor Attack,* part 19, p. 3461.
37. Langer and Gleason, *Undeclared War,* p. 451.
38. *Pearl Harbor Attack,* part 16, pp. 2229–30.
39. Ibid., p. 2231.
40. Ibid., pp. 2163–64.
41. Memo: Director, War Plans Division, to Chief of Naval Operations, 10 April 1941, NHD: Dir., WPD Special File.
42. Ibid.
43. *Pearl Harbor Attack,* part 16, p. 2168.
44. Ibid., p. 2238.
45. Memo: Captain Kirk to Chief of Naval Operations, 16 June 1941, NHD: CNO A8-5/EF 37.
46. Hull, *Memoirs,* 2:1012.
47. Ibid.

NOTES TO CHAPTER 10

1. Memo: Lieutenant Commander W. S. Scobey, USA, Secretary, Joint Board, to Chief of Naval Operations, 9 June 1941, NHD Misc. File 1, case 802, #5.

2. *Pearl Harbor Attack,* part 16, p. 2175.

3. Memo: Director, War Plans Division to Chief of Naval Operations, 11 July 1941, NHD: Dir., WPD Special File.

4. Letter: Director, War Plans Division to Chief of Naval Operations, 19 July 1941, NH A11-A15, case 804, bottom.

5. Hull, *Memoirs,* 2:1013.

6. Memo: Admiral Turner to Chief of Naval Operations, 21 July 1941, NHD: Dir., WPD Special File.

7. *Pearl Harbor Attack,* part 16, p. 2172.

8. Ibid., part 14, p. 1401.

9. Ibid., part 16, p. 2239.

10. Ibid.

11. Ibid., p. 2240.

12. Ibid., p. 2174.

13. Ibid., p. 2242.

14. Letter: Hart to Stark, 31 July 1941, NHD: Dir., WPD Special File.

15. Ibid.

16. Langer and Gleason, *Undeclared War,* p. 657.

17. *Pearl Harbor Attack,* part 20, p. 3998.

18. Ibid., p. 4000.

19. Hull, *Memoirs,* 2:1018.

20. Ibid.

21. Ibid., pp. 1019–20.

22. *Pearl Harbor Attack,* part 20, p. 4001.

23. Watson, *Chief of Staff,* p. 438; Matloff and Snell, *Coalition Warfare,* pp. 67–68.

24. Telegram: Ambassador Gauss to Secretary of State, 16 August 1941, NA 811.30 AF/941.

25. Memo: Unidentified author, probably Walter Adams, State Department, 20 August 1941, Ibid.

26. Letter: Commander in Chief, Asiatic Fleet, to Chief of Naval Operations, 28 August 1941, NA 811.30 AF/954.

27. *Pearl Harbor Attack,* part 16, pp. 2183–90.

28. Ibid., p. 2451.

29. Hull, *Memoirs,* 2:1021.

30. Ibid., p. 1022.

31. *Pearl Harbor Attack,* part 16, p. 2450.

32. Ibid., p. 2208.

33. Ibid., part 20, p. 4006.

34. Ibid.

35. Ibid., part 16, p. 2210.

36. Ibid., p. 2248.

37. Unpublished Hart monograph, NHD.

38. *Pearl Harbor Attack,* part 16, p. 2213.

39. Ibid.

40. Ibid., pp. 2213–14.

41. Ibid., p. 2210.

NOTES TO CHAPTER 11

1. *Pearl Harbor Attack,* p. 2211.

2. Ibid., pp. 2211–12.

3. Memo: Director, War Plans Division, to Chief of Naval Operations, 29 September 1941, NHD: Dir., WPD Special File.

4. *Pearl Harbor Attack,* part 20, p. 4009.

5. Ibid.

6. Letter: Chief of Naval Operations to Secretary of State, 10 October 1941, NHD: Pacific-Far East U.S. Joint Staff Correspondence #2.

7. *Pearl Harbor Attack,* part 16, p. 2216.

8. Ibid., p. 2217.

9. Ibid.

10. Ibid., part 14, p. 1402.

11. Ibid.

12. Ibid.

13. Ibid.

14. Ibid.

15. Ibid., part 16, p. 2214.

16. Ibid., pp. 2215–16.

17. Ibid., p. 2249.

18. Ibid., part 14, pp. 1062–63.

19. Ibid.

20. Ibid., pp. 1064–65.

21. Ibid.

22. Ibid., p. 1062.

23. Ibid.

24. Ibid.

25. Ibid., part 19, p. 3467.

26. Ibid., part 16, pp. 2451–54.

27. Ibid., part 11, p. 5396.

28. Winston Churchill, *The Grand Alliance* (Boston: Houghton Mifflin Co., 1950), p. 594.

29. *Pearl Harbor Attack,* part 16, p. 2220.

30. Ibid., p. 2456.

31. Ibid., p. 2252.

32. Ibid., p. 2253.
33. Ibid., p. 2224.
34. Hull, *Memoirs,* 2:1067.
35. *Pearl Harbor Attack,* part 12, p. 165.
36. Ibid., Report of Joint Committee, p. 367.
37. Ibid., part 14, pp. 1104–5. Cf. Langer and Gleason, *Undeclared War,* pp. 876–77, for an excellent summary of the White *Outline.*
38. Ibid., p. 1142.
39. Ibid., p. 1405.
40. Ibid., Report of Joint Committee, p. 374.
41. Ibid., part 16, p. 2224.
42. Ibid., part 15, pp. 1771–72.
43. Letter: British Chief of Staff to British Joint Staff for passing to Chief of Naval Operations, 22 November 1941, NHD: Pacific-Far East British Joint Staff Correspondence #1.
44. *Pearl Harbor Attack,* part 14, p. 1300.
45. Ibid., Report of Joint Committee, p. 379.
46. Ibid., pp. 382–384. The proposed *Outline* and the withdrawn *modus vivendi* appear in Appendix B.
47. Ibid., part 14, p. 1406.
48. Ibid., p. 1083.
49. Ibid., part 20, p. 4487.
50. Ibid., Report of Joint Committee, p. 394.
51. Watson, *Chief of Staff,* p. 448.
52. Ibid., p. 451.
53. *Pearl Harbor Attack,* Report of Joint Committee, p. 401.
54. Ibid., part 14, p. 1300.
55. Ibid., Report of Joint Committee, pp. 403–4.
56. Ibid., part 15, p. 1768.
57. Ibid., Report of Joint Committee, p. 413.
58. Memo of conversation, Hamilton with Schuirmann, 1 December 1941, NA 811.30 AF/965.
59. *Pearl Harbor Attack,* part 14, p. 1407.
60. Ibid., part 15, p. 1769.
61. Ibid., Report of Joint Committee, p. 412.
62. Ibid., part 16, p. 2255.
63. Ibid., p. 2254.
64. Ibid., p. 2256.
65. Ibid., Report of Joint Committee, p. 418.
66. Ibid., part 14, p. 1408.
67. Ibid., part 15, p. 1773.
68. Ibid.

69. Hull, *Memoirs,* 2:781.

70. *Pearl Harbor Attack,* part 11, p. 5472.

71. Ibid., part 2, p. 493.

72. Cf. R. Esthus, "President Roosevelt's Commitment to Britain to Intervene in a Pacific War," *Mississippi Valley Historical Review* (1963): 28–39, for an analysis of events confirming the Creighton-Hart dispatch.

73. *Pearl Harbor Attack,* part 11, p. 5514.

74. Ibid., Report of Joint Committee, p. 429.

75. Ibid., part 12, p. 245.

76. Ibid., Report of Joint Committee, p. 439.

77. Hull, *Memoirs,* 2:787.

NOTES TO CHAPTER 12

1. Hull, *Memoirs,* 1:457.

2. Letter: Statutory Board on Submarine, Destroyer, Mine and Naval Air Bases, 1938 (Hepburn Board Report), 1 December 1938, p. 66, NHD Hepburn Board.

3. Stimson was Secretary of State under President Herbert Hoover.

4. Memo: William D. Leahy to the President, 15 December 1938; *Roosevelt Papers,* Secretary's Files; I Dip. Correspondence, 1933–37, 1939–41, Box 11. FDR Memorial Library.

5. Memo: War Plans Division to Chief of Naval Operations, 1 September 1939, NHD A16/Mobilization.

6. Memo: Captain Crenshaw to Admiral Stark, 9 December 1939, NHD EA-EZ.

7. Memo: Hornbeck's evaluation of letter from Admiral Hart to Admiral Stark, 13 November 1940, NA 740.0011 P.W./72.

8. Letter: Chief of Naval Operations to Secretary of the Navy, 17 January 1941, NHD A16-3/of 37, 15 January to 24 December 1941.

9. Supplement to narrative of Admiral Thomas C. Hart, USN; on file in the NHD.

10. Memo: Admiral Yarnell to Secretary of the Navy, 15 January 1941, NHD: same as note 8 above.

11. Letter: Chief of Naval Operations to Secretary of the Navy, 17 January 1941; NHD: same as note 8 above.

12. *Pearl Harbor Attack,* part 16, p. 2222.

13. Ibid., part 14, p. 932.

14. Ibid., p. 943.

15. Ibid., p. 962.

16. Langer and Gleason, *Challenge to Isolation,* p. 597.

17. *Pearl Harbor Attack,* part 14, p. 971.

Bibliography

PRIMARY SOURCES OF ORIGINAL MATERIAL

Naval History Division, Office of the Chief of Naval Operations, Navy Department; Washington, D.C.

Naval Records Branch, National Archives; Washington, D.C.

State Department Records, National Archives; Washington, D.C.

SECONDARY SOURCES OF ORIGINAL MATERIAL

President Franklin D. Roosevelt Memorial Library; Hyde Park, New York.

Naval War College Library, Newport, Rhode Island.

PUBLIC DOCUMENTS

Code of Federal Regulations of the United States of America.

Foreign Relations of the United States; Japan, 1931–1941. Department of State Publication No. 2016, United States Government Printing Office, Washington, D.C., 1943. 2 vols.

Hearings before the Joint Committee on the Investigation of the Pearl Harbor Attack, Seventy-ninth Congress, United States Government Printing Office, Washington, D.C., 1946. 39 vols.

Navy Regulations 1920, Navy Department, United States Government Printing Office, Washington, D.C., 1920.

Oil in Japan's War, Report of the Oil and Chemical Division, United States Strategic Bombing Survey, Washington, D.C., 1946.

United States Navy. Senate Document 35, Seventy-fifth Congress, first session. United States Government Printing Office, 1937.

BOOKS

Beard, Charles A. *President Roosevelt and the Coming of the War, 1941.* New Haven: Yale University Press, 1948.

Braisted, William Reynolds. *The United States Navy in the Pacific, 1897–1909*. Austin: University of Texas, 1958.

Bywater, Hector C. *Sea-Power in the Pacific*. Boston: Houghton Mifflin Co., 1934.

Churchill, Winston S. *Their Finest Hour*. Boston: Houghton Mifflin Co., 1949.

———. *The Grand Alliance*. Boston: Houghton Mifflin Co., 1950.

Cline, Ray S. *Washington Command Post: The Operations Division*. In the series *United States Army in World War II*. Washington: Office of the Chief of Military History, Department of the Army, 1951.

Eden, Anthony. *Memoirs: Facing the Dictators*. Boston: Houghton Mifflin Co., 1962.

Feis, Herbert. *The Road to Pearl Harbor*. Princeton: Princeton University Press, 1950.

Furer, Rear Admiral Julius Augustus. *Administration of the Navy in World War II*. Washington: Department of the Navy, 1959.

Grew, Joseph C. *Ten Years in Japan*. New York: Simon and Schuster, 1944.

Griswold, A. Whitney. *The Far Eastern Policy of the United States*. New York: Harcourt, Brace and Company, 1938.

Hull, Cordell. *The Memoirs of Cordell Hull*. New York: Macmillan Company, 1948. 2 vols.

Jones, Francis Clifford. *Japan's New Order in East Asia; Its Rise and Fall, 1937–45*. London: Oxford University Press, 1954.

Kimmel, Admiral Husband E. *Admiral Kimmel's Story*. Chicago: Henry Regnery Company, 1955.

Knox, Dudley W. *A History of the United States Navy*. New York: G. P. Putnam's Sons, 1948.

Langer, William L. and Everett S. Gleason. *The Challenge to Isolation*. New York: Harper and Brothers, 1952.

———. *The Undeclared War, 1940–1941*. New York: Harper & Brothers, 1953.

Livezey, William E. *Mahan on Sea Power*. Norman: University of Oklahoma Press, 1947.

Mahan, Alfred Thayer. *The Influence of Sea Power upon History, 1660–1783*. Boston: Little, Brown and Company, 1890.

———. *The Interest of America in Sea Power, Present and Future*. Boston: Little, Brown and Company, 1897.

———. *The Problem of Asia*. Boston: Little, Brown and Company, 1900.

————. *From Sail to Steam: Recollections of Naval Life.* New York and London: Harper and Brothers, 1907.

————. *The Interest of America in International Conditions.* Boston: Little, Brown and Company, 1910.

Matloff, Maurice and Edwin M. Snell. *Strategic Planning for Coalition Warfare, 1941–1942.* In the series *United States Army in World War II.* Washington: Office of the Chief of Military History, Department of the Army, 1953.

May, Ernest R. *The World War and American Isolation, 1914–1917.* Cambridge: Harvard University Press, 1959.

Mitchell, Donald W. *History of the Modern American Navy.* New York: Alfred A. Knopf, 1946.

Morison, Elting E. *Admiral Sims and the Modern American Navy.* Boston: Houghton Mifflin Company, 1942.

Morison, Samuel Eliot. *The Battle of the Atlantic, September 1939–May 1943.* Boston: Little, Brown and Company, 1947. (Volume I of *History of United States Naval Operations in World War II.*)

————. *The Rising Sun in the Pacific, 1931–April 1942.* Boston: Little, Brown and Company, 198. (Volume III of *History of United States Naval Operations in World War II.*)

Morton, Louis. *The Fall of the Philippines.* In the series *United States Army in World War II.* Washington: Office of the Chief of Military History, Department of the Army, 1953.

Sprout, Harold and Margaret. *The Rise of American Naval Power, 1776–1918.* Princeton: Princeton University Press, 1946.

————. *Toward a New Order of Sea Power: American Naval Policy and the World Scene, 1918–1922.* Princeton: Princeton University Press, 1946.

Stimson, Henry L. and McGeorge Bundy. *On Active Service in War and Peace.* Harper and Brothers, 1947.

Watson, Mark S. *Chief of Staff: Prewar Plans and Preparations.* In the series *United States Army in World War II.* Washington: Office of the Chief of Military History, Department of the Army, 1950.

PERIODICALS

Esthus, R. ————. "President Roosevelt's Commitment to Britain to Intervene in a Pacific War," *Mississippi Valley Historical* Review (1963): 28–29.

Morton, Louis. "American and Allied Strategy in the Far East," *Military Review,* December 1949, Vol. XXIX No. 9 .

UNPUBLISHED MATERIAL

Hart, Admiral Thomas C. "Narrative of Events Leading up to War;" and "Supplement to Narrative." On file Naval History Division.

Kittredge, Tracy C. "Monograph: United States Navy in World War II." On file Naval History Division.

OTHER SOURCES

Biographies Branch, OI-430, Office of Information, Navy Department; Washington, D.C.

Churchill, Winston S. *The Grand Alliance.* Boston: Houghton Mifflin Co., 1950.

Index